Philip Sheldrake

SPIRITUALITY AND HISTORY

Questions of Interpretation and Method

ORBIS BOOKS

Maryknoll, New York 10545

First published in Great Britain 1991
SPCK
Holy Trinity Church
Marylebone Road
London NW1 4DU

Revised edition 1995

Published in the USA 1998
Orbis Books
P.O. Box 308
Maryknoll, New York 10545-0308 U.S.A.

ISBN 1-57075-203-6

Cataloging-in-Publication Data for this book
is available from the Library of Congress

Printed in Great Britain by Biddles Ltd
Guildford and King's Lynn

Contents

TO MY PARENTS

who taught me to
love history

Preface

I am grateful to SPCK for the opportunity provided by a second edition to make some revisions in response to developments in the field of spirituality since 1990. This edition has a revised Introduction, which includes reference to many significant new writings in the field, an updated Bibliography, and some revisions to the Index. I have been encouraged and stimulated by reactions to the original book, especially the forum provided by the new scholarly Society for the Study of Christian Spirituality which discussed the book at its first annual conference in San Francisco in 1992.

Philip Sheldrake

Preface to the First Edition

Some four years ago, it was suggested that I should write a general introduction to contemporary spirituality. It soon became clear that this would be a very lengthy task if I were to do justice to the complexity of the subject without being either too diffuse or too simplistic. I decided that a more precise focus, concerning new approaches to the history of spirituality, would enable me to produce a more coherent study and would, in any case, answer a need of which I had become aware through my teaching in university and adult education courses. With the change of focus also came a change of style and what had begun as an attempt at an intelligent introductory survey to fairly well-known material ended as an academically much more demanding and original text.

In 1987 I was privileged to be invited to the Jesuit 'American Assistancy Seminar' in St Louis to hear a paper by Philip Endean (now published, and cited in this study) on the dangers of historical fundamentalism in spirituality. Another participant, John Staudenmaier of the University of Detroit, suggested that some of the questions he had raised in a book on the history of technology might further help my reflections on the history of spirituality. He subsequently sent me the relevant material which I would not, otherwise, have seen. Both the seminar and John Staudenmaier's book were an important stimulus to my own thinking.

I am also grateful for other conversations, and suggestions for further reading, that assisted me along the way. In particular, I would like to thank John O'Malley of the Weston School of Theology, Cambridge Mass., for helpful references and articles, and my colleagues at Heythrop College, Anne Murphy and Michael Barnes, for their tolerance and suggestions during various conversations over the last few years.

I am indebted to John O'Malley and Anne Murphy for reading a draft of the book. Others who kindly agreed to do the same were: Thomas Clarke, Associate Editor of *The Way* for many years; Anand Chitnis, lecturer in history at the University of Stirling; and Frances Teresa of the Convent of Poor Clares, Arundel. Michael Barnes made helpful criticisms of the Introduction and Chapter

One. Lavinia Byrne, my colleague at the Institute of Spirituality, read chapters 5 and 6. I am grateful to all these for their encouraging response and for their astute criticisms, suggestions and further historical examples, which have helped to improve the structure and content of the book. They cannot, of course, be held responsible for any imperfections that remain.

More general thanks are due to a number of people. David Lonsdale and Mary Critchley of the Institute of Spirituality contributed greatly to the supportive atmosphere that has made it possible to work on this book in the midst of so many other tasks. Philip Law and Brendan Walsh of SPCK contributed a great deal of helpful advice and support. The ecumenical community at Hengrave Hall, Suffolk, by their generous hospitality during the Spring of 1989, restored the energy I needed to complete the final chapters. I am also grateful to them for permission to use, as a cover illustration, a photograph by David Lonsdale of a medieval window in their chapel which depicts God breathing the world and history into being. The members of the Jesuit community at South Woodford, where I have lived for the last few years, have encouraged me by their interest and good-humoured comments. Finally, this book would never have been completed without the affection and support of a few close friends and relatives – not least in the aftermath of family bereavement. This brief acknowledgement is an inadequate return for all that they have given me.

Philip Sheldrake
June 1990

Introduction

A paradoxical feature of contemporary western culture, particularly in the English-speaking world, is that alongside a decline in traditional religious practice there exists an ever-increasing hunger for spirituality.[1] One obvious manifestation is the explosion of publications on the so-called New Age, humanistic psychology, the new science, mysticism, ritual and meditation; and these subjects are now stocked in general bookshops as well as specialist ones.[2] Popular editions of some Christian classics, such as the medieval English *The Cloud of Unknowing*, rub shoulders with Sufi mysticism and the occult. Celtic spirituality and the medieval women known as Beguines have been enthusiastically 'rediscovered'.[3] Certain Christian figures, such as Julian of Norwich, Hildegard of Bingen or Meister Eckhart, have achieved an almost cult status. Music too plays a part in the spiritual quest, as demonstrated by the fact that recordings of Gregorian chant appear in CD bestseller lists.

Pluralism and the crisis of postmodernity

This contemporary interest in spirituality is frequently accompanied by what might be called a theological vacuum. Even Christian communities can no longer take for granted the old consensus about the language of faith that lies behind classical spiritual traditions. It may be that a great deal of variety always existed in practice, but a quite radical pluralism is now an undeniable reality within all the major western denominations. When we reflect on current experience within the Church it is less easy to speak of 'Christian spirituality' than in the past, and more accurate to speak of 'the spiritualities of Christians'. Exclusive systems are increasingly giving way to an eclectic approach to spirituality that is prepared to 'borrow' not only across denominational boundaries, but also from other world faiths.[4]

The possibility of fruitful interaction between Christian spirituality and other world faiths has been popularized by the writings of William Johnston in Japan and Bede Griffiths in India. The

1

issues involved in interfaith conversation are complex, and the literature is already vast. Interfaith spirituality is set to become a major area of development. There are complicated issues involved – such as the fact that not all world faiths use the concept 'spirituality' or the category 'God' – but there are also untold possibilities.[5]

In addition, many of the seekers who look partly to Christian spiritualities for enlightenment are no longer committed to the central religious truths assumed by those traditions. In many quarters, there is a suspicion of religious dogma in general, and a coherent system of belief is not presumed necessary for a valid spiritual quest.[6] Western cultures now exist in what is frequently referred to as a postmodern world. The precise meaning of 'postmodernity' varies among theorists, depending on their interests and perspectives. Yet one aspect about which there appears to be broad agreement is that the enthusiastic modernity of the Enlightenment no longer seems viable. A belief in human self-sufficiency, the primacy of reason, the possibility of achieving totally objective knowledge, and assumptions about inevitable progress now appear simplistic and over-optimistic. Western culture overall has lost faith in simple explanations or universal certainties.

Why is this so? In one sense, this shift of attitude has taken place because we have learned too much about nature and humanity. We can no longer afford to be naïve. As I have suggested elsewhere,[7] we are at a particularly crucial point in the history of western consciousness, comparable to the Renaissance, the Reformation, the Enlightenment or the Industrial Revolution. Traditional patterns of thought and behaviour, as well as institutions of all kinds (including religious ones), are under continual pressure. They are struggling to deal with a surrounding reality that is impervious to the answers of the past, and that presents an apparently overwhelming number of new questions. There are several general factors that have served to undermine the world-view that we have inherited from the past, and that traditional spiritualities took for granted. Some of these originated in the nineteenth century, but have only slowly percolated into the consciousness of society at large.

First, our understanding of the universe of which we are a part has changed substantially as a result of such things as developments in cosmology and quantum physics. Our little world and the human race can no longer be seen as giving unique meaning to the whole of creation. Second, evolutionary theory of some kind is now accepted without question, except by some religious fundamentalists. The evolution of humanity is understood to be one of life's processes that can neither be separated from, nor understood as inherently superior to, others. Third, we now live in a world that generally accepts psychology as a respectable science. This reveals a vast and complex inner world that calls into question the straightforward objectivity of human perceptions and values. Fourth, developments in economics and political theory, as well as the birth of the social sciences, challenge traditional conceptions of human society. Finally, events in this century such as the Holocaust or Hiroshima, and the present realities of widespread hunger and poverty, have irrevocably undermined overconfidence in human progress. Equally, the unexpectedly rapid collapse of the Soviet empire calls into question the long-term stability of even the most monolithic of human institutions.

Alongside the breakdown of former certainties, there has also been a fragmentation of the collective consciousness. This tends to inhibit a sense of community and to encourage a concentration on interiority and purely personal development. Spirituality easily becomes a private affair. Some theorists of postmodernity would even suggest that overarching frameworks of explanation and values (or meta-narratives) of any kind are now impossible. This leaves us with no agreed criteria for evaluating human experiences and actions. Thus, some might argue, we are only able to say that an event such as the Holocaust was 'what people chose to do'.

The critique of traditional approaches to spirituality proposed by this book implicitly accepts certain central features of postmodernity. However, a key part of my thesis is based on a rejection of the radical version of postmodern theory that I have just outlined. In simple terms, I believe that it is impossible to escape from value-judgements. To deny that committed standpoints on human events are valid or viable is not simply a statement of 'the way things are'; it is itself an interpretation based on theoretical assumptions and value-judgements. This book therefore does not simply attempt to criticize traditional explanations of the history of spirituality. It proposes alternative frameworks – not least ones that are based on a commitment to rehabilitate traditions and people that have usually been marginalized.

Postmodernity and spirituality

It is important to note that, despite the breakdown of many traditional collective frames of reference, contemporary western approaches to spirituality are not entirely individualistic. There is also a widespread desire for a recovery of public and social values

3

in response to what is widely interpreted as the rampant material-ism and individualism of the 1980s. The word 'postmaterialism' is becoming more common among people who discuss the future of western society. 'Spirituality' and 'community' are again being described as vitally important. It is encouraging that the debate about reconstruction is no longer confined to theoretical positions espoused by neo-conservative groups.

However, it does seem inevitable that attempts to arrive at a reconstructed adult faith in this climate cannot avoid the painful loss of our 'first innocence'. Faith is no longer a simple matter of passing a received wisdom from generation to generation. Most people these days who define their lives spiritually have been through a 'dark night' in which, for example, the familiar images of God are stripped away. Perhaps this partly explains the popu-larity of modern religious poets such as R. S. Thomas or mystics such as Meister Eckhart, who use the language of 'unknowing' or darkness.

The specific connection between postmodern culture and mysticism is one that was noted by the great French intellectual, the late Michel de Certeau. He suggested that postmodern expe-rience of the world is a kind of movement of perpetual departure, dissatisfaction and inability to settle on any one moment, structure or system of explanation as 'truth'. Traditional Christian mystics, too, are wanderers and pilgrims who are caught up in 'an eternity without shores' and become lost 'in the totality of the immense'. Mystics are people of insatiable desire and so, de Certeau sug-gested, are the inhabitants of contemporary western culture:

> He or she is a mystic who cannot stop walking and, with the cer-tainty of what is lacking, knows of every place and object that it is *not that*, one cannot stay *there* nor be content with *that*. Desire creates an excess. Places are exceeded, passed, lost behind it. It makes one go further, elsewhere. It lives nowhere.[8]

More precise connections between postmodern culture and spirituality have yet to be thoroughly explored. This is undoubtedly not helped by the fact that both 'spirituality' and 'postmodernity' can be such fluid terms. However, there have been some useful attempts at sketching out an approach.[9]

One aspect of postmodernism that is very relevant is that it encourages us to uncover the social and cultural agendas that underlie particular ideas and approaches – not least to spirituality. I would suggest that the subversion of ideologies is actually inherent in the Christian tradition. The experience of postmodern culture may remind us of this in exciting ways, and particularly that the mystery of God, and God's action within human experience, always transcends our human capacity to comprehend it.[10] In this context, tools provided since the Second World War by what might be called the 'new history', and reflected in this book, are highly relevant. This view of history rejects a simple narrative approach that would reduce human experience to neatly ordered categories. It is itself partly a reaction against Enlightenment views of knowledge, and is in some respects an expression of postmodern experience.

Spirituality and the academy

Alongside the cultural situation, we should note a second important development since this book was written five years ago. A great deal has happened in those years to spirituality as an academic discipline. Within the English-speaking world, three features stand out. First, a major annual journal has appeared, *Studies in Spirituality*, with the explicit aim of encouraging a thoroughly scholarly and multidisciplinary approach.[11] Second, an increasing number of universities and colleges are offering spirituality within their theology syllabuses or are developing separate graduate programmes in the field. Third, an international scholarly society for the study of Christian spirituality has been founded in relationship with the American Academy of Religion. Through its conferences and bulletin, this has encouraged a great deal more reflection on the meaning of spirituality and the definition and content of the academic field.[12]

The present academic debate about the nature of spirituality has by no means reached a definitive conclusion. There seem to be three major points of consensus at present. First, spirituality is both multidisciplinary and an interdisciplinary field. Second, there is a need for a proper understanding of the historical process. Third, historical-contextual, hermeneutical and theological approaches to the field cannot claim to be exclusive, but are mutually complementary. I would identify two major areas where views continue to differ, and sometimes quite sharply. These questions are closely related. First, what is the precise relationship between spirituality and theology? Second, can spirituality be theologically non-thematic?

With regard to the overall relationship between spirituality and theology, there are a number of problems. It is important to recognize the limitations of abstract theological concepts to express the nuances of the spiritual quest. In doing so, however, we also need to remember the major shift that is still taking place in theology itself towards a less deductive and more experiential method. The academy frequently still sees theology as essentially informative rather than performative, and theologians as experts in analysis. However, 'being a theologian' is as much a quality of 'being' in relation to the reality we reflect upon as a concern for the technology of a specific discipline. This view brings the nature of theology and of spirituality much closer together. Both are self-implicating yet critical. In both disciplines, some kind of transformation is implied by the search for knowledge.[13]

The second debated question concerns our understanding of spirituality itself. For example, it has been suggested that North American nature literature is characterized by what might be called an implicit or oblique evocation of the transcendent.[14.] Some of its exponents, such as Annie Dillard,[15] may be described as quasi-mystical. However, it is not easy to define the spirituality that is said to emerge from this literature because it is outside conventional religious or theological frameworks. Without denying the possibility of using the word 'spirituality' of some examples of this genre, it is difficult to pin down precisely what is the something that makes for 'spirituality', and how that is different from any strikingly evocative nature or travel writing.

Another example is provided by the valuable 'World Spirituality Series' that continues to be published on both sides of the Atlantic. Because of the breadth of the series, the editors have been careful not to impose a narrow definition of spirituality on the contributors. One recent volume is entitled *South and Meso-American Native Spirituality*.[16] This includes essays on Mayan Faith and Andean Religion. Some of these essays might be expected in any volume of religious anthropology. Clearly, the social sciences (including anthropology) have a contribution to make to the field of spirituality. However, the question remains as to what makes for merely good anthropology, and what the something is that qualifies as spirituality. Unless we are careful, 'spirituality' can all too easily become just another word for almost every human experience. All of this indicates that the debate about the nature of spirituality and its relationship to theology is still, in many ways, at an early stage.

6

The structure of the book

The present approach to the field of spirituality is increasingly interdisciplinary. We need to draw not only upon history and theology, but also on the human and social sciences as well as literary theory. This book does not pretend to offer a map of the whole field. Arguably, it is premature to attempt one and, given the complexities of the subject, it is unlikely to be written by a single author. My aim is more limited, as I confine my attention primarily to the role of historical method and secondarily to changing approaches to the relationship between spirituality and theology.

The new edition of this book continues to offer, as far as I am aware, something new in the contemporary study of spirituality. It combines three principal and closely related elements. First, it aims to present a coherent statement not only of the weaknesses of traditional approaches to the history of spirituality, but also of the kind of questions that will help us to create an alternative perspective. Second, it introduces much contemporary literature in the field, particularly the most creative or provocative writing. For this reason, there are detailed endnote references as well as a revised Bibliography of works cited or consulted. There are some citations of primary sources where this seemed especially appropriate, but most references are deliberately confined, as far as possible, to studies written in English or to texts available in translation. This approach obviously has its limitations, but my concern in this book is not to concentrate on detailed study, but on more general questions about the nature of the historical process and about the assumptions behind historical interpretation in the area of spirituality. In this sense, the book does not replace works of detailed scholarship about texts or events, but hopefully encourages a reading of such works with fresh eyes and a more critical perspective.

Finally, the book seeks to synthesize the methodological considerations that relate to history and spirituality. In doing this, particular attention has been given to the recovery of the 'underside of history', to the way in which western spirituality has been dominated by certain spiritual, cultural and social élites, and how our historical method has tended to highlight these. In this sense, the study has a committed standpoint. My premises and method are shaped by post-Vatican II ecclesiology, spirituality and hermeneutics. As we shall see, commitments, as opposed to uncritical or unconscious bias, are valid entry points into historical knowledge.

In general, the book tries to move away from the rather in-house focus of many of the works on the history of spirituality written from the perspective of my own Roman Catholic tradition, not only by giving greater attention to other Christian traditions, but, where possible, by stepping off the beaten track and exploring some less familiar paths. While my perspective is a modern Roman Catholic one, I argue that traditional understandings of the supposed great divide between a 'Catholic mentality' and a 'Protestant mentality' need to be questioned.

Although the focus of the book is primarily historical, it is an interdisciplinary study which brings together the issues that are relevant to history, those suggested by the emerging discipline of spirituality and contemporary theological horizons. Because the inspiration for the book originated in my experience of teaching spirituality in various academic contexts, the needs of students, many of whom are not historians, have been much in mind. However, because of the interdisciplinary nature of the book, and the kind of questions that such a synthetic approach raises, the result has been of interest to specialists. I hope that the book will also be useful to general readers who, while not experts, have some background, as well as interest, in the relationship between history and spirituality.

The first four chapters, which form Part One, set out the essential programme and provide a framework for reconsidering our approach to the history of spirituality. Chapter 1, on the nature of history, has proved to be quite demanding reading for those not familiar with historical theory and method. However, for students of spirituality, the issues it discusses are a vital introduction to shifts in historical thinking in recent years. The second chapter clarifies what is meant by spirituality and charts the way in which the term has been given different meanings, and how the breadth of human experience and practice to which it refers has varied throughout history.[17] Chapters 3 and 4 turn in more detail to the history of spirituality. First, I address some questions to the process of history, and then I turn to the way in which the history of spirituality has subsequently been described and used. My contention is that 'what happens' in history takes place within value-structures, whether spiritual, theological or social. The process of history is itself selective, and this is not necessarily a story of inexorable progress.[18] The ways in which we subsequently analyse and use the past in the present are even more selective because of our models of history as well as of spirituality. Both of these factors suggest the need for a much more critical approach to the history we believe we have inherited, and to which we seek to be faithful.

These chapters in Part One provide a selection of appropriate historical illustrations as they proceed. However, chapters 5 and 6 in Part Two ground some of the questions of analysis and inter-pretation in a more detailed examination of two case studies. Religious life suggested itself as the first study because it became such a dominant force in western spirituality, and lies behind many of the spiritual traditions upon which contemporary Christians, of different backgrounds, seek to draw.[19] The second study, of the medieval women's movement, the Beguines, recommended itself because, in recent years, it has moved from being a little-known and marginalized tradition to a new prominence as its lay, femi-nine and radical spirit is rescued from obscurity and repossessed.[20]

The two final chapters of this book, in Part Three, address issues that are central to much of the contemporary interest in spirituality, whether theoretical or practical. Chapter 7 acknowl-edges the remarkable popularity of spiritual classics. However, whether our aim is historical knowledge or practical use, to read a text from one age and culture in another, far removed from it, raises acute questions of interpretation. This is not merely an issue of the integrity of a text and respect for the standpoint of the orig-inal author. In the context of the contemporary spiritual quest there may be very practical dangers involved if we read our own assumptions into a text or, on the other hand, adopt the author's teaching in an uncritical way. The chapter, therefore, offers some guidelines about interpreting historical spiritual texts, and con-cludes with brief considerations of two sample texts, *The Cloud of Unknowing* and the *Spiritual Exercises*, which enjoy a vogue at the present time. Finally, all historians use organizing frameworks. One that is particular to spirituality is the categorization of spiri-tual traditions into different 'types'. This is to be found not only in histories of spirituality, but also in books on prayer and medita-tion. Chapter 8 examines whether Christian spirituality should be viewed as one or many, and how useful or legitimate are some of the attempts to describe different spiritual traditions in terms of basic types.

An interdisciplinary overview, such as this book, does not offer definitive conclusions concerning the issues it addresses. Much of the book consists of suggestions or postulations. This is quite deliberate, as my aim is to provoke questions about traditional interpretations of evidence and to open up contentious areas to further reflection. Until recently, the study of spirituality, and especially the well-known general histories of the subject, focused almost exclusively on the communication of historical *information* as a background to what was perceived as the main task: an exposition of the teachings of particular traditions. Historical factors, in other words, were largely at the service of the concerns of traditional spiritual theology. This book takes a quite different line. It does not only argue that history should be treated seriously as a discipline in its own right when we try to make sense of our inherited spiritual traditions – a point developed further towards the end of chapter 1. While not denying the importance of information, this book also concentrates on exposing the discipline of spirituality to the contemporary concern with historical skills and interpretation – something that has rarely been done, in my experience, in studying spirituality. In particular, it seeks to alert readers and students to the importance of understanding spiritualities in their full historical settings, to the complex issues raised by seeking to organize the details of history into an intelligible pattern, to the need to grasp differences in interpretations of history, and the need to use our sources in a more sophisticated way. My main hope is that readers who feel that history, even of spirituality, is a dry and dusty discipline, or of merely peripheral interest, may discover some of the excitement that can be generated by a more questioning and adventurous approach.

Notes

1. Wade Clark Roof has written a landmark study of the new generation of spiritual seekers in the USA, and the impact that this is likely to have on social and cultural values. See his *A Generation of Seekers: The Spiritual Journey of the Baby Boom Generation* (New York 1994).

2. The 'New Age' phenomenon tends to provoke strongly negative reactions among some traditional Christians. *The Way* journal has attempted to encourage a more balanced evaluation. A complete issue was dedicated to essays on 'New Age Spirituality' in July 1993. See also Siddika Angle, 'Beyond Familiar Shores: New Age Spirituality', *The Way* (April 1993), pp. 138–47. On the contemporary fascination with the relationship between mysticism and science, see the essays by Ross Thompson and Robert Russell in 'Mysticism, Spirituality and Science', *The Way* (October 1992).

3. I have tried to address some of the complex issues of interpretation as we approach the history and spirituality of Celtic Christianity in my *Living Between Worlds: Place and Journey in Celtic Spirituality* (London/Boston 1995), especially the Introduction and ch. 1.

4. See Walter Principe, 'Pluralism in Christian Spirituality', *The Way* (January 1992), pp. 54–61.

5. There is a useful collection of essays called *Interfaith Spirituality*, published as *The Way Supplement* 78 (Autumn 1993).

6. See Peter H. Van Ness, 'Spirituality and Secularity', *The Way Supplement* 73 (Spring 1992), pp. 68–79. Van Ness is also editor of the forthcoming *Spirituality and the Secular Quest* to be published by Crossroad in their World Spirituality Series.

7. See Philip Sheldrake, *Images of Holiness* (London/Notre Dame 1987), pp. 3 and 7–8.

8. Michel de Certeau, *The Mystic Fable*, vol. 1 (ET, Chicago, 1992), p. 299. The emphases are the author's.

9. See, for example, a useful essay on postmodernism by Michael Downey in a new dictionary of spirituality: Michael Downey, ed., *The New Dictionary of Catholic Spirituality* (Collegeville 1993), pp. 746–9. The language of postmodernism tends not to be very accessible, but a good summary of the issues it provokes for theology can be found in the collection of essays by Frederic B. Burnham, ed., *Postmodern Theology: Christian Faith in a Pluralist World* (New York 1989).

10. *The Way* journal for July 1996 will address in detail the relationship between postmodernism and spirituality.

11. *Studies in Spirituality* was founded in 1991 and is edited from the Titus Brandsma Institute in Nijmegen. While produced in The Netherlands and accepting articles in a number of European languages, it is predominantly published in English. It has an international board of editorial advisers.

12. A major collection of essays on the nature of modern spirituality produced by the American Academy of Religion appeared just after the first edition of this book went to press. See Bradley Hanson, ed., *Modern Christian Spirituality: Methodological and Historical Essays* (American Academy of Religion Studies in Religion no. 92, Atlanta 1990). The Society for the Study of Christian Spirituality, founded in 1992, produces a biannual *Christian Spirituality Bulletin*. On the definition and methodology of the field, see Bernard McGinn, 'The Letter and the Spirit: Spirituality as an Academic Discipline', and Sandra Schneiders, 'Spirituality as an Academic Discipline: Reflections from Experience', *Christian Spirituality Bulletin* 1/2 (Fall 1993), pp. 1–9 and 10–15 respectively. Also, the *Bulletin* 2/1 (Spring 1994) consists of three papers and the response from the 1993 conference: Walter Principe, 'Broadening the Focus: Context as a Corrective Lens in Reading Historical Works in Spirituality', pp. 1–5; Bradley Hanson, 'Theological Approaches to Spirituality: A Lutheran Approach', pp. 5–8; Sandra Schneiders, 'A Hermeneutical Approach to the Study of Christian Spirituality', pp. 9–14; Philip Sheldrake, 'Some Continuing Questions: The Relationship Between Spirituality and Theology', pp. 15–17.

13. The question of this relationship underlies all the recent writing on the method and content of the spirituality field. For some reflections on the terms of the debate, see my response 'Some Continuing Questions'

in the *Bulletin*, as note 12 above. See also my chapter, 'Spirituality and Theology', in Peter Byrne and Leslie Houlden, eds, *Companion Encyclopedia of Theology* (London 1995).

14. See, for example, Douglas Burton-Christie, 'The Literature of Nature and the Quest for the Sacred', in *Spirituality, Imagination and Contemporary Literature, The Way Supplement* 81 (Autumn 1994), pp. 4–14.

15. For example, her *Pilgrim at Tinker Creek* (London/New York 1977).

16. Garry H. Gossem, ed., *South and Meso-American Native Spirituality* (New York/London 1993).

17. Professor Bernard McGinn of the University of Chicago has undertaken a major four-volume history of western Christian mysticism, and study of how mysticism has been interpreted theologically, philosophically and comparatively, entitled 'The Presence of God'. The first two volumes have already appeared, and have established the series as one of the most significant recent projects in the field of spirituality: *The Foundations of Mysticism: Origins to the Fifth Century* (New York 1991/London 1992); and *The Growth of Mysticism: From Gregory the Great to the Twelfth Century* (New York 1994/London 1995).

18. The literature of images of sainthood has expanded considerably in recent years. See, for example, Thomas Heffernan, *Sacred Biography: Saints and Their Biographers in the Middle Ages* (New York/Oxford 1992); Renate Blumenfeld-Kosinski and Timea Szell, eds, *Images of Sainthood in Medieval Europe* (Ithaca/London 1991); Richard Kieckhefer and George Bond, eds, *Sainthood: Its Manifestations in World Religions* (Berkeley/London 1990). There has also been a growing appreciation of popular spirituality beyond specialist texts. See, for example, Miri Rubin, *Corpus Christi: The Eucharist in Late Medieval Culture* (Cambridge 1991), and the highly stimulating Part 1 of Eamon Duffy, *The Stripping of the Altars: Traditional Religion in England 1400–1580* (New Haven/London 1992). Caroline Walker Bynum has continued to write provocative and scholarly studies on the spirituality of women. See her *Holy Feast and Holy Fast: The Religious Significance of Food to Medieval Women* (Berkeley/London 1988), and *Fragmentation and Redemption: Essays on Gender and the Human Body in Medieval Religion* (New York 1992). Bynum has also recently produced a more general study of religious attitudes to the body and asceticism: *The Resurrection of the Body in Western Christendom, 200–1336* (New York 1995). Other significant contributions to the debate about the spirituality of women include Elizabeth Petroff, *Body and Soul: Essays on Medieval Women and Mysticism* (New York/Oxford 1994), and a number of essays in W. J. Sheils and Diana Wood, eds, *Women in the Church*, Studies in Church History 27 (Oxford 1990). There have also been significant new studies on individuals (including Julian of Norwich) which are too numerous to mention. We cannot overlook the contribution to religious history of the milestone five-volume general study *A History of Women in The West*, edited by Georges Duby and Michelle Perrot (Cambridge, Mass./London 1992–4).

19. There have been a number of new historical studies of the development of women's monastic life in the Middle Ages to join that by Elkins. This has done something to correct the imbalance in earlier histories (such as those by David Knowles) that largely excluded women. See, for example, Sally Thompson, *Women Religious: The Founding of English Nunneries after the Norman Conquest* (Oxford 1991). Roberta Gilchrist's *Gender and Material Culture: The Archaeology of Religious Women* (London/New York 1994) uses the theory of gender archaeology to provide a fascinating revisionist study of the lives of monastic and other religious women in England during the Middle Ages. Also, I omitted from the first edition of this book an important study of the eleventh-century monastic reform movement: Henrietta Leyser, *Hermits and the New Monasticism* (London 1984).

20. I have confined my attention to the Beguines in northern Europe, although some recent studies appear to have demonstrated their presence in Italy and Spain. This, however, is a controversial matter, because the new female community life and spirituality that appeared in the early thirteenth century differed significantly in expression between northern and southern Europe. Many authorities would continue to limit the title 'Beguines' to northern groups. See, for example, Brenda Bolton and Paul Gerrard, 'Clare in Her Time', in *Contemporary Reflections on The Spirituality of Clare, The Way Supplement* 80 (Summer 1994), pp. 42–50. For an important new study of Beguine mysticism, see Bernard McGinn, ed., *Meister Eckhart and the Beguine Mystics* (New York 1994/London 1995). For some recent translations of Beguine texts, see Ellen Babinsky, ed., *Marguerite Porete: The Mirror of Simple Souls*, Classics of Western Spirituality (New York 1993); also, *The Life of Christina Mirabilis* (1989), *The Life of Juliana of Mont-Cornillon* (no date), *The Life of Margaret of Ypres* (1990) and *The Life of Marie d'Oignes* (1993), all published in the Matrologia Latina Series by Peregrina Publishing Company, Toronto.

PART ONE

Reconsidering History

CHAPTER ONE

The Nature of History

Many of the critical questions raised throughout this book are provoked by changes of emphasis in historical study over the last few decades. Because these have not yet greatly influenced popular understandings of history, nor the study of spirituality, it seems helpful to begin by examining some common assumptions about historical knowledge and how we may need to revise them. Henry Ford, the founder of the famous automobile empire, is supposed to have said that history was bunk. The fascination with tracing 'family trees' is evidence that, on a personal level, many people do not share this dismissive attitude. We interpret the present in terms of our individual or family history. The stories of our family past feed our sense of identity because they bring us into contact with our roots. The need for an identifiable history is even more striking in groups such as the Church where tradition plays an important role. Most of us would probably say that history is 'what happened'. This assumption has two major elements. Firstly, we can have direct contact with the past. Secondly, it is possible, at least in principle, to establish 'the facts' in a relatively simple way. History books then order these facts in a proper sequence by reference to dates and periods.

Contact with the past

Do we, in fact, have direct contact with the past? Our first encounter with history is usually at the level of what is offered by historical writers, in children's stories, school textbooks or in more scholarly volumes. These accounts of history are, in reality, several steps removed from what actually 'happened'. Let us focus for a moment on an example which every English child of my generation, and many others in the English-speaking world, learnt in school. The story of the victory of the English barons over the king, and the signing of the Magna Carta in 1215, was portrayed as the origin of our democratic way of government, freedom of speech and civil liberties. In the popular understanding of the story, the noble barons were the heroes and King John was, in every way, 'a bad thing'. Such a picture was reinforced by the well-known myth of Robin Hood which characterised John as evil and unjust in contrast to his heroic brother, Richard the Lion-Heart. However, modern reassessments indicate that, in the confrontation between John and the barons, the labels 'hero' and 'villain' are less easy to place than once seemed possible. The barons were concerned to preserve traditional feudal privileges rather than to further the cause of human rights. John may have been a more effective king and Richard less attractive than traditionally thought.

The point is that the attitudes of hostile chronicles, combined with legend, had created a negative image of King John which survived until recently even in sophisticated histories. This reflected what might be called the point of view of the winning side – in this case the nobility and the Church which, under Pope Innocent III, was keen to establish its supremacy over secular rulers and which had also been in conflict with King John. Ultimately, the reputation of the king suffered from the fact that he lost – to the barons, to the Church and also, territorially, to the French who were allied to the papacy. More popularly, his image suffered in comparison to that of his more dashing crusader brother. In general, the history which is remembered, and which continues to survive in subsequent historical accounts, reflects the interests of those who possess power after the event.

A belief in direct contact with the past is undermined by the fact that historical accounts, whether contemporary chronicles or later textbooks, are always partial in two senses. They offer only part of the whole story and, at the same time, they express the values or assumptions of the person writing. The example of King John also highlights the way in which we have limited our accounts of history by assuming too readily that official records provide objective documentation. There has, consequently, been an in-built bias towards the viewpoint of the powerful, or 'the winners', and we have largely ignored the powerless, or 'losers'. Even in more scholarly writings, and however broad the historian's conception of evidence, the result is never a complete account nor a direct contact with the past. Historical accounts necessarily produce a refined, edited, and interpreted version of 'what happened'. This is true of older interpretations of King John as well as modern reassessments. They seek not merely to describe events but also, implicitly or explicitly, why they occurred, what the consequences were and what their meaning was. For 'history' on this level, hindsight and present values are crucial.

Traditional historical method was, until recently, 'teleological'. That is, it approached the past in order to explain the results that we supposed that it produced. The danger was that such a version of 'hindsight' over-emphasised elements in a story (for example of King John and the barons) which anticipated the result sometimes to the point where not only the story was misunderstood but, consequently, the result as well. However, in attempting to correct such an approach, we need great care. Historical revision may conclude that previous accounts reached conclusions for unsound reasons and yet we cannot simply *assume*, from the start, that the conclusion was undoubtedly false. All that can be said initially is that there are new questions which must be asked. We can never anticipate fully the result of such a process of revision.

In the history of spirituality there are similar problems. The spread of Latin values and Roman forms of religious life from the South has usually taken pride of place in descriptions of the development of English Christianity during the Anglo–Saxon period. The great Celtic movement of evangelisation from the North, with its own rich spiritual culture, was presented as little more than an eccentric introduction to the main story.

Furthermore, the historical accounts of spirituality also concentrated their attention on the development of relatively sophisticated ideas about the Christian life. A spirituality of ideas is inherently élitist and so the religious world of the ordinary Christian scarcely found a place in such accounts.

What has been described, up to this point, is the surface level of 'history'. If we dig a little deeper, we find a second level, that of the primary evidence. Aspects of the original historical process live on in documents, art, archeological remains and, sometimes, in collective memories or oral history. Despite its range, the evidence is never complete. Accessible history on this second level is also partial. Only parts of the whole are documented, and only certain artifacts survive. The process of history also tends to produce dominant groups and others that are subordinate. It is the values of the élites that inevitably gain greatest exposure in the records, literature and structures of their time. Relatively few people attain the status of historical figures and a limited range of happenings are deemed to be significant events. The written sources are necessarily affected by the intentions of the authors and their cultural assumptions.

It is fair to say that, in the case of documents and records, this second level of history is already *controlled* history which begins to divide and limit because of the interests of the chroniclers. For example, as those concerned with the revision of women's spiritual history have pointed out, much of our information about the religion of women in the Middle Ages comes from male biographers or chroniclers. Thus, much of what was recorded as fact, or whose significance was explained, was conceived in terms of what men understood about the spiritual and, as a consequence, admired or disliked about women.[1] More critical historians, therefore, look beyond the explicit meaning of texts. They note the assumptions or bias and, as far as they can, make allowances.

Finally, there is the primary, bedrock, level of history. This is the universal historical process ('what happened' in its broadest sense) which is the creation of all who participate in it. This total history is, in practice, never completely accessible even at the time an event occurs. No one can possibly grasp all the causes, all the inter-relationships, all the meaning. This total process is, despite the development of more refined interpretations of evidence, even less accessible to subsequent generations.

Establishing the facts

Even if direct contact with the past is not feasible, is it possible to establish 'the facts' of history in a relatively straight-forward way? The way in which we assume that the names we attach to particular events are simply factual descriptions provides an excellent starting point. For example, British school-children learnt that what happened in 1857 was The Indian Mutiny. In reality, the 'facts' are not as simple as that because the name we give to those events is an interpretation of them. Some years ago I visited a museum in India which portrayed the history of the country in a series of murals. There, the events of 1857 were described not as 'The Indian Mutiny' but as 'The First War of Independence'. To change the title of a well-known event meant that the history of India ceased to be a justification of an imperial past and became the explanation of, and basis for, an independent present. This revision was as valid, if also as limited, as the naming and, therefore, the interpretation of 1857 in traditional British school textbooks.

The problem of names or titles affects the great processes of history as well as individual events. On a recent journey by train, I overheard a young boy asking his father for help with a history quiz which he had been given at school. 'Who discovered America?' The boy replied, 'Christopher Columbus of course.' 'Correct!' said the father. But is this correct? On one level, those with a little more knowledge might want to ask what exactly it was that Columbus discovered. 'America' is a rather elastic term. Alternatively, the case for much earlier visits to North America by stray Vikings might be advanced. However, at another level, the very concept of 'discovery' is questionable. For one thing, it depends on our geographical perspective. The peoples of North and Central America already knew their own land and would have found it odd to be told that they had just been 'discovered' and, as a result, permitted to have a place in world history. Probably the native peoples would have understood the word 'conquest', or even 'destruction', better than 'discovery'. In a sense, a whole process of history, known as 'the Age of Discovery' is revealed to be not a simple fact but an artificial concept. Was there ever such a thing? That depends entirely on which set of presuppositions we work from and the (literal, geographical) position where we stand. To reduce 'what happened' to such concepts would be very limiting if not positively inaccurate.

These examples highlight the complications involved whenever historical accounts adopt conceptual categories such as 'The Indian Mutiny' or 'Discovery of America'. However, a degree of structuring seems unavoidable if we are to make the past intelligible. Some would say that we need a theory before we can give meaning to the past. This is a controversial issue which will be discussed presently. However, in religious history and spirituality we use some familiar conceptual structures, such as movements like 'the Counter-Reformation' or 'the twelfth-century Renaissance', and groupings such as 'the Rhenish mystics', the 'Christian humanists' and so on. This raises the question of whether everything in our accounts of history is equally real. For example, are Eckhart, Tauler and Suso more or less real than a concept such as 'Rhenish mysticism'? If we are historical realists, we might argue that the first are real because we know that they existed, and the latter is merely something we construct. We have established that names for events or conceptual structures are a form of interpretation. This is perfectly valid, and inevitable in historical accounts and so we cannot reject the value of structures entirely, even though we must take care to submit the presuppositions behind them to critical scrutiny lest they seriously inhibit our appreciation of 'what happened'.

On the face of it, the clearest historical facts are dates and periods. Most of us learnt at school to memorise important dates. This may have been a tedious and rather unimaginative way to learn history, but, nonetheless, it left us with a general sense of where a particular event or person fitted into the overall pattern of history, leading to the present moment. We are also used to thinking of the past in terms of centuries and periods. We can grasp what it means when someone or something is called 'medieval', and this provides us with a sense of historical distance and perspective. To divide time into manageable portions enables us to exercise a degree of control over an inexorable force, particularly because dating seems to be descriptive and objective rather than a matter of interpretation.

However, an event cannot be isolated in a simple way by providing a date for it. If we return to our memories of the schoolroom, we probably learnt that the Norman Conquest of England 'happened' in 1066. In that year, Duke William of Normandy (the Conqueror) somewhat fortuitously won a significant battle, and formally gained the English throne. However, apart from the quite complicated process which led up to 1066, the 'conquest' of England as a whole was by no means settled in one day, and on a single battlefield. Historical events exist in a continuum of time rather than in an isolated moment. People live in a continuum of events, rather than in this age or that. We also need to be aware that the sequence of events is not one-dimensional but has a structure. As the French *annales* school of historians reminds us, there is short-term time (the time span of individuals or of specific events); medium-term time (the life-span of religious, social or political organisations of which individuals are a part); and long-term time (the overall conditions of material life or states of mind in which organisations find their broad context). The practical problem is to make a plurality of time-scales co-exist intelligibly in our descriptions of a single moment of history such as 1066.

We do not merely date individual events but also package time into segments such as centuries or periods. If these are too watertight, we lose a proper appreciation of the continuities between events, the extension of movements and of their broader significance. Historians recognise that although we are bound to divide time for the sake of convenience, our attempts frequently leave us with awkward questions. How do we begin and end the time-span of such a complex phenomenon as the Reformation

22

'period'? To say that it 'began' with the posting of Luther's ninety-five theses in 1517 is a cliché of popular history which raises more questions than it answers. The time-scales we use are not merely descriptive but involve interpretation.[2]

Finally, while the questions of conceptual structures and dating are central to our understanding of 'facts', two other issues can be summarised briefly. Firstly, some historical texts present themselves as factual in a way that is questionable in modern terms. For example, medieval hagiography used the genre of 'factual' biography but contemporary historians are more interested in what such texts reveal about the religious values and presuppositions of an age.[3] Hagiographies may therefore offer some factual insights, but this does not demand that we accept as 'fact' every last, extraordinary detail. Further, the people of the past understood reality in a different way from ourselves. For example they might describe demonic possession. Are the historical 'facts' what we now believe to have been present in the past, or are they what the people of the period under examination believed to be the case? Secondly, historical accounts do not, in practice, use all the 'facts' available but select in the light of the questions we have in mind when we analyse historical events. No one has a completely open mind because we undoubtedly have unconscious assumptions, whether historical, religious or social. Historical knowledge cannot rigidly separate fact from values. In this sense, historical accounts are never purely objective in that they are not simply empirical. In order not to be arbitrary, we have to assess our assumptions and attitudes before we can come to any conclusion about the real status of historical knowledge.

Many of our common assumptions about history, and particularly the belief that we can establish 'what happened' and recover, in a straight-forward and accurate way, the reality of the past, its facts, events and personalities, is the result of an important shift in historical perspectives which took place in the nineteenth century. The movement that arose at that time in Germany, and which is known as 'historicism', gave birth to some of the most influential features of subsequent historical enquiry and to the kind of historical consciousness in which we share.

Historicism

To an extent, historicism represents a conservative reaction to the rationalism of the Enlightenment model of history, which viewed it as a story of inexorable progress, and to the French Revolution, a child of the Enlightenment, which had attempted to turn its back on the past with apparently disastrous consequences. The historicists' attempt to re-establish the past involved a notion of its inherent distance and difference from the present and yet, at the same time, a belief in the possibility of achieving objective knowledge of it. The most prominent exponent of historicism, Leopold von Ranke, was not a pure antiquarian who cut history completely adrift from purpose and usefulness. However, he did not look for simple, practical lessons from the past. He, and the other historicists, believed that each age was unique. The past was recoverable, but a record of facts or events could only have meaning if the full context or mentality of another age were reconstructed as well. Consequently, to understand the past we have to step outside our own values and assumptions in order to step inside an earlier age.

A number of the central ideas of historicism are still generally accepted in historical enquiry. Firstly, we must take the past seriously on its own terms. An unbalanced emphasis on the primacy of contemporary interests leads us to subordinate history to present meaning and significance. This is generally termed 'presentism'.[4] Secondly, we need to be aware that our present age owes its own distinctive character to the way it has grown out of those past circumstances and mentalities. Finally, proper attention to the particularity of different periods reinforces a sense that human mentalities and achievements have an extraordinary variety. Thus, the sense of possibility and potential in the present and future is broadened.

However, pure historicism also has striking weaknesses. Firstly, because it values history for its own sake and canonises the 'past in its pastness', it tends to avoid critical judgements and to accept the past simply 'as the case'. The belief that we can recover 'what happened' without any inconvenient contemporary overlay ignores the necessity, as well as the validity, of contemporary questions and horizons as sources of knowledge. Secondly, because each period is seen as unique, there was a tendency to view periods in isolation and thus to exaggerate discontinuities. For example, to view the origin of the friars as a thirteenth-century phenomenon would be to ignore the fact that the broad lay poverty-movement, which was the wider context for the emergence of the mendicant orders, began in the late eleventh and early twelfth centuries. We would gain a very limited perspective on the significance of the friars if we imprisoned ourselves within a narrow periodization. Thirdly, historicism's desire to enter into the subjective experience of protagonists of a past age is open to certain a-historical temptations. Psychological theories may be useful to historians as sources of interesting questions. However, we cannot simply explain the complexities of Luther's life and thought, for example, in terms of psychoanalytic theory without acknowledging its limited character. The absence of the 'patient' makes this approach, used in isolation, a blunt instrument and highly unreliable. Finally, historicism tends to limit the meaning of documentary or literary evidence to the authors' original intentions and to the reception of texts by an original audience.

Paradoxically, for all its attempts to free the 'objective' past from the bias of the present, the logic of thorough-going historicism produced the opposite effect. The belief in the possibility of achieving objective knowledge of the past, and of describing how things really were, involves a judgement about the nature of reality. Although historicism appeared to react against the Enlightenment, it was a child of its age when it posited a form of historical precision which was based on scientifically-grounded canons of what was real. Only those aspects of the past that were perceived as compatible with such an understanding of reality could be designated as 'what happened' or 'fact'. Assumptions which remain unacknowledged have a more powerful and insidious influence on the selection and reconstruction of the past than the honest admission of the validity, as well as the limitations, of contemporary questions. This can be seen in the historical-critical approach to Scripture in the nineteenth century, which was in many respects a product of historicism. The search for the historical Jesus, by peeling away the layers of interpretation, and by a rigorous demythologisation in pursuit of a more 'scientific' approach, tended to reject miracles, the empty tomb and even the divinity of Christ as 'inappropriate ideas' and therefore non-factual. By extension, historicism can lead to a similar reductionism in our approach to a classical spiritual text from another age.

Historical knowledge: the new history

While some aspects of historicist theory, and those approaches to history that derive from it, retain their validity, it is inadequate on its own for purposes of historical interpretation. Since the Second World War, a variety of revised approaches, collectively termed the 'new history', have emerged. These have begun to influence specialist Church history but not the study of spirituality to the same degree. They have also not yet passed into our general historical consciousness. Perhaps the greatest revolution has been in the approach to historical evidence. The minutiae of life in the past, in all its aspects, are now increasingly felt to provide the vital context for understanding traditions, personalities and theories. Reliance on single sources, or one kind of source material has been effectively questioned. Historians, above all, have learnt to be much more critical of their sources. Contemporary documentation cannot simply be taken on face value. It must be validated and then assessed in the light of particular questions. In general terms, evaluation and judgement have become more respectable.

The 'new history' also challenged the primacy of élite structures or privileged groups. Ordinary people were drawn for the first time, on their own terms, into the historians' view. The new history thus led to an interest in the retrieval of lost traditions or ideas. Every period, or historical moment, is a time of choice and thus we need to pay attention not merely to options that were actually taken, or to perspectives and values that won the day, but also to those opposing viewpoints which did not win universal acceptance. The 'new history' also marked a movement away from conceiving history purely in terms of significant individuals and towards serious consideration of groups or classes. When the history of institutional structures was studied, it became important to gauge the extent to which particular social groups participated in and influenced them, reacted to them, ignored them or were in any way affected by them.

The common assumption that 'history' is only what is documented means that its distribution is very uneven. As new groups emerge into self-consciousness, or those who have been marginalised recover their sense of identity (for example, the indigenous Christians of Latin America or the laity in the Church), they demand not only a present but also a history. As a consequence, there were also changes in methodology. Unwritten evidence was increasingly used: for example, art, or archeology, and there were also advances in the use of oral history. In general terms, one of the effects of this approach to history has been to emphasise its complexity and variety and to question the older, chronological or narrative approach. It is important, however, not to lose sight of the need to respect the particularity of the past and not to move away entirely from traditional documentary sources, even if we need to examine them in new ways.

Historical explanation: recreation and analysis

Even if we seek to portray the past on its own terms, our descriptions of 'what happened' can scarcely avoid questions of explanation. If we believe that evaluation and judgement have a legitimate place in historical enquiry, explanation will be even more central. Historical enquiry has different literary forms (for example, description, narrative and analysis), based on the different purposes of enquiry and the tension between the need to recreate the past and to interpret it. Recreation involves the reconstruction of the historical moment. Here, the attempt is to describe, and to give us some direct experience of the past, by setting the scene or evoking the spirit of the age. This has to be framed within a story or narrative form lest it be incoherent. The problem is that the motivations associated with past events are harder to grasp than their sequence and can usually only be inferred from fragmentary evidence. Equally, recreation on its own tends to treat events or periods in isolation. But the very concept of 'history' presupposes that there is a before and an after, as well as connections with other contemporary events. In practice, 'what happened?' is preliminary to 'why?' and 'with what results?' In other words, we recreate and narrate in order to explain.

Nineteenth-century historians, following von Ranke, frequently employed narrative directly as the means of explanation. But this imposes limitations on any systematic attempt to explain. Simply to place events in the correct time sequence does not in itself settle the relationship between them. That X comes before Y does not necessarily mean that X caused Y. Causation is also many-layered. To explain events involves examining all the possible causes and then placing them in some order of priority. Narrative alone cannot do this. Thus, there is also the need for analysis, and historical enquiry has become much more analytical than it was in the time of von Ranke, with a greater emphasis on the significance and inter-relationship of events.

Within historical analysis, there is a tension between what might be called the footnote approach and the overview approach to history. If we confine ourselves to a detailed mastery of primary sources our knowledge may become so fragmentary as to appear meaningless. Detailed analysis of particular moments or events is vital, but the sum-total of such details does not of itself make a history. However, when we stand back to obtain an overview we also face acute problems of interpretation. How do we combine the many strands into a coherent account? How do we determine the relative weight of this factor or that? How do we avoid over-simplification?

Overviews, or thematic studies, are particularly vulnerable to criticism because they stand at one remove from a detailed concentration on primary sources. Yet they have a vital purpose. They are perhaps one of the most fertile sources for new questions, in particular concerning explanation, which have an importance in their own right. Only within the wider context of an overall explanation of a period or movement does the detailed analysis of parts make sense. For example, a detailed knowledge of a spiritual text such as the Spiritual Exercises or the writings of one of the fourteenth-century English mystics, and the particular problems of interpretation, depends not only on an understanding of literary questions and of the mentality of the author but also on a broad sense of a period or movement as a whole.

Overviews also open up the possibility of comparison. No society or event should be viewed in isolation because, historically, they did not so exist. For example, within roughly the same period of Iberian culture, we may find it illuminating to compare the different spiritual horizons of Ignatius of Loyola and John of the Cross. Equally, we may gain some useful insights by comparing Ignatius of Loyola with Martin Luther as different responses to the problem of reform within the Church in the sixteenth century. We may indeed cross the boundaries of periods altogether and examine Dominicans and Franciscans in the thirteenth century, and the Jesuits in the sixteenth century, in terms of two key-moments in the development of ministry and a more actively engaged religious life and spirituality.[5]

Underlying the contrast between 'historicism' and the 'new history', in their approaches to historical knowledge, is the question of whether, in any sense, there is an objective history. How definite is our knowledge of the past? An important question here is whether we view history as a science. This continues to divide historians. The scientific view valued a careful observation of reality by a disinterested and passive observer. Generalisations are valid only if they flow directly and naturally from the data. Historians should avoid preconceptions and be without moral involvement in their enquiry. By contrast, others rejected these fundamental assumptions. Human events can only be understood by means of a dialogue between our contemporary horizons and values, and the intentions, feelings and mentality of the historical protagonists. Historical knowledge, therefore, is in part subjective.

Theory and the interpretation of history

Our approach to the past is moulded by our social as well as personal experience. Thus, to an extent, history is rewritten by each generation. In other words, historical interpretation involves value-judgements created by prevailing moral, religious, social or political attitudes and experiences. Present-mindedness is inevitably part and parcel of historical enquiry. To that extent, theory is implicitly involved. As I have already suggested, contemporary historians are divided over whether theory may legitimately play an explicit role in the formulation of historical hypotheses. As a matter of fact it is increasingly used, but the remaining caution is caused largely by the fact that much historical theory is derived, in varying degrees, from Marxism, and the remainder is borrowed from other disciplines, such as sociology, about which traditional historians are suspicious.

The application of explicit theory to historical enquiry is attractive for several reasons. Firstly, we face a considerable difficulty in grasping the inter-relatedness of every dimension of experience at a given time. To the degree that total history is obtainable, it is so only if we have some conception of how the various components of the 'historical moment' form a whole. Secondly, without theory it is difficult to analyse and explain the central fact of history which is change. Do major transitions in history display common features? And if so, how does change generally proceed? Thirdly, we not only have the problem of change but also of where change leads to, if anywhere. The Divine Providence model of human destiny no longer recommends itself as a *practical* historical tool (that is, history is a simple linear movement from Creation to Judgement under continual guidance of God). However, some modern historians still seek an organising form through which we can interpret human destiny by giving some overall meaning to history in itself.

There are obvious dangers in the application of theory. The clearest problem is that theory may take over from facts. It is always possible to marshal sufficient instances to support the desired pattern. The past may even be crudely ransacked or falsified for ideological purposes. Stalinism and extreme ultramontane Catholicism have a number of features in common in this respect. A more general problem is that any theory can over-simplify the irreducible diversity of particular epochs and cultures. Frequently this affects the perfectly legitimate interest in the historical origins of modern values and trends – for example, lay ministry, women's religious experience and changes in religious life. Yet theory, while it has its dangers and cannot produce *the* ultimate explanation, is productive of stimulating hypotheses and alerts us to new questions.

The historical enterprise is thus not a simple question of 'looking at the facts'. We cannot distinguish between facts 'out there' and value-judgements 'in here' (that is, within my subjective consciousness) as if facts were unquestionably objective and values always dubious or misleading. Even statements of fact presume judgement, not least that *these* facts are significant in the first place or that, for example, the events of 1857 constituted 'The First War of Independence' rather than 'The Indian Mutiny'. So, even descriptive statements move within value-judgements. History will simply become antiquarianism, and therefore an empty enterprise, unless, in some way, it is in continuity with the present and constitutive of our future. This connection with contemporary interests and values means that we inevitably select in order to interpret. It is also important to understand that values are necessary if we are to make any statement at all. It is not that there is something called factual knowledge which may or may not become distorted by interests and judgements. Rather, interests are *constitutive* of knowledge and not merely prejudices which imperil it. In other words, history is effectively dependent on our interest in it and our use of it.

In practice at least, the search for a fully objective, scientific, history which just exists apart from our interest in it or interpretation of it, which will be complete and about which there will be no more questions or issues of interpretation, is a chimera. In fact, the more we know, the less we can be certain of, the more evidence, the bigger the questions. For every side of history there is always another. All interpretations of history are partial in both senses, that is, incomplete and at the same time interest-related.

There is an obvious danger in admitting the appropriateness of contemporary perspectives. To allow our perfectly justifiable horizons and interests to have an unbalanced priority becomes 'presentism'. We have the right to ask critical questions of the past. However, the starting point for such questions must be a serious and honest attempt to contextualize the past, to establish the original context of classical spiritual texts or particular ideas and emphases. On the other hand, 'presentism' collapses the past into the present, thus refusing to let the past be the past or to acknowledge, in the process, the relativity of all facts.

If fact and value are so bound together, are we able to distinguish authentic from inauthentic history? Can we ultimately establish nothing and are we, therefore, forced to remain in a permanent state of agnosticism? There is a danger that our awareness of the impossibility of distinguishing fact from interpretation, coupled with a realisation that all interpretation is value-conditioned, may lead us merely to a critical undermining of past certainties about historical periods, figures or movements. However, my point in questioning simple understandings of 'history', 'fact' and 'time' is not to establish that we know nothing, rather it is to rehabilitate interpretation as a necessary entry point into the past.

What historians must do is to try to ensure that, in their selection and evaluation, they remain as true to the available reality of the past as possible. They must scrutinize their values to see how these relate to the enquiry they are undertaking. They should frame their interpretations as hypotheses which once again need to be tested by the evidence. And they must submit their work to the discipline of historical context. In these ways, present-mindedness and theory need not imply anything as crude as historical anachronism or falsification.

True to which past?

If being true to the past is a central value in historical enquiry, the problem is precisely which past we are talking about. Certainly, historians have a responsibility to ensure that the historical perspective that they provide assists debate rather than serves a particular ideology. However, it is open to us to retrieve aspects of the past, long forgotten and even deliberately submerged, which may speak to us once again in the present. Present perspectives may establish the questions we ask but not the answers we obtain. Some critical questions concerning the process and the use we make of history will be suggested in chapter 3 and chapter 4. However, at this point it is possible to summarise some general emphases in contemporary spirituality which relate to the question: true to which past?

Firstly, the contemporary sense of the unity and equality of the Christian call to holiness inevitably calls into question the clerical and monastic élitism that has frequently been present in spiritual traditions, at least in the Catholic tradition. So, there may be an attempt to retrieve those groups or traditions which offer some kind of historical model for lay life or for women's roles in the Christian community. Secondly, and related in some respects to the equality of Christians, there is a social perspective which will lead us to ask who lost out in history and how the process took place. Such a perspective will be concerned to examine the ways in which spiritualities encapsulate particular social, as well as religious, values. Thirdly, the Christian Church is far more aware, than hitherto, of being multi-cultural. In what ways, therefore, did particular cultural perspectives become predominant? Positively, this will enable us to pay attention to minority cultures. It will also serve, in the present, to reinforce a healthy sense of cultural and spiritual pluralism and to move us away from a eurocentric understanding of the Church. As a specific example, this perspective provides a different standpoint from which to examine such controversial historical issues as the adaptation of the Roman liturgy and Catholic spirituality, in the seventeenth century, to Chinese and South Indian culture and the eventual condemnation of this process.

A fourth dimension of contemporary Christian consciousness, which provides a crucial standpoint from which to re-examine our history, is ecumenism. This questions traditional polemical approaches to historical enquiry, and will lead us to examine more critically the ways in which we have automatically opposed Catholic and Protestant traditions thus preventing us from discerning the continuities and parallels. Finally, the contemporary interest in the wisdom of the past, as the source of insights into the life of prayer and the spiritual journey in general, means that we will need to develop an appropriate theory of interpretation in order to re-read classical spiritual texts in a helpful as well as an accurate way.

Is history relevant?

If contemporary questions provide a means of interpreting our past, that same past has frequently been employed as a framework for interpreting our present. History is often used to sustain desirable forms of social, political or religious consciousness. The emergence of the nation-state, in the later Middle Ages and early modern period, meant that a sense of national history proved a strong bond in uniting the political community and this has had some influence on religious history as well. Arguably a sense of shared history is as vital as a common language in creating a sense of national identity. Nations, such as Poland or Ireland, that have been oppressed, conquered or divided over the centuries retain a feeling of common identity through the potent force of a historical consciousness, often with strong religious overtones. A thorough revision of historical perspectives has played an important role in creating and sustaining a sense of national identity in post-colonial Africa and Asia. The state, particularly when of a totalitarian hue, has never had any doubts about the power and usefulness of history in the service of ideology. Equally, history has its dangers: to know the past is to know that things have not always been as they now are and that, presumably, they need not remain the same in the future. To know the past is also to know the limited and flawed nature of leaders and legislators. For this reason the control of history has been an important issue. The current revisionism in Soviet society is slowly revealing to the people a quite different picture of history since the 1917 Revolution. The disastrous and brutal social and economic policies under Stalin have begun to emerge from the closet. The past, for so long controlled in the name of the State, is being recovered in a new richness.

I do not wish to paint too close a comparison between the institutional Church and totalitarian states! However, the role that Church history played for so long within Christian apologetics meant that it often gave in to the temptation to offer optimistic, pious or uncritical interpretations of the past. The 'acceptable face' of the Church needed to be presented at all times in order to preserve a sense of its essentially other-worldly character.[6] Equally, each division in the fabric of Christendom, whether between East and West or between Protestant and Catholic subsequent to the Reformation, has encouraged people to interpret history, prior to the divisions, in a way that justifies their sectarian perspective. Finally, the stories of origin of particular spiritual traditions have also been susceptible to naïve or fundamentalist interpretations or even to subtle manipulation because they articulate a distinctive identity and spirit as well as furnish a source of precedents.[7]

Thus history has frequently served religious authority but, equally, the sanction of the past has sometimes been enlisted in support of dissent from the established consensus. In this context, the appeal to a more distant past has a dual role. Firstly, the recent past has presumably been controlled by those who have power. The more distant past is therefore viewed as a potent source of liberation. It may also become the symbol of some kind of original purity, prior to more recent corruptions. However, in the Christian context, the rediscovery of purity and claims to be faithful to 'real' history have a second element. Because the deeper meaning given by Christians to a series of particular historical events in first-century Palestine makes them the ultimate reference point for the significance of history as a whole, the stories of origin in Christianity play a more than ordinarily normative role. Dissenting or reformist movements, therefore, have always sought to recapture the apostolic period in some form or other.

However, we need to take seriously the fact that the motivation for dissenting or reformist spiritualities frequently involves a sense not only that the present status quo is unfaithful to Christian origins, but also a belief that it unjustly excludes certain groups. Dissent and reform do not depend solely on the finely-tuned theological sensitivities of some but on the ability of the dissenting view to capture the imagination of a wider public. The attraction of dissenting movements, therefore, lies not simply in their preaching of a purified call of the gospel but also in their capacity to liberate people from concrete burdens, or to enhance their sense of value in the here and now. Certainly, movements of Christian dissent and reform are strikingly unified throughout history by an appeal to the gospel call to discipleship (the *vita apostolica*) and sometimes to the (supposed) structures of the Early Church.

Thus, history becomes a battleground. The sanction of the past seems to be vital both to those who stand for the status quo and for those who question or subvert it. In the Church, to the same degree as in society at large, different histories contend for attention as conservatives, liberals, and radicals ground their perceptions about the identity of the Church, or the nature of the Christian life, in the authority of the past.

All of this raises the question of whether we can learn from history. Those who answer in the affirmative often see the lessons of history in one of two ways. In the one case, what has happened before guides us in our actions now. In the other, to view our present in historical perspective offers a greater sense of 'where we are' and consequently of the directions which may lie ahead. The first has rather obvious dangers. The past as a practical lesson for the present has a long pedigree, especially among those who lived consciously within a historical spiritual tradition. So, if you want to know how to be a Franciscan, simply look at the life pattern of St Francis and his early followers. The problem is that this approach shows scant respect for historical context – that of St Francis and our own. For a historical precedent to be valid, in a straight-forward way, precisely the same conditions would have to apply. Old problems or familiar possibilities, on more careful investigation, will turn out to be different because circumstances have necessarily changed, in subtle or even quite dramatic ways.

What of the second common approach to the lessons of history? Can future possibilities be discovered from the movement of history up to the present? The trouble here is that all grand designs which, in their different ways, view history in terms of destiny have elements of wishful thinking or even manipulation. While precedent and prediction cannot be entirely excluded from the usefulness of history, historical enquiry must avoid either a stress on superficial similarities between the past and the present or a tendency to manipulate the past from the point of a priori assumptions.

Although the question of historical precedent has its pitfalls, and potential naïveties, a critical use of historical analogies may be illuminating if we take care to be aware both of what is recurrent (basic values), and what is new (context and specific choices), in our comparisons. Another approach offers even greater possibilities. The popular tendency is to see historical prediction in repetitive or recurrent terms (history repeating itself). Of course, we can never say that history precisely repeats itself, if only for the reason that our actions are affected by our knowledge of what happened the first time round! However, if we view prediction in *sequential* terms this has other possibilities. Here we seek to identify past trends, their actual projection into the present, and their possible projection into the future. I say 'possible' because we are not here concerned with models of history as 'inevitable progress' or as 'the working of Divine Providence in visible form'. We must be aware of the crucial historical precedent that history is unpredictable! However, to be aware of the long-standing nature and strength of a trend which stretches forwards from the past into the present and which will have to be faced in the future has an undoubted value.

Perhaps history's claim to relevance is associated less with prediction and precedent and more with what tends to be called a 'historical perspective'. In other words, history may convey a greater awareness of what is enduring in the present and what is not. This counteracts a common tendency to take for granted everything that exists in our present experience. A healthy sense of contingency, reinforced by history, makes it easier to estimate how

35

easily or otherwise change can be brought about and how helpful or otherwise change may be.[8]

History in the Church

These are general issues but, in the context of spirituality, a further problem remains. Many Christians appear to be impatient with history altogether. I think that this is not merely a contemporary phenomenon but is part of an inherent tension in the very nature of the Christian community and its self-understanding. In a sense, the Church exists at the intersection of two worlds – the world of contingent reality or events and the world of the transcendent. For the believer, the Church is never *purely* a sociological fact. The problem with this tension is that it can easily overbalance in the direction of the transcendent. For, it is uncomfortable to be caught between an understanding of history as touched by Divine Providence and the ambiguity of human events. As a consequence, we may begin to see the Church as autonomous, as something that cannot be compared to any other kind of historical reality. The history of the Church thus becomes a special case that is obedient to laws of its own. The Christian community, and the spiritual traditions that arise within it, act upon, and are sometimes in conflict with history but history does not act in or upon the Church.

In fact, the prevailing attitude until recent years was that while history might be a source for theology this was so only in the subordinate sense that it provided material for theological argumentation. The fundamentals of Christian faith, based on revelation rather than natural knowledge, followed a law of their own, characterized by assent to an external authority. History, insofar as it was useful, was employed for largely apologetic purposes. That is, history was really the proof of what was already known. This reflected a generally negative judgement on the process of modern history which was seen as corrupt. Many of the older histories of spirituality firmly reflected these standpoints. A recent review of a book about *Opus Dei* notes that the subordination of historical facts to orthodoxy involves the danger that facts, such as the dating of spiritual writings, may be changed to suit currently perceived needs. 'The process of becoming is irrelevant. It is the final product that matters and that is timeless. It is divine and thus eternal. It has always been there. Why worry about dates?'[9]

The turning point in the Roman Catholic attitude to history came with Pope John XXIII and with the Second Vatican Council. Pope John's use of the phrase 'signs of the times', and its repetition in Council documents, was highly significant. It constituted a *recognition* of history – that every historical moment has a dynamic of its own which is of value and is a place where the imminent presence of the Kingdom of God may be perceived. History is not an accidental or extraneous fact but is constitutive of the salvation that Christians proclaim. This fundamental change in the approach to history had several implications which are relevant to our study of spirituality. Firstly, the recognition of history and the location of faith within it, rather than alongside it or in opposition to it, meant a renewal of true historical memory rather than mere adaptation. Secondly, a respect for history makes it impossible to reduce diversity and plurality to certain universal formulae. Finally, no separation is possible between religious history and the history of the world at large. We can no longer use the categories which help to distinguish between the sacred and the profane.[10]

There is also a pragmatic, pastoral reason which suggests that history is not particularly relevant. There seems to be such a pressing need to concentrate on the Church, and its proclamation of the Christian message in the here and now, that to hark back to the past is a distraction. However, the contemporary weariness with history has deeper roots in society at large. Firstly, rapid social changes, and the decline of traditional communities, have broken most people's living bonds with the past and with tradition. Secondly, there appears to be a positive desire to break free from history, which is perceived as a conservative force, in order to create a more rational society. We need to work out our future, untrammelled by the tiresome burden of a historical consciousness. These sentiments are reflected in parts of the Christian community as much as in wider society. However, an orientation towards the present and the future demands a sense of the past. Without a consciousness of the past we cannot have a sense of time – 'there is no future without history.'[11] An account of the past, as we have seen, is essential to the life of any culture. Stories are fundamental because without storytelling we put ourselves out of contact with the basic realities in our world. In other words, it is only through stories that we can situate and understand our existence in time. To be human is to be part of a story and to be Christian is to recognise a story within a story.

37

Notes
1. See Caroline Walker Bynum, 'Religious Women in the Later Middle Ages' in Jill Raitt and John Meyendorff, eds, *Christian Spirituality: High Middle Ages and Reformation* (London/New York 1987), pp. 136–7.
2. The problem of how to divide periods, with particular reference to the placing of Reformation spirituality alongside that of the High Middle Ages, is addressed in the introduction to Raitt, *Christian Spirituality*. An example of how the adoption of a particular time-scale may reinforce a specific interpretation of events is provided by a recent history of the English Catholic community by Edward Norman, *Roman Catholicism in England from the Elizabethan Settlement to the Second Vatican Council*, Oxford/New York 1985. To begin with the Elizabethan Settlement emphasises discontinuity with the pre-Reformation Church and new beginnings. To end with the *calling* of the Second Vatican Council would seem to coincide with the author's dislike of tendencies in the Church since the Council.
3. For example, see D. Weinstein and R. Bell, *Saints and Society: The Two Worlds of Western Christendom, 1000–1700*, Chicago 1982.
4. For example, see John Tosh, *The Pursuit of History* (London/New York 1988), pp. 119–20.
5. For example, see John O'Malley, 'Priesthood, Ministry and Religious Life: Some Historical and Historiographical Considerations', *Theological Studies* 49 (1988), pp. 231–48.
6. See John Kent, *The Unacceptable Face: The Modern Church in the Eyes of the Historian* (London 1987), ch. 1.
7. See Philip Endean, 'Who do you say Ignatius is? Jesuit fundamentalism and beyond', *Studies in the Spirituality of Jesuits*, 19:5 (1987).
8. Readers who wish to explore further some of the ideas in this chapter may find the following volumes on the theory of history or on historiography helpful: Michael Stanford, *The Nature of Historical Knowledge* (Oxford/New York 1987) identifies the structures involved in history and how they relate. He also examines the role of models in historical understanding and the function of historiography. Tosh, *The Pursuit of History*, is the best short introduction for the general reader to the aims and methods of modern history that I have come across. Ernst Breisach, *Historiography: Ancient, Medieval and Modern* (Chicago 1983) provides a comprehensive treatment of the history of 'ideas about history' and historical interpretation; see chapter 15 onwards for the development of theories about historical enquiry from Ranke to the present day.
9. See Giuseppe Ruggieri, 'Faith and History' in Giuseppe Alberigo, Jean-Pierre Jossua and Joseph A. Komonchak, eds, *The Reception of Vatican II* (ET, Washington DC 1987), pp. 92–5; see also the review by Vladimir Felzmann in *The Month* (December 1989), p. 491.
10. Ruggieri, 'Faith and History', pp. 95–104.

11. For some comments on the contemporary liberation from historical consciousness and its implications for a necessary reorientation of Church history, see Anton Weiler, 'Church History and the Reorientation of the Scientific Study of History', *Concilium* 7:6 (1970), pp. 13–32.

CHAPTER TWO

What is Spirituality?

Spirituality, as an area of study, must be capable of definition. If it has no conceptual limits, effectively it means nothing. In recent years the criticism has sometimes been levelled at spirituality that it is an artificial entity that relies for its existence on a variety of other disciplines without having anything that it can call its own, or that it 'enjoys an unlimited wealth of resources but possesses no tools for getting those resources organised'.[1] Undoubtedly a cursory glance at the different kinds of writing which appear under the label 'spirituality', whether popular or more scholarly, reveals that it may cover history, psychology and theology as well as devotional works. It appears that spirituality is one of those subjects whose meaning everyone claims to know until they have to define it. At the very least, contemporary spirituality has emerged as a cross-disciplinary subject which, on the face of it, has considerable problems of coherence.

The reference to 'contemporary' spirituality highlights an important issue. Throughout Christian history, 'spirituality' has changed shape, often subtly but sometimes substantially. The word itself, as we shall see, has a relatively short pedigree. Our understanding of what the word broadly seeks to express (that is, the theory and practice of the Christian life) has evolved as individuals and historical or cultural environments change. Because our thinking about God, Church and the human person necessarily develops under the influence of theology as well as human knowledge and historical events, every generation has to redefine what precisely spirituality is meant to encompass. The approach of traditional ascetical-mystical theology, or spiritual theology, over the last hundred years or so implied an agreed theological language in reference to the Christian life which no longer applies. The universal categories of the old theology textbooks were based largely on an approach to the truths of the Christian faith that was framed within logical and rigorously constructed theses. In other words, theology was a stable body of knowledge, rich in the tradition of the past and secure enough to answer the questions of the present and future.

This detached, and a priori, approach to doctrine gave birth to a similarly structured theory of the spiritual life which was separated from the core of human experience and consequently was largely alienated from, for example, nature, the body and the feminine.

In recent decades, there has been a paradigm shift in the general approach to theology towards a greater reflection on human experience as an authentic source of divine revelation. Not surprisingly, this has brought about substantial changes in the way that the study of the Christian life has been conducted and, in particular, has facilitated a movement from the static concept of 'spiritual theology' to the more fluid 'spirituality'. If the frontiers of theology increasingly seek articulation in a process and method that is experiential, spirituality has followed suit by becoming more of a dialectical tension. On the one hand, there is the historical concreteness of revelation in Jesus and subsequent Christian tradition, and, on the other, there is the personal assimilation of salvation in Christ by each person within changing historical, cultural and social circumstances that demand new approaches to Christian conduct.

As a result of these shifts of perspective, the realisation has emerged that specific spiritual traditions are initially embodied in people rather than doctrine and grow out of life rather than from abstract ideas. Thus they may be described as *secular-dialogic* – secular because they take the everyday world as the proper starting place for spiritual experience and reflection; dialogic because spiritual theory and practice operate on the frontier between contemporary experience and the tradition and do not simplistically apply the latter as the measure of the former.[2] In short, part of the contemporary problem with defining 'spirituality' is associated with the fact that it is not a single, transcultural, phenomenon but is rooted within the lived experience of God's presence in history – and a history which is always specific. Indeed, our basic understanding of what is 'spiritual' and what is 'the Christian life' depends, in part at least, on particular experiences rather than merely on a theological language given for all time.

I propose, first of all, to survey briefly the history of the word 'spirituality'. Then the way will be open for us to examine how the theory and practice of Christian living (or what we nowadays refer to as spirituality) has been differently understood and defined over the centuries. Because it is difficult to define 'spirituality as such' in abstract terms, apart that is from historical questions and attention to changes in theological presuppositions, the remainder of this chapter as a whole may be understood as a discussion of what spirituality is. However, the final section, 'From spiritual theology to spirituality' offers a brief discussion of contemporary approaches to questions of definition and a summary conclusion.

The history of the term 'spirituality'

The word 'spirituality' is used so frequently nowadays that it comes as a surprise to find that its pedigree is very short both in theological and secular writing.[3] A comparison of *The Catholic Encyclopedia*, published between 1912–15, with the revised *New Catholic Encyclopedia* of the 1970s is revealing. In the first there are no references to 'spirituality', while in the second there are eight articles that employ the word. Secular usage, however, remains conservative. In the *Oxford Dictionary*, and in the *Websters International Dictionary* of 1961, six meanings are given. Five of these do not correspond to 'spirituality' as a religious area of study: three definitions refer to incorporeal beings or volatility, and two to the obsolete social class of 'persons spiritual', that is, ecclesiastics. The sixth definition, while related to the contemporary religious meaning, is firmly dualistic: the condition of being spiritual, or regard for things of the spirit as opposed to material interests.

The Latin root of the word 'spirituality', *spiritualitas*, attempts to translate the Greek noun for spirit, *pneuma*, and its adjective *pneumatikos* as they appear in the New Testament Pauline letters. Thus, 'to be united to Christ is to enter into the sphere of the Spirit' (1 Cor. 6, 17), or 'faith in the Lord is from and in the Spirit' (1 Cor. 2, 10f.). This is not the place to enter into debate about more complex issues of Pauline scholarship. However, at the risk of simplification, it is important to grasp that, in Pauline theology, 'Spirit' and 'spiritual' are not contrasted with 'physical' or 'material' (for which the Greek *soma*, in Latin *corpus*, is the root) but rather with *all that is opposed to the Spirit of God* (for which the word *sarx*, in Latin *caro*, is used). What is opposed to the Spirit may as well be the mind or the will as the body or material reality. The contrast that emerges is therefore between two ways of life or attitudes to life. The 'spiritual' is what is under the influence of, or is a manifestation of, the Spirit of God. A dualistic contrast between 'spiritual' and 'physical', or body and soul, is not part of the Pauline understanding of the human person or of created reality in general. There is therefore no justification for using the Pauline contrast as the basis for a denial of the flesh or a rejection of materiality as some classical Christian spirituality subsequently did. The 'spiritual person' (e.g. 1 Cor 2, 14–15) is *not* someone who turns away from material reality but rather someone in whom the Spirit of God dwells.[4]

In fact the abstract Latin noun *spiritualitas* (spirituality), as opposed to the adjective *spiritualis* (spiritual), did not make its appearance until the fifth century. A letter once ascribed to St Jerome exhorts the reader so to act as to advance in 'spirituality' (*ut in spiritualitate proficias*). As the context is living within the power of the Holy Spirit this continues to reflect the basic theology of the Pauline letters. The reference to life in the Spirit is constant in further usage of the word up to the twelfth century.

It was the influence of a new philosophical trend in theology, known as scholasticism, which began in the twelfth century, that led to a sharper distinction between spirit and matter. The word 'spiritual' began to be applied to intelligent creatures (that is, humankind), as opposed to non-rational creation. Thus it lost its Pauline moral sense and took on a meaning more radically opposed to corporeality. Here, then, lie the intellectual roots of that disdain for the body that sometimes appeared in later spiritual writing. However, the new meaning of 'spirituality' did not completely replace the former Pauline emphasis. In the thirteenth century the two meanings stood side by side. Thus Thomas Aquinas used both the Pauline and the anti-material senses. A third juridical sense, 'spirituality' as the clerical estate, also came into being at this time and, from the thirteenth to sixteenth centuries, is in fact the most frequent usage.

It was only in the seventeenth century that the word became once again established in France in reference to the spiritual life. In a positive sense it was used to express a personal, affective relationship with God. However, this new meaning was also used pejoratively of enthusiastic or quietistic movements and here it was contrasted with words such as 'devotion', which seemed to preserve a proper emphasis on human co-operation. For example Voltaire used the word in his violent attacks on the 'salon mysticism' of Madame Guyon and Fénelon, which appeared too refined, rarified and separated from ordinary Christian life. In fact a variety of words were used in the seventeenth and eighteenth centuries to express life in the Spirit: 'devotion' in Francis de Sales or the Anglican mystic William Law; 'perfection' in John Wesley and the early Methodists; 'piety' among Evangelicals. The word 'spirituality' virtually disappeared from the religious and theological vocabulary of Roman Catholic circles in the early eighteenth century and this undoubtedly had a great deal to do with a suspicion both of religious enthusiasm and quietism. In the nineteenth century the use of the word 'spirituality' was confined mainly to free religious groupings outside the mainline Churches.

In the early decades of the present century, 'spirituality' once again appeared among Roman Catholics in France and then passed into English through translations of French writings. The use of 'spirituality' was closely tied to the debate concerning the nature of the spiritual life in itself. Those who saw a continuity between the 'ordinary' and 'extraordinary' (that is, mystical) dimensions of Christian living preferred the word 'spirituality' because of its comprehensiveness. Its increased use was also associated with attempts to distinguish between dogma and the study of the spiritual life as well as with an increasing emphasis on religious consciousness and the experiential. The foundation of the much respected *Revue d'Ascetique et de Mystique* in 1920, and the beginning of the continuing *Dictionnaire de spiritualité* in 1932 further established the respectability of the term. In the years after the Second Vatican Council, the theological dictionary *Sacramentum mundi*, and its one-volume popular edition, included a comprehensive article on the subject. More recently a dictionary and a general introduction to the subject have been published in English as the result of ecumenical collaboration.[5]

The history of 'spirituality', as a subject for reflection

Precisely because the word 'spirituality', in its present sense, has a relatively short history, we are faced with a problem of 'translation' when we attempt to explore how spirituality was viewed in different periods of Christian history. What precisely should we look for and how can we avoid an unhelpful imposition of contemporary assumptions on the evidence we find? If we look back merely over the last hundred years, it soon becomes apparent that 'spirituality' is not simply coterminous with older concepts such as 'spiritual theology' or 'ascetical-mystical theology'. If we extend our exploration further into the past, we will soon realise that defined concepts of any kind with regard to 'the spiritual life', let alone with reference to a distinct discipline, have a limited history. Translation, therefore, is not merely a question of looking for terminology equivalent to 'spirituality' in different ages.

Yet to write in any way about 'spirituality' in the history of the Christian tradition means that we must have some working model or framework for interpretation. I would suggest that what the word 'spirituality' seeks to express is the conscious human response to God that is both personal and ecclesial. In short, 'life in the Spirit'. Within this simple working definition, we may then approach particular periods with a number of questions in mind. Was there in fact a body of literature that dealt specifically with the 'spiritual' life? More broadly, how was the relationship between the intellectual, affective and ethical dimensions of Christian existence viewed and was there, in practice, a distinction between what we now think of as doctrine, spirituality and ethics? This necessarily brief overview will be limited to three major periods: the patristic, the High Middle Ages in the West, and finally the (mainly Roman Catholic) concern for an explicit theology of the spiritual life in the period from the late nineteenth century to Vatican II. I will also consider some particular emphases in the Anglican tradition and point, in broad terms, to the major differences in approach between the Eastern Orthodox tradition and that of the West.

The patristic period

There is disagreement about how long this period may be considered to have lasted. Some would limit it to the earliest centuries of the Christian era – so, for example, the Protestant tradition has tended to accept the Council of Chalcedon in 451 C.E. as an approximate end. The Eastern Orthodox would include such figures as Gregory Palamas who lived from 1296–1359. Others use the term, somewhat broadly, to describe the whole period up to the development of the 'new theology' of scholasticism in the West in the twelfth century. While we may feel that such a broad definition of the term 'patristic' raises awkward questions, there is some validity in it, at least as far as the general *style* of theology in the West is concerned. Until the rise of scholasticism, 'life in the Spirit' continued to be viewed as something which was applicable to all the baptised, even though there was already a *de facto* division between 'states of life' in the Church. Theology was also conceived as a unity to which later divisions (into, for example, doctrine, ethics and spirituality) were entirely foreign. The unifying feature was the Bible, and theology was generally what we nowadays think of as biblical theology – that is to say, an exegetically-based interpretation of Scripture aimed at producing

45

both a fuller understanding of Christian faith and a deepening of the Christian life in all its dimensions.

Thus, patristic theology encapsulates an idea of Christian knowledge in which biblical exegesis, speculative reasoning and mystical contemplation are fused into a synthesis. Because patristic theology was primarily a way of looking at the Bible, the most common written genre was scriptural commentary. The 'Fathers' did not neglect a methodical study of texts within the limits of their time, but their interest was primarily theological and their theology, while rigorous, was fundamentally pastoral. In other words, they placed the Bible in the context of the Christian life and their theology was involved in the life of the Church.

The patristic period, in the limited sense of the early Christian centuries, was a formative time both for the fundamentals of doctrine and for what has been called 'mystical theology'. It is no accident, therefore, that the two aspects of Christian knowledge are intimately bound up with each other. 'The basic doctrines of the Trinity and Incarnation, worked out in these centuries, are mystical doctrines formulated dogmatically.'[6] In other words, 'mystical theology' aimed to provide a context for the direct apprehension of God who is revealed in Christ and within us as the Spirit. Doctrinal theology attempted to incarnate these apprehensions in precise and objective language which in turn inspired a mystical understanding of the God who has been revealed. Thus the polemical writings of this period, for example, should not be separated from the homilies and scriptural commentaries. A more fruitful approach would be to study the 'mysticism' of the Fathers as the very *heart of their theology*.[7]

When we talk of the 'mystical theology' of this period, we must be careful not to confuse it with the later medieval fascination in the West with subjective experience or with the development of a detailed itinerary for the spiritual journey. Patristic 'mysticism' is neither abstract nor systematic. It refers to the personal life of the Christian who knows God as revealed in Christ by belonging to the fellowship of the 'mystery'. This means the mystery of Christ as expressed in the Bible and the liturgy as well as in personal Christian living. Living the mystery begins with our incorporation into Christ in baptism and comes to fruition in us through the sacramental life and by growth in virtue. In this sense, all believers are mystics in that they are plunged into the mystery of Christ.

In the late fifth or early sixth century, this fundamental insight flowed together with certain Neo-Platonic elements in the writings

46

of a theologian commonly known as Pseudo-Dionysius who, for many centuries, was thought to be the Pauline convert known as Denis (or Dionysius) the Areopagite. However, even though this author does appear to offer a 'mystical theology' that is closer to later western emphases, he in fact sums up the patristic tradition. His *Mystical Theology* was not concerned with enumerating the means towards spiritual progress or with the technicalities of mystical union but rather explored the nature of the soul's surrender to God as the person passed beyond sign and concept to be fully grasped by the mystery of love and so transformed. The later interest in subjective experience is not present, for 'the mystery' is still the objective fact of God in Christ into which all are drawn through Scripture and liturgy. To take the writer's *Mystical Theology* out of the context both of his other writings and of his overall theological horizons would be to ignore the fact that he continued the general patristic understanding of 'mystery' and 'mysticism'.[8]

What is the context within which the Fathers created their synthesis? There seem to be four important factors. First of all, the general setting for the spiritual message of the Fathers is the atmosphere created by the doctrinal polemics of the early centuries, as the Christian community worked out the central features of its understanding of God, Christ and redemption. It is these same Fathers whose style of theology chiefly contributed to the Orthodox formulation of the data of faith. So, for example, Athanasius' rejection of the Arian view of salvation may appear biased in some respects, but it was the medium through which he became a champion of the renewed doctrine of the incarnation and its spiritual implications. It is Augustine's refutation of Pelagian ethics which was the medium for the forceful exposition of his own spirituality.

Secondly, nearly all of the major writers were bishops. Therefore, it was entirely natural that their theology should be involved in the life of the Church. In a real sense, all of their theology was pastoral – that is to say, for the upbuilding of the community. Their pastoral work put them in contact with the life of ordinary Christian communities. Preaching was understood as the action of the living Word of God in the congregation. So the explanation of the sacraments had a privileged place in their teaching.

Thirdly, a large proportion of the writers had been monks or were responsible for encouraging the development of celibate community life (for example, John Chrysostom, Basil, Jerome and Augustine). It is not surprising, therefore, that they saw theological speculation and contemplation as closely associated nor that they placed a strong emphasis on the Christian life as a call to holiness and on themes drawn from the ascetical trends of their time.

Finally, the intellectual pattern of the patristic theologians was necessarily forged, in part, by their social origins and education. In fact, apart from Athanasius and Augustine, all the outstanding spiritual and theological leaders seem to have been born into the élite classes and all were men. So their spirituality which was inherited and relied upon by succeeding generations for almost a thousand years needs to be relocated within its social milieu – that is, the estates of landowners or the sophisticated upper-class circles of the leading cities of the Roman Empire. In practice, this meant a grafting on to the biblical vision of Christianity of the humanistic values and traditional philosophical attitudes of the contemporary upper-class and male élites.[9]

The High Middle Ages

In the West, from the seventh to the twelfth centuries, theology developed almost exclusively within the confines of male religious houses. Although one might expect some interest in spirituality as a familiar area of experience and therefore reflection, in practice the patristic synthesis continued to dominate. There seems little evidence, from the sources, for any interest in mysticism as a subjective experience, or in the kind of spiritual-mystical states which dominated the lives of many saints as well as the treatises of the High and late Middle Ages.[10] The monastic style of theology, as it continued until overtaken by that of the schools from the twelfth century onwards, drew its inspiration from the traditional meditative reading of Scripture, or *lectio divina*, and monastic liturgy. Indeed, it was this fact that led the new breed of thinkers to criticise the proponents of the old theology. That is, that their theological method was limited to reading, reflecting and commenting on traditional sources. In contrast, the new theologians were concerned to develop a more systematic and precise method of research based upon the increasing availability of the Greek philosophy of antiquity. So the twelfth century, and even more strikingly the thirteenth, witnessed the birth of a more 'scientific' understanding of the theological enterprise.[11]

Until the twelfth century, therefore, what we might call 'spiritual theology' or 'mystical theology' had continued, in the main, to appear in the context of collections of homilies or scriptural and patristic commentaries. There were some exceptions to this general rule. Firstly, some writings appeared that were associated specifically with religious life, particularly with the new monastic or canonical communities which arose in the eleventh and twelfth centuries. These promoted a series of reflections on the way to God appropriate to reformed religious life. For example, there were the *Customs* of Guigo I composed for the Grande Chartreuse during the years 1121–28 as well as his *Reflections* on the interior life of the solitary. There were also Cistercian texts, such as the *Carta Caritatis* of Citeaux in 1114 and St Bernard's *Apologia* for the Cistercian emphasis on detachment and spiritual simplicity. Secondly, there were a small number of treatises on specifically spiritual topics which, however, also came into existence predominantly within the context of monastic renewal. For example, Guigo II of Chartreuse produced the *Scale of Perfection* which was a fairly systematic approach to the traditional monastic *lectio divina*. William of St Thierry, a Benedictine turned Cistercian, wrote his *Letter to the Brethren of Mont-Dieu* (often known as the *Golden Epistle*) for the Carthusians but it also encapsulates a vision of mystical theology. Although St Bernard wrote on prayer and asceticism, and saw his teaching as valid for all Christians, we need to remember two things: that his spiritual doctrine cannot be separated from his overall theology, which is all of a piece; that he took for granted that the monastery was the best place to put his teaching into practice. He remains, as Jean Leclercq describes him, essentially a *doctor monasticus*.[12]

From the twelfth century onwards, writing on the spiritual life began to take new directions as the result of several factors. Firstly, there was the gradual separation of considerations about the spiritual life from the rest of theology although this process took some time. This related to the fact that theology as a whole began to be organised into its different components. For example, in the thirteenth century, St Thomas Aquinas (who tried to retain the unity between loving contemplation and theological speculation) divided his *Summa theologiae* into parts. The first dealt with God as first principle, the second with God as the 'end' of creation, the final part with the Incarnate Word as the way to that 'end'. In other words, he effectively established the classical scholastic divisions of theology into dogma and moral theology. Most of what he had to say about the Christian life appeared in the second part as an aspect of moral theology.[13] Secondly, there was a recovery of interest in the mystical theology of Pseudo-Dionysius.

A combination of these two factors bore fruit in the writings produced by the school of theology associated with the Canons Regular at St Victor in Paris, especially Hugh of St Victor and Richard of St Victor, which exercised such an influence on subsequent directions in medieval spiritual theory. Richard of St Victor, in particular, seemed equally at home with speculation and contemplation and made a distinct spiritual theology his speciality. He condensed his spiritual doctrine especially into two works, *Benjamin minor* and *Benjamin major*, which describe the journey of the soul towards contemplation. Although, like Hugh, he was influenced by Scripture, Richard and his disciples in the Victorine school increasingly opened the way to an emphasis on the teachings of Pseudo-Dionysius as the yardstick by which to judge the spiritual and specifically mystical way of life. Some commentators would now consider this emphasis to be unbalanced and, in any case, to be based on a selective reading and understanding of Pseudo-Dionysius, taken out of context. Richard had considerable subsequent influence, not least on St Bonaventure's *Journey of the Mind/Soul into God*, and the fourteenth-century English text, *The Cloud of Unknowing*.[14]

A third factor was the growth of affective mysticism and subjective mystical experiences and the birth of a new literary genre based upon these. The shift of emphasis in medieval mysticism away from participation in the objective mystery of Christ towards the experiences of *mystics*, as an identifiable group, was clearly, in part, a result of the interest in Pseudo-Dionysius. However, there seem to be other reasons for this development. Some medievalists have noted the emergence, from about the twelfth century onwards, of a new religious sensitivity of which practical, experiential mysticism was merely the most marked expression. The major intellectual and cultural movement, known as the 'twelfth-century Renaissance', which divides the early from the High Middle Ages also involved a shift of feeling and sensitivity which was at least as important as its new intellectual content. Peter Dinzelbacher, for example, writes of 'the nearly synchronous discovery of divine and of human love as expressed in experienced mysticism on the one hand and courtly love on the other'. In general terms, the twelfth century witnessed a striking increase in the cultivation of the theme of love both in religious circles and in secular culture. The degree to which the latter influenced religious writing or developments in mysticism cannot be settled definitively. Whatever the case, a preoccupation with the romantic love of men and women, its emotions and gentle expression, was encouraged by the poetry and song of troubadors, by the Arthurian myths and other romances. At the same time, love became a central theme for religious writers, particularly in the new Cistercian order. Many, like St Bernard, turned their attention to the Old Testament book, the Song of Songs, as a contemplative text which offered a ready expression for a spirituality of intimacy. The Song of Songs became a major source of imagery for mystics and writers of mystical theology.[15] Other medievalists have concentrated their attention on an increasing interest in the individual and in the realm of subjective feelings where individuality was most apparent. However, this needs careful qualification. The individual, in the modern sense of a unique person in isolation from group membership, was not discovered at this time. Yet there does seem to have been a new sense of *the self*, or of the inner mystery and 'inner human landscape'.[16] The development of spiritual guidance was another phenomenon associated both with the rise of affective mysticism and with the proliferation of new forms of Christian life, eremitical or community-orientated. Several important texts on the mystical way, such as *The Cloud of Unknowing*, were written (or purported to be) as treatises by directors for those under their guidance. Much of the writing which is known as the Rhineland school of mysticism arose from the developing ministry of guidance by Dominican friars among communities of contemplative women.[17]

A further factor, in the growth of interest in a distinct body of knowledge associated with the spiritual life, was the gradual systematization of meditation and prayer. Although people such as John of Fécamp and St Anselm, in the eleventh century, produced collections of meditations, these were still aimed at providing material for traditional monastic *lectio divina*, or free-flowing ruminative and prayerful reading of Scripture. There was no attempt to be methodical. It was really the Canons of St Victor in the twelfth century, already noted for their promotion of the influence of Pseudo-Dionysius, who tried to describe and formalize meditation, as one of the activities of prayer, with much greater precision than the monastic tradition up to that date. This gradually led to several ways of classifying meditation which became more and more systematic but which, as yet, did not include a *method* in the strict sense. However, it was as a result of these distinctions and schemes that there later developed the interest in methods of prayer and meditation.[18] Writings on methods of prayer rapidly increased, from the fourteenth century onwards, in the context of the movement of spiritual renewal in Germany and the Low Countries known as the *devotio moderna*. Its leading figure, Gerard Groote, composed a systematic treatise on 'the four kinds of things to be meditated'. Other representatives of this movement, such as Florent Radewijns, Gerard of Zutphen and Jan Mombaer, further developed the 'science' of meditation and structured prayer, arranging it into groups of exercises day by day, week by week and month by month. This tradition of methodical prayer gave rise to a considerable literature over the next few centuries – not merely in the Roman Catholic Church but, after the Reformation, in some Reformed communities as well.[19]

In summary, the period from the twelfth century onwards in the West saw a process of development in the approach to the spiritual life which may be characterized as one of separation and division. There was, first of all, a division of spirituality from theology, of affectivity from knowledge. Secondly, there was a gradual limitation of interest to interiority or subjective spiritual experience. In other words, spirituality became separated from social praxis and ethics. And finally, although it has been touched upon only indirectly, there was a separation of spirituality from liturgy, the personal from the communal, expressed most graphically by a new attention to the structures of personal prayer and meditation. The practical context, of course, for the late-medieval believer was not to face God in isolation, but through communal experience, for example in the numerous religious confraternities. Through these divisions and separations, an interest developed in specific experiences and activities: prayer, contemplation and mysticism. This was increasingly linked to theories about spiritual progress and growth. And growth was conceived more and more in terms of ascent, whereby the active life was merely a preparation for the contemplative and was thus viewed as a 'lower' way. By the end of the Middle Ages, the 'spiritual life' had increasingly moved to a marginal position in relation to culture as a whole. A more internalized, personal religious practice assumed an existence of its own and therefore demanded a new, specialized language.

Towards a systematic spiritual theology

To some extent the division between a 'science' of the spiritual life and doctrine or ethics, begun in the later Middle Ages, was already well-entrenched by the sixteenth and seventeenth centuries. We only have to contrast the approaches of Thomas Aquinas and

Bonaventure, on the one hand, and the Carmelites Teresa of Avila and John of the Cross, Ignatius of Loyola and Francis de Sales, on the other, to realise that, while the latter did not use the precise terms 'ascetical' or 'mystical' theology, they certainly showed clear signs of subscribing to a new discipline, separated from academic theology.

It was the intense interest in the life of Christian perfection that developed in the course of the seventeenth century, especially in France, that led to this becoming an object of detailed study in the eighteenth and nineteenth centuries. It appears that the Jesuit Giovanni Battista Scaramelli (1687–1752), with his *Direttorio ascetico* (1752) and *Direttorio mistico* (1754), was the first to establish the titles of 'ascetical' and 'mystical' theology in a way that subsequently became firmly established in Roman Catholic circles. During the following hundred and fifty years or so the vocabulary of 'Christian perfection' stabilized and a field defined as 'spiritual theology' became well-established. This was classically divided into ascetical theology, which dealt with the form and progress of the Christian life up to the beginnings of passive contemplation, and mystical theology which analysed further stages up to mystical union.

The approach of the manuals of ascetical and mystical theology was to seek to reduce the study of the Christian life to manageable categories, precise distinctions and reliable definitions. This accorded with the static approach to theology in general which applied during the period up to the Second Vatican Council. The method used was primarily deductive because divine revelation and rational knowledge were assumed to be its principal sources. Unless universal principles governed the study of the spiritual life it could not claim to be scientific, within a scientific theology. The classical works of this genre tended to be divided between 'principles' and 'applications'. Although defended as a distinct branch of theology, spiritual theology was in practice subordinate to dogmatic theology, from which it derived its principles, and was frequently thought of as a subdivision of moral theology. The latter was primarily concerned with what was 'of obligation' for all Christians, and the subdivision of spiritual theology went on to discuss what was 'additional'.

There were, in fact, a large number of different manuals of spiritual theology in this period. Perhaps the most familiar were those written by A. A. Tanquerey (the most common textbook in Roman Catholic seminaries in the period before Vatican II), J. de Guibert and R. Garrigou-Lagrange.[20] There was a difference of opinion with regard to whether the spiritual life was fundamentally a unity or not. In the debate about the distinction or continuity between the 'ordinary' (ascetical) way of Christian living and the 'extraordinary' (mystical) way, Tanquerey and Garrigou-Lagrange may be taken as representatives of the two contrasting views. For Tanquerey there was a fundamental division between ordinary growth in the moral life and the extraordinary gifts of mystical prayer. Ordinary life passed through stages, in a gradual progression towards the fulfilment of the counsels of perfection, by means of observing the commandments and of ascetical practices. The mystical state was reserved for a very few and the study of it focused on special experiences and extraordinary phenomena. In contrast, Garrigou-Lagrange emphasized the unity and continuity of the Christian life in all its aspects. Mystical prayer was thus a goal to which all were called and for which they were offered God's grace. He agreed that mystical phenomena were extraordinary, but was not happy with the limitation of mysticism merely to these.[21]

The phrase 'spiritual theology' came into vogue, for example with de Guibert, precisely to bypass this controversy about continuity or discontinuity. Such a term appeared more comprehensive than 'ascetical' and 'mystical' and yet it is questionable whether it does justice to what most people understand by spirituality today. Whether distinguished as ascetical and mystical theology or united as spiritual theology, the approach to the spiritual life which held the field up to the Second Vatican Council had several features with which a contemporary theology would be uncomfortable. Firstly, while not crudely dualistic, this approach often conceived of the supernatural life as distinguishable from, or grafted on to the natural. As a consequence it was possible to identify specifically spiritual areas for exclusive treatment. Secondly, while differing on the classifications and distinctions in the spiritual life, spiritual theologians saw the journey towards perfection in terms of degrees and consecutive or separate stages. Thus, the ultimately mysterious nature of human experience and existence was reduced to detailed analysis according to predetermined general laws. Finally, there was a tendency to be individualistic, to ignore the social dimensions of Christian spiritual life and to reduce the ecclesial aspects of spirituality to participation in the sacraments. Although in general, this approach withered after Vatican II, there appeared as late as 1980, rather surprisingly, an English-language volume of spiritual theology on the old model which differed little from Tanquerey and which, apart from some references, appeared to ignore any developments in theology since the Vatican Council.[22]

A writer such as Louis Bouyer must be distinguished carefully from this kind of manual theology. His approach is illustrated mainly through *An Introduction to Spirituality*.[23] Bouyer differed substantially from the older manuals in recognizing developments in liturgical theology and biblical study, and in his impatience with a multitude of classifications and distinctions. He was also more open to the spirituality of traditions other than the Roman Catholic one. Although Bouyer's approach is now dated, it formed an important bridge between the constraints of a narrow neo-scholastic theological approach to spirituality and a more scriptural, liturgical and ecumenical approach after Vatican II.[24]

The Anglican tradition

Many people would single out the Anglican tradition as different from the Churches of the Reformation as a whole because it continued to take an interest in the spiritual guidance of individuals. As a consequence, it produced a body of literature which sought to frame a pattern for the development of the Christian life. Much of this guidance was not systematic but was dispersed in sermons, collections of prayers or devotions and even poems. Equally, because the Anglican tradition was based so strongly on a collective liturgical life, inspired by the Book of Common Prayer (which itself may be considered a work of 'spiritual guidance'), many of the writings which dealt explicitly with the spiritual life were, in effect, companions to the Prayer Book and were strongly liturgical and sacramental in flavour. Until the twentieth century, it seems fair to say, there was no real attempt to compile a coherent spiritual theology which precisely paralleled the ascetical-mystical theology of the Roman Catholic tradition. However, from the seventeenth century through to the twentieth, there were various attempts to provide guidance in the life of prayer or Christian virtues. One of the most notable aspects of this Anglican approach to the spiritual life was that it was frequently linked to moral theology.

There is some evidence for the continued popularity among Anglicans of such late medieval English spiritual treatises as Walter Hilton's *Ladder of Perfection* which was reprinted several times in the seventeenth century. In the seventeenth century, a number of books appeared on meditation or on practical rules for prayer, such as Bishop Hall's *The Arte of Divine Meditation*. There were also pastoral treatises on the Christian life as a whole, such as

Bishop Bayley's *The Practice of Piety: Directing the Christian how to Walk that he may Please God*, Jeremy Taylor's highly influential *Rules and Exercise of Holy Living*, and the anonymous *Whole Duty of Man* with its emphasis on proper conduct and 'the plain way of holiness'. Importantly, there were also attempts to provide some guidance for clergy in the art of spiritual direction. George Herbert, in his treatise on the priestly life, *The Country Parson*, included some hints in chapters 15 and 34, but these are not much developed. A major work in this area was Gilbert Burret's *Discourse on Pastoral Care* and Jeremy Taylor also addressed the practicalities of spiritual direction in *Doctor Dubitantium*.

Of the eighteenth-century works, undoubtedly the best known is William Law's *A Serious Call to a Devout and Holy Life*, a guide to the counsels of perfection addressed to all 'serious' Christians. The nineteenth century continued to see new treatises on the life of prayer and virtue such as *A Treatise on Prayer* by the Evangelical, Edward Bickersteth, which included a summary theology of prayer. Strangely perhaps, the Tractarians did not on the whole write spiritual treatises but frequently confined themselves to translating contemporary French Roman Catholic works on confession. Arguably, the Tractarians tended not to distinguish their treatment of a theology of the Christian life from other theological considerations such as the liturgy, the sacraments and the nature of the Church.

It was only in the 1930s that the beginnings of a school of spiritual theology emerged with the work of F. P. Harton. In his *The Elements of the Spiritual Life*, Harton provided Anglicans with a structured treatise similar in some respects to contemporary Roman Catholic ascetical theology, though with a somewhat greater emphasis on liturgy and sacraments and a less legalistic approach. This development corresponds to a period when Anglo-Catholicism, once barely tolerated, was becoming a central force within the Church of England and when a revival of Thomism offered an attractive new theological ground plan. At much the same time there appeared the authoritative classic by Evelyn Underhill, *Mysticism*, and Bede Frost's *The Art of Mental Prayer*. Finally, in the 1950s and 1960s, Martin Thornton attempted a properly Anglican approach to the theory of spirituality with his *Pastoral Theology*, *Christian Proficiency* and *English Spirituality*. More recently, it seems fair to say, the Anglican contribution to the theory of the spiritual life has, like its Roman Catholic counterpart, blended into a more ecumenical, multi-disciplinary approach to spirituality.[25]

The Eastern Orthodox tradition

The Eastern Orthodox tradition, unlike western Christianity in the Middle Ages, did not suffer a separation between theology and spirituality or mysticism. In other words, when the Eastern tradition uses the phrase 'mystical theology', it does not mean a division of practical theology as in the West, but something which, on the patristic model, closely relates the Christian moral life and experience of God with doctrine. Because the subjective spiritual experience of individuals is comparatively hidden in eastern Christianity, it possesses very few autobiographical accounts of the interior life in contrast to the development of a certain spiritual individualism or interest in subjective experience in the West.

The classical treatment of Eastern mystical theology by Vladimir Lossky defines it as a spirituality which expresses a doctrinal attitude. On one level, all theology is mystical in that its aim is to show forth the divine mystery. There is therefore no opposition between theology and a mysticism that is something inaccessible to understanding or lived rather than known. Mysticism and theology support and complete each other. On the one hand, mystical experience, while personal, is nevertheless the working out of a common faith. Theology, on the other hand, is an articulation of something which can be experienced by everyone. Theology could not be merely a rational deduction from revealed premises because *theologia* was inseparable from *theoria* or contemplation. Rather, theology is a vision experienced by saints whose authenticity was checked against the witness of Scripture and tradition. True theologians were those who saw and experienced the content of their theology.[26]

From spiritual theology to spirituality

It was suggested at the beginning of this chapter that there has been a major shift in western theology towards a more serious reflection on human experience in its cultural particularity and therefore pluriformity. This in turn provoked a movement away from a static approach to the Christian life, embodied in an analytical and abstract spiritual theology, and towards a more dynamic and inclusive concept, namely 'spirituality'. I would also add that this new concept has gained considerable ecumenical acceptance and so spirituality now tends to be eclectic in its approach as it seeks to draw upon the riches of a shared Christian heritage rather than to limit itself to a sectarian understanding of 'life in the Spirit'. Spirituality, in other words, is a far better expression of Catholicity than any previous spiritual theology.

The differences between the spirituality that has emerged in the last twenty years within western Christianity and the older spiritual theology may therefore usefully be summarized by four central characteristics. Firstly it is not exclusive – certainly not associated exclusively with any one Christian tradition, nor even necessarily with Christianity as a whole. Secondly, while if anything more, rather than less, associated with solid theology than in the recent past, it is not simply the prescriptive application of absolute or dogmatic principles to life. Thirdly, it does not so much concern itself with defining perfection as with surveying the complex mystery of human growth in the context of a living relationship with the Absolute. Finally, it is not limited to a concern with the interior life but seeks an integration of all aspects of human life and experience.

The last characteristic underlines the importance of issues of life-style within Christian spirituality. While not pointing to a return to the categories of scholastic theology, this has stimulated some reflection on the relationship between spirituality and ethics or moral theology. Moral theology has moved away from a concern primarily with the quality of actions to a much greater interest in people's dispositions of character. In other words, there has been a shift from human actions to human agent and the beginnings, at least, of an awareness of the basic unity of the moral and spiritual life. Many would now consider that the joint task of spirituality and contemporary moral theology is to explore renewed definitions of 'virtue' (that is, what enables a person to become truly human within a commitment to Christ and the action of grace) and 'character' (or what we should *be* if we are to become fully human persons).[27]

These changes in perspective are at the heart of questions of definition. The broader the perspective, the greater the issue of coherence and the danger of subsuming spirituality into an interest in religion in general.[28] Many contemporary writers would explicitly reject the limitation of spirituality to interiority. Rather, 'the spiritual life is the life of the whole person directed towards God.'[29] The British theologian Rowan Williams rejects the notion that spirituality is merely the science of interpreting exceptional private experiences and suggests that 'it must now touch every area of human experience, the public and social, the painful, negative, even pathological byways of the mind, the moral and relational world.'[30] Contemporary theorists accept that once we cease to drive a wedge between sacred activities and the secular, or between the spiritual dimension of human existence and materiality, the issues become more complex. However, whatever the problems, contemporary spirituality is characterized more by an attempt to integrate human and religious values than by an exclusive interest in the component parts of 'spiritual' growth such as stages of prayer.

A notable liberation of women's spiritual experience has been associated with the shift towards a more human, inclusive and experiential approach to spirituality. This is important not only for women but ultimately for Christian spirituality as a whole. A disembodied spirituality which had problems not only with the body and material reality but with the feminine in particular (that most potent symbol of embodiment, not to say of sexuality), was firmly rooted in theological concepts. These, as we have seen, were dogmatic and thus free from emotion, objective, rational and logical in contrast to the muddy waters of personal experience. To say that women's religious experience was caged within a male theology is more than to note that theological teaching was for so long dominated by men. Although, theoretically, theology was a priori, in practice the categories and tone expressed a male mentality.

The result was a spirituality whose values included the individual and separateness and the quest for achievement, self-determination associated with dominance, control and conquest – of the self and of the world. Such values inevitably led, it seems to me, to a hierarchical conception of the human and spiritual life. Consequently the language of traditional spiritual theology tended to prefer images of ladders of perfection, the language of 'stages' and detachment achieved by rules and formulae. The end in view was undivided love of God which, in fact, implied being divided from large parts of the self and separated from created reality.

In contrast, the liberation of women's experience has meant the reinforcement of other values such as subjectivity, feelings, the relational, nurture, reverence, compassion, the sacredness of all life and the earth. Although the shift in contemporary spirituality is not simply the result of this liberation (indeed is, to a degree, a precondition of it) there is no doubt that the explicit contribution of women to the debate about spirituality has offered a great deal to the whole field.[31]

For some, the emphasis on experience as the starting point for spirituality is associated with what is perceived as a tendency to define it in generic terms, that is, 'spirituality as such' or 'in general'. In practice, spiritualities are specific and have particular religious or doctrinal referents. This is what makes it possible to sift the authentic from the inauthentic in spirituality. Every religious tradition has tests for the authenticity of spiritual experience based not only on human considerations but also on the revelation or foundational beliefs of the tradition. Without specific points of reference, it is difficult to say precisely what is spirituality and what is not, and what is appropriate or not. Criticisms of generic definitions of spirituality are undoubtedly valid because spirituality is unavoidably conditioned by historical and religious contexts and embodies thematically explicit commitments and distinctive symbols – in other words, the language of a tradition. However, it is not clear that the vagueness of some contemporary definitions in Christian circles (for example, 'one typical way of handling the human condition' or 'becoming a person in the fullest sense') indicates more than a recognition that there are people who live consciously within a horizon of absolute value, or who seek genuine self-transcendence, but who do not describe this in specifically Christian terms or even within religious language as traditionally conceived.[32]

Certainly, when it comes to defining contemporary Christian spirituality, the emphasis on the experiential does not in practice exclude specific reference to tradition. Even if there is common ground between different faith traditions regarding the meaning of spirituality, that is, the development of the human capacity for self-transcendence in relation to the Absolute (however this is named), nevertheless the specifically Christian approach is increasingly related to theological themes rather than otherwise. While spirituality, in Christian terms, is not about some other *kind* of life but about *the whole of human life at depth*, our understanding of what this might mean cannot avoid questions posed specifically by the Christian tradition of revelation about the nature of God, human nature and the relationship between the two. Spirituality is understood to include not merely the techniques of prayer but, more broadly, a conscious relationship with God, in Jesus Christ, through the indwelling of the Spirit and in the context of the community of believers. Spirituality is, therefore, concerned with the conjunction of theology, prayer and practical Christianity. A central feature is that spirituality derives its identity from the Christian belief that as human beings we are capable of entering into a relationship with God who is both transcendent and, at the same time, indwelling in

60

the heart of all created things. This relationship is lived out, not in isolation, but in a community of believers that is brought into being by commitment to Christ and sustained by the active presence of the Spirit of God in each and in the community as a whole. In Christian terms, the self-transcendence involved in referring life to something beyond is a gift of the Spirit of God which establishes a life-giving relationship with God, in Christ, within a believing community. In other words, contemporary Christian spirituality is explicitly Trinitarian, Christological, and ecclesial.[33]

Notes

1. See Edward Kinerk, 'Towards a method for the study of spirituality', *Review for Religious* 40: 1 (1981), p. 3.
2. See Avery Dulles, *Models of the Church* (Dublin 1974), p. 86.
3. For surveys of the history of the word, see Walter Principe, 'Towards Defining Spirituality', *Sciences Religieuses* 12: 2 (1983), pp. 130–35; Sandra Schneiders, 'Theology and Spirituality: Strangers, Rivals or Partners?', *Horizons* 13: 2 (1986), pp. 257–60, and 'Spirituality in the Academy', *Theological Studies* (December 1989), pp. 680–84; Jon Alexander, 'What do Recent Writers Mean by Spirituality?', *Spirituality Today* 32 (1980), pp. 247–56; Jean Leclercq, 'Introduction' in E. Rozanne Elder, ed., *The Spirituality of Western Christendom*, Cistercian Studies, 30, Kalamazoo 1976.
4. For a good summary of the issues, see Thomas Deidun, 'Beyond Dualisms: Paul on Sex, *Sarx* and *Soma*', *The Way* (July 1988), pp. 195–205.
5. See Josef Sudbrack, 'Spirituality', in Karl Rahner, ed., *Encyclopedia of Theology: a Concise Sacramentum Mundi*, London 1975; Gordon Wakefield, ed., *A Dictionary of Christian Spirituality*, London 1983; Cheslyn Jones, Geoffrey Wainwright and Edward Yarnold, eds, *The Study of Spirituality*, London New York 1986.
6. See Andrew Louth, *The Origins of the Christian Mystical Tradition* (Oxford 1981), introduction, p. xi.
7. See Louth, ibid., for a general background to the origins of the Christian mystical tradition in the patristic period.
8. For a development of this point see, Louis Bouyer, 'Mysticism – an Essay on the History of the Word', in Richard Woods, ed., *Understanding Mysticism* (London 1981), pp. 52–3.
9. For a brief overview of the meaning of patristic theology see J. Daniélou, 'Patristic Literature', introduction, J. Daniélou, A. H. Couratin and John Kent, *The Pelican Guide to Modern Theology*, 2 (Harmondsworth 1971), pp. 30–2. For a survey of the main lines of patristic spirituality, see Charles Kannengeisser, 'The Spiritual Message of the Great Fathers', in Bernard McGinn and John Meyendorff, eds, *Christian Spirituality: Origins to the Twelfth*

Century (London/New York 1986), pp. 61–88. A good introduction to the theology of Pseudo-Dionysius is provided by Paul Rorem, 'The Uplifting Spirituality of Pseudo-Dionysius' in the same volume, pp. 132–51. Bouyer, 'Mysticism', offers a corrective to an unbalanced approach to Dionysian mysticism.

10. For some illuminating suggestions concerning the origins of an interest in subjective mystical experiences see Peter Dinzelbacher, 'The Beginnings of Mysticism Experienced in Twelfth-Century England', in Marion Glasscoe, ed., *The Medieval Mystical Tradition in England*, Exeter Symposium IV, Woodbridge, Suffolk, 1987.

11. The classic analysis of monastic theology is Jean Leclercq, *The Love of Learning and the Desire for God* (ET, London 1978), ch. 9. For comparisons between this and the 'new' scholastic method see E. Rozanne Elder, ed., *From Cloister to Classroom: Monastic and Scholastic Approaches to Truth*, Cistercian Studies 90 (Kalamazoo 1986), especially essays by Thomas Renna, Michael Strasser, Jean Leclercq and Luke Anderson.

12. A useful summary of writings associated with the new religious orders is in Jean Leclercq, chapter 6, 'The new orders', and chapter 8, 'The school of Citeaux', in Louis Bouyer et al., *A History of Christian Spirituality 2: The Spirituality of the Middle Ages*, ET, London 1968. See also John Sommerfeldt, 'Bernard of Clairvaux: the Mystic and Society'; E. Rozanne Elder, 'William of St Thierry: Rational and Affective Spirituality'; and Keith Egan, 'Guigo II: the Theology of the Contemplative Life', in Elder, *The Spirituality of Western Christendom*.

13. For a recent edition of the *Summa*, with English translation, see that published by Eyre & Spottiswoode/McGraw-Hill from 1963 onwards.

14. On the Victorine school and its influence, see François Vandenbroucke, 'The Schoolmen of the Twelfth Century', in Bouyer, *The Spirituality of the Middle Ages*, ch. 1; and Grover A. Zinn, 'The Regular Canons' in McGinn, *Christian Spirituality*, pp. 218–227. *Benjamin Major* and *Benjamin Minor* were commonly referred to in the medieval period as *The Mystical Ark* and *The Twelve Patriarchs* respectively. Recent English translations have appeared in the volume on Richard of St Victor, edited by Grover Zinn, in the series The Classics of Western Spirituality (London/New York 1979).

15. Dinzelbacher, 'The Beginnings of Mysticism', p. 126. On the popularity of the Song of Songs in monastic, and particularly Cistercian, circles and on the importance of the imagery of the book in contemplative and mystical works, see Jean Leclercq, *The Love of Learning and the Desire for God* (New York 1974, London 1978), pp. 106–109, and Caroline Walker Bynum, *Jesus as Mother: Studies in the Spirituality of the High Middle Ages* (Berkeley 1982), chapter 4. For a brief sketch of the cultivation of the theme of love in both secular and religious circles in the twelfth century, see the Preface by Ewart Cousins in G. R. Evans, ed., *Bernard of Clairvaux: Selected Works* (New Jersey 1987), pp. 7–8. For a selection of sermons

on the Song of Songs by St Bernard, see the same volume, pp. 209–78.

16. See Bynum's illuminating survey of this question in *Jesus as Mother*, chapter 3, 'Did the Twelfth Century Discover the Individual?', pp. 82–109. She also has many fresh insights on mysticism in chapter 5, 'Women Mystics in the Thirteenth Century', pp. 170–262. A good general collection of essays on mysticism would be Paul Szarmach, ed., *An Introduction to the Medieval Mystics of Europe*, New York 1984, and see also Alois Maria Haas's chapter, 'Schools of Late Medieval Mysticism', in Jill Raitt et al., (eds.), *Christian Spirituality: High Middle Ages and Reformation* pp. 140–75.

17. See Haas, pp. 143–55.

18. See Jean Leclercq, 'Prayer and Contemplation: 2, Western', in McGinn, *Christian Spirituality*, pp. 427ff. For the development of an approach to imaginative prayer using Scripture, see Ewert Cousins, 'The Humanity and Passion of Christ', in Raitt, *Christian Spirituality*, pp. 375–91.

19. For two modern overviews of the *devotio moderna* and its approach to prayer, see Otto Gründler, 'Devotio Moderna', in Raitt, *Christian Spirituality*, pp. 176–93; and John Van Engen, ed., *Devotio Moderna: Basic Writings*, New York 1989.

20. A. A. Tanquerey, *The Spiritual Life*, ET, Tournai 1930; J. de Guibert, *The Theology of the Spiritual Life*, ET, London 1954); R. Garrigou-Lagrange, *Christian Perfection and Contemplation*, ET, St Louis, 1937.

21. Tanquerey, pp. 5–6; Garrigou-Lagrange, pp. 27–43.

22. J. Aumann, *Spiritual Theology*, London 1980.

23. Louis Bouyer, *An Introduction to Spirituality*, ET, New York 1961.

24. For a survey of developments in spiritual theology from the High Middle Ages to the immediate aftermath of Vatican II, see Eugene Megyer, 'Spiritual Theology Today', *The Way* (January 1981), pp. 55–67.

25. For references and general background, see John Moorman, *The Anglican Spiritual Tradition*, London 1983; Kenneth Leech, *Soul Friend* (London 1977), Ch. 3; and the appropriate sections in Jones, *Study of Spirituality*. For background on the advance of Anglo-Catholicism, see Adrian Hastings, *A History of English Christianity, 1920–1985* (London 1986), ch. 11.

26. For summaries of the nature of 'mystical theology' in the Eastern tradition, see Vladimir Lossky, *The Mystical Theology of the Eastern Church* (ET, London 1973), ch. 1; John Meyendorff, *Byzantine Theology* (London 1975), introduction.

27. For a brief summary of the overlap between ethics and spirituality and the issues facing them, see the review essay by James A. O'Donohoe, 'A return to virtue', *Church* (Spring 1987), pp. 48–54.

28. See comments on this problem in Principe, 'Towards Defining Spirituality', pp. 137–41.

29. See Leech, *Soul Friend*, p. 34.

30. Rowan Williams, *The Wound of Knowledge* (London 1979), p. 2.

31. See, for example, Margaret Brennan, 'Women and Theology: Singing of God in an Alien Land', *The Way Supplement* 53 (Summer 1985), pp. 93–103.

32. For critical surveys of contemporary attempts to define spirituality, see Principe, 'Towards Defining Spirituality'; Alexander, 'What do Writers mean by Spirituality?', pp. 247–56; Sandra Schneiders, 'Theology and Spirituality', pp. 253–74 and 'Spirituality in the Academy', pp. 687–97.

33. For a useful attempt to define the Christian understanding of spirituality in contemporary terms, see Joann Wolski Conn, *Spirituality and Personal Maturity* (New York 1989), ch. 1.

CHAPTER THREE

Spirituality and the Process of History

Who is permitted to have a history and who is not is a vital issue because those who have no memories or story have no life. In André Brink's powerful novel *Looking on Darkness*, the South African 'Coloured' actor Joseph Malan, awaiting execution for the murder of his white lover, recalls his own life-history and that of his family. He is proud because they *have* a story – so many 'Coloured' people do not. Joseph has vivid memories of his mother's firm views on this matter. 'You must look up, Joseph. Remember your Fa'er and his peoples. I'm nothing, I'm an orphan born and bred. But he's different, he's got a hist'ry jus' like enny white man. Don' forget that.'[1] But there is another side to this story. While recalling the poverty of his ancester Dlamini, who struggled to survive as a blind musician in the last part of the nineteenth century, Joseph reflects, 'Strange to think how little of the country's official history appears in my chronicle as if we've always existed apart from it.' During Dlamini's lifetime all kinds of 'significant historical events' took place – for example the Great Trek, the Zulu Wars, the evolution of the Cape from representative to reponsible government, the first Boer War . . . yet, 'Of all that there is no mention in my chronicle. It surrounds our story but forms no part of it. For my tale is not history, but, at most, the shadow-side of history.'[2]

Joseph's dreams graphically illustrate the difference between a universal historical process, which involves everyone, and recorded history in which only *some* people are active participants. Recorded history, imposed from above, is controlled history beyond whose boundaries are silence and darkness. The bias of traditional history towards the viewpoint of the powerful, and the fact that the values of these élite groups gain the greatest exposure, has led some contemporary historians to seek to retrieve the story of those who are overlooked in traditional history and to offer a substantial revision of our perceptions of particular periods or movements.

These considerations have a number of consequences for the study of spirituality. First of all, we need to come to a realization that all human attempts to respond to the initiative of God, that is the different spiritual traditions, are to some extent limited by particular historical, social and cultural contexts and that spiritualities embody specific social values and commitments. For example, the emergence of mendicant spirituality in the thirteenth century represented both an evangelical and a *social* reaction to the wealth and power of society and of a Church that all too frequently aped the values of 'the world'. Francis of Assisi's choice of radical poverty as *the* gospel value was not a-historical but was a rejection of what were understood to be the characteristic sins of his time. Without entering into the debate about the originality of Francis's vision, it seems fair to say that Francis's vision is symptomatic of a wider spiritual movement in the late eleventh and twelfth centuries, known as the *vita apostolica*. The emphasis on poverty, as the literal imitation of the poor and homeless Jesus, was central to this. The mendicant movement also reflects a partly conscious and partly unconscious attempt to break free from the dominance of a monastic élite in spirituality. 'Flight from the world' had already, by the early thirteenth century, begun to move outward from the stability and separation of the cloister into a broader unsettlement of crusade and pilgrimage. Francis embraced this instability of life on the road. The phrase in his *Later Rule*, 'as pilgrims and strangers in this world who serve the Lord in poverty and humility, let them go begging for alms with full trust', expresses an understanding of discipleship that accords substantially with the evangelical and penitential movements of his age.[3]

A revisionist approach to history also underlines the need for a critical awareness of the way in which traditions, as they developed, often spiritualized and formalized the original values and treated the structures that expressed them as absolute or normative. For example, we would have a quite unhistorical picture of the origins of the Franciscan movement if we accepted, in an uncritical way, St Bonaventure's portrayal of St Francis's decision to lead a life of radical poverty as *solely* the result of a sudden inspiration at Mass while listening to a reading of Matthew, chapter 10.[4]

A further issue is that certain individuals are given star quality in traditions as they develop not merely in accordance with spiritual criteria but also for more worldly motives – for example, they support an acceptable understanding of the tradition. Thus, while, at first glance, our spiritual inheritance may appear to offer impressive variety and breadth, there is in fact an 'underside' to that history. We are largely unaware of this because it has been screened out as traditions establish themselves and move in particular directions rather than others.

There seem to me to be certain fundamental priorities which have to a great extent controlled the development of spirituality and how it was viewed or recorded. One overall priority really summarizes the remainder – that of the *institution and authority structures*. However, it is possible to distinguish some subsidiary features. Firstly, the value of *orthodoxy* frequently meant the priority of majority over minority, 'winners' over 'losers', those who get their ideas across over the less articulate. *Conformity to the centre* valued uniformity over pluralism, Establishment over new ventures, a universal culture over local experience. Finally, *the clerical-monastic* tone gave priority to special 'ways' over normal Christian life and spiritual over material reality. These priorities point to a number of questions about history which may help us to focus our attempts to look more critically at the past and to revise our vision of it. Who was holy and what was holy? Who creates or controls spirituality? What directions were not taken? Where are the groups that did not fit? Taken together, these questions focus on one basic issue: the ways in which certain groups become insiders, and others outsiders, in the history of spirituality. As a consequence it also seemed useful to summarize a few reflections on the process of dissent and oppression.[5] Although the main emphasis of this chapter concerns a framework for understanding the underside of history, it concludes with the kind of organising structure which may assist us to understand how spiritualities which become well-established develop and also, perhaps eventually, decline.

The chapter focuses predominantly, but not exclusively, on the Middle Ages, partly for the sake of greater coherence, but also because it was during this long period that so many of the theories and values that affected the directions taken by western spirituality for centuries were formulated. This includes important schools of spirituality that continue to influence us today. The Middle Ages also witnessed a much greater monastic and clerical dominance of spirituality which produced a legacy that is only now in process of being dismantled – not without struggle. For those in the Catholic tradition, the period saw the development of a theological method which ultimately gave birth to the tradition of ascetical and mystical theology within which the study of spirituality was framed for so long. For many Catholics (and, in the aftermath of the Oxford

Movement, many Anglicans as well), the Middle Ages signified an almost dreamlike undivided Christendom, a golden age. So much so, that the period became a kind of 'symbol of return' and thus a particularly fertile breeding ground for myths. Our understanding of medieval Christianity has been substantially challenged over the last few decades. This is partly the result of considering new kinds of evidence, but even more of new questions which have shifted our perspectives. While some new approaches can fall into the trap of replacing the old, romantic, view with new dogmatisms, there does seem to be a value in recovering spiritual traditions beyond those recorded, or supported, by clerical-monastic élites.[6]

Who was holy and what was holy?

In defining holiness, an outstanding priority in western Christianity has been what may be called the *clerical-monastic* one, that is 'special ways' as opposed to Christian life as a whole. From the early centuries of the Church, the development of a hierarchy and the differentiation of charisms gradually set apart those who had chosen the 'better part' or who were deemed more whole-hearted in their discipleship – in practice the clerics and the celibates-ascetics. Such élitism was also related to a priority of 'spiritual' over 'material' reality, often linked to a suspicion of human sexuality. This was partly the legacy of Platonism, as well as of aristocratic social principles in Graeco-Roman culture, which found a later echo in the development of monarchy among the Christianised Germanic tribes once their nomadic days were over.[7]

Another factor was just as ancient. The first language of Christian perfection was that of martyrdom. The detachment from the world that made Christians different was manifested particularly in confrontations with the power of the pagan state and with public history. The martyr witnessed to the transformation of the self by losing life in order to gain it through victory over death. With the conversion of the Roman Empire to Christianity, this language of perfection was necessarily translated into something different. The emergence of monasticism from the fourth century onwards may be related partly to this movement by Christianity from marginalization to respectability and, indeed, official status. Monasticism did two things. It continued the martyr model of holiness and developed it from victory over physical death to victory over the world as death-dealing. Secondly, monasticism, not inherently but effectively, abandoned the idea of perfection for the ordinary Christian. Thus a division was created within the Church between the perfect and the imperfect, symbolized by physical withdrawal.[8]

Because sanctity is not a completely independent category, unconnected to a wider context of values, it is reasonable to ask *what* as well as who is being canonised. The priority of spiritual élites frequently merges with social élitism. At its crudest this reinforces prejudices against certain kinds of people. Thus, the popular cult of Little Hugh of Lincoln (never officially sanctioned, but nevertheless long-standing) as a martyr to Jewish avarice, as well as to the supposed magical and satanic practices of that community, reinforced a powerful and unpleasant strand of anti-semitism in England throughout the Middle Ages. Again, the kind of violent death that we interpret as martyrdom is partly a *political and social decision.* We are much less likely, today, to be inspired by the martyrdom of an inquisitor who was killed by the relatives of his victims – particularly when we now know a great deal more about the ambiguities surrounding supposedly heretical groups or movements in the Middle Ages and their repression.[9]

Social élitism has also been present in perceptions of holiness. It is interesting to note that, between about 1000–1700, saints appear in a ratio of approximately three to one in favour of élite classes. There was a disposition to equate moral with social nobility. Because holiness involved a dimension of sacrifice and the reversal of worldly status, the surrender by an upper class saint of social position and riches appeared more impressive than the poverty and nothingness of the already poor. This tendency to prefer a 'riches to rags and thus back to spiritual riches' journey to holiness appears in religious traditions other than the Christian one – we only have to reflect on the legendary life of the Buddha.

It is true that there was a tradition of 'servant-saints' in the Middle Ages but this does not necessarily reflect a more democratic approach to sanctity! The stereotypical servant-saint was a young female living in servitude. It is probable that these servant-saints were a spiritual solace to their class. They stood as a criticism of the worst excesses of the master-servant relationship, particularly sexual harassment. Through their stories, the life of virtue was made imaginable even in servile circumstances. Frequently, in contrast to their aristocratic masters, these saints manifested the true signs of nobility, particularly through a care for those poorer than themselves. Sometimes, in their legends, the cruelty of wicked masters was confounded or repaid in miraculous form.

69

Thus Gunthild of Suffersheim (died around 1057) managed to combine 'noble' charity and retribution by giving her master's milk to the poor despite his opposition and also arranging for his remaining supply to turn to ashes. However, the servant-saint model was hardly subversive. In several ways it reinforced the status quo. This is not surprising when we consider that the advancement of the causes of servant-saints seems to have had more to do with the patronage of powerful families than popular cultus. It is likely that the origins of the promotion of such saints reflected a desire to maintain the allegiance of a marginal class. Equally, their virtue revealed what true nobility was. In fact several servant-saints were described as socially noble in origin but fallen on hard times. In this sense too, the motif served the noble rather than the servile class. Finally, the model, with its emphasis on a strict curb on natural sensuality, also embodied the Church's ambivalent attitude to women. Woman's natural tendency to be 'temptress' was further compounded by the corrupted morals of the servile state.[10]

An underlying assumption behind spiritual élitism was that the flesh and involvement in material things were associated with original sin. It was difficult to conceive of the possibility of saintliness *through* marriage or labour in the fields! In the Middle Ages representations of heaven as idealized in art tended to reproduce the hierarchies of society and Church. Peasants did not sit with kings or monks. On the west front of Chartres Cathedral:

> Elongated figures of 'saints' thinned out of the world to reach a God above, and stout, stocky figures of this-worldly artisans and peasants supporting with the sweat of their brows that other 'leisure class' who have all the time and energy for liturgies and mystical contemplation, point to a conception of spirituality indelibly sculptured in the cathedrals of our collective unconscious.[11]

The traditional approach also reinforced an individualistic understanding of discipleship and holiness, rather than communal or social dimensions, by emphasizing the attainment of outstanding personal virtue. In contrast, the approach of contemporary liberation theology reminds us that there is a holiness appropriate to a *people as a whole* which of its nature cannot be understood as outstanding moral virtue but which is, at root, the holiness which is a gift of the indwelling Spirit in the midst of the messiness and imperfections of human society.[12]

Who creates or controls spirituality?

Because of these models of holiness, the priority of the institution and its representatives as the creators and controllers of spiritual traditions was firmly established. Two subsidiary priorities, those of the *clerical over lay* and *majority over minority* (in the sense of those who get their ideas across), may also be distinguished. For example, the spirituality of the medieval West frequently appears to be confined, with few exceptions, to religious orders, the theologically literate and to mystics. Apart from a clerical-monastic élite there was also a bias in favour of those who, in terms of a traditional ascetical-mystical theology, were deemed to have reached a higher level of spiritual enlightenment. Superficially this is understandable because in a period when literacy was not widespread the spirituality of ordinary people, in contrast to that of élites, is less likely to have travelled beyond its original context, to have developed the articulation needed for permanence, or to have captured the centre stage. Thus the fact that creators of spirituality were not to be found exclusively in cathedral, cloister and university was effectively ignored.

To express this in a different way, there was an inherent tendency towards excessive 'refinement' conceived in hierarchical terms: the spiritual was above the material, withdrawal was superior to engagement, contemplation a better way than activity. It was inevitable that such a hierarchy of values meant that only a small minority of the Christian community had access to those contexts where the higher way was possible. Classical spiritual texts, such as the fourteenth-century English mystical work, *The Cloud of Unknowing*, assume a conscious choice of the contemplative life over the active, and use the story of Martha and Mary as a symbol of the contemplative way as 'the better part' (chapter 21 in standard texts). *The Cloud* warns at the outset, and repeats at the end, that the teaching is only suitable for those called to the contemplative life – although, rather grudgingly it seems, the author admits in the Foreword that *some* in the active life may be preparing to 'grasp the message of this book'.[13] The origin of this emphasis lies in the concept of union with God as wisdom (*gnosis*), based on a Platonic ascent away from the natural world towards the purity of ideas or intelligibility which is God. This passed into later western tradition mainly through the influence of the works of the fifth-or sixth-century writer known as Pseudo-Dionysius.

In recent years some historians have suggested that the period from about 1100 to the Reformation, and particularly the thirteenth and fourteenth centuries, witnessed the emergence of a distinctively lay spirituality. That is, there was an increasing diffusion outward from the cloister into society of religious practices and values as well as a new willingness to give religious significance to roles 'in the world'. This view, however, needs considerable qualification. While certain features of this period may have prepared the way, in the long term, for a proper evaluation of the secular, in the short term the period was one of increased prominence for the clergy. The Gregorian reforms of the mid-eleventh century began the process of centring supernatural power in a clerically-controlled Eucharist and the roles of clergy and laity were more and more clearly distinguished. It is true that there was also a great spiritual revival, centring around a desire for the 'apostolic life' of poverty, mendicancy and preaching, which attracted large numbers of lay adherents. However, in the first place, this new religiosity was, at least in part, a reaction against increasing clerical domination of official Church life and piety. Secondly, the lay share in this spiritual revival did not go unchallenged and by the early fourteenth century was effectively condemned.[14]

Finally, while by the fourteenth century a higher proportion of the recognized saints than previously were either laypeople or religious who tried to serve their needs, no new models of holiness emerged to support a greater exaltation of marriage or work. Lay saints simply imbibed the spirituality of the cloister: strict asceticism, absorption in prayer and alienation from the world around them. The point was that an élitist monastic spirituality had for so long defined what a saint was that such conceptions were not easily superceded. It may seem, on the face of it, that the emergence of the monastic reform of the Cistercians in the early twelfth century contradicts, to some degree at least, my assertion that spirituality remained in the hands of an educated élite. The order, after all, stressed the importance of manual labour and incorporated a class of lay-brothers, or *conversi*, into monastic life. In an over-view study such as this, which uses historical instances as illustrations of broad, critical questions, it is impossible to do proper justice to such a complex organisation as the Cistercians. At the risk, therefore, of simplification I would simply raise three questions concerning the degree to which the order truly departed from the established élitism in spirituality. Firstly, given that the monasticism of the Rule of St Benedict originated as an essentially *lay* movement, was not the creation of a distinct *class* of lay-brethren from about the eighth century onwards, and refined by the Cistercian usages, an indication of the degree to which religious life and its government had become clericalised? Secondly, was it not the case that the broadening of the social base in their monasteries by the incorporation of lay-brethren in some senses *reinforced* a spiritual élitism because the underlying assumption was that it was somehow better for *all* manner and conditions of person to belong to religious life? The incorporation of lay-brethren, in itself, was not evidence of an increased valuation of ordinary Christian living, outside the cloister, but was, if anything, the opposite. Thirdly, the manner of incorporation of lay-brethren needs to be understood within a feudal, socially hierarchical mentality. *Conversi* were required to remain illiterate, were used predominantly as the means to develop and sustain a highly developed agrarian economy, enabled the literate choir-monks to remain largely free from the need to become involved in work beyond the cloister, and were prevented from full participation in community life and decision-making.[15]

Indentured servitude or equals?

What directions were not taken?

In the story of directions taken and not taken the priorities of *orthodoxy* and *conformity to the centre* were particularly powerful.[16] The history of spirituality easily becomes merely a record of success stories and uniformity if our attention is concentrated only on those who created the majority of literature or institutional structures. However, we receive a quite false impression if we look at history simply from the angle of the winning side. The institutional version of events needs 'goodies and badies' and tends to oversimplify issues or even, more crudely, to rewrite history. It is now apparent that the medieval women's movement, known as the Beguines, was not as inherently unorthodox as it was portrayed in many official accounts. Rather, a discomfort with independent groups of women who read Scripture, were not subject to the usual canonical restraints, who did not rely sufficiently on the clergy for appropriate guidance and preferred a more affective piety had much to do with the suppression of the movement. It is possible that some Beguines were associated with heretical groups, such as those dubbed the Free Spirit (which it was thought justified nihilism, megalomania and amorality), but most were not. The problem was really a suspicion of the trend known as *vita apostolica* which sought a life-style of poverty and preaching close to that of the first followers of Jesus.[17]

The fate of the *vita apostolica* movement as a whole is a good illustration of what can happen to new and challenging directions in spirituality. Were its values, in any sense, absorbed into the bloodstream of mainline spirituality in the late Middle Ages? Ultimately the mendicant movement *did* find an accepted place through the formal recognition of the way of life of the friars, and especially of the Franciscans. However, motivation is always a complex matter. To an extent the Church sought to neutralize the charismatic attraction of popular leaders, or to make it routine, by taking from the movements the typically evangelical elements, such as poverty. As a consequence, it may also be argued that *vita apostolica* spirituality was not so much accepted as channelled into acceptable directions. Many wandering preachers, such as Norbert of Xanten, eventually settled down to a fairly orthodox monastic life. Even the mendicant orders, while retaining a certain mobility, simplicity and emphasis on popular preaching, took on a recognisably conventual life-style. The tension that was thus created between the original vision and the constraints of traditional religious life continued to cause problems to the mendicants throughout their subsequent history.

The monasticization of spirituality, while challenged during the thirteenth century, in fact continued to dominate the Church for some time to come. It was not until the sixteenth century, with the creation of such orders as the Jesuits, that a fully non-monastic religious life emerged. However while the sixteenth and seventeenth centuries saw major shifts within spirituality away from an exclusively monastic model, religious life *as such* remained the dominant force. The acceptance of significant lay movements within the Church was delayed for several more centuries. Ignatius Loyola and his first companions spent a great deal of time wondering about their future. However, their desire for some permanent framework for their vision ultimately, and inevitably in the context of their time, led them to accept both ordination and the structures of religious life although they had begun as a much more informal group. Women suffered even more from the dominant monastic emphasis in spirituality. Attempts during the sixteenth and seventeenth centuries to form groups, albeit within formal religious life, that would parallel the style of the Jesuits and other new communities of men largely foundered. For example, the radical vision of the Englishwoman Mary Ward, in the early seventeenth century, was condemned by the official Church and her Institute of the Blessed Virgin Mary was, until modern times, unable to live the mobile and fully uncloistered life envisaged by the foundress.[18]

Where are the groups that did not fit?

It is not surprising that the directions taken by institutional spirituality inevitably created individuals or groups that did not fit. Apart from the priority of *orthodoxy*, that of *conformity to the centre*, and especially the repression of pluralism, is particularly evident. This is often reflected in the disappearance of certain traditions and individuals from history, or at best their continuation as a kind of marginal embarrassment to the mainline story. Once again, one only has to think of Mary Ward who, after her condemnation by Church authorities, was made a non-person and written out of the record by ceasing to appear as foundress of her Institute in official documents until her rehabilitation in the present century. Other examples would be the way in which the experience of lay Christians in general, in the Catholic tradition, was ignored in the formulation of spiritual theory, or the process by which the insights of the radical Reformation (e.g. the Anabaptists) were marginalised by the large, territorial, Protestant Churches.[19] It is interesting that both Mary Ward and Anabaptist radicals have been rediscovered in recent years and are seen by many as speaking directly to late-twentieth-century experience.

Another way of seeing the question is to think of spiritualities as cultures, and therefore to examine examples of marginalisation in terms of cultural conflicts. The effect of such conflicts emerges in a clash between the values of a predominant culture and a subordinate one. The history of the Church in England provides some examples. We can think of the gradual erosion of the Celtic tradition, in the face of Latin cultural and religious hegemony, during the seventh and eighth centuries or the clash between older Anglo-Saxon forms of the clerical life and new reformed continental models after the Norman Conquest which were imposed in the name of greater 'spiritual observance'. In both these cases, of course, the culture clash involved more than differences in religious values in isolation.

The suggestion that the great 'monastic reformation' of the tenth century was a culture clash is perhaps more controversial. The eventual success of the reformers, and the important long term developments in English Church life which followed from this, have coloured the subsequent interpretation of the period even to the present day. The straight-forward, 'spiritual', account, classically expressed by David Knowles, whereby a fervent movement of clergy and monks reformed cathedrals and restored monasteries after the depredations of the Scandinavian invasions, is questionable.[20] Firstly, Knowles' own evidence for what existed prior to the invasions makes a simple picture of restoration difficult to sustain. Monastic life had been pluriform and individual houses were mixed in inspiration. Some of the former communities had not been monastic (despite the imprecise usage of words like *monasterium* or *abbas*) so much as conventual or canonical. On the other hand, what was 'restored' in the tenth century was more uniform, self-consciously monastic and Benedictine. Further, Knowles' own analysis of the central reform document, *Regularis Concordia*, suggests that it was based largely on imported continental models rather than conceived as a return to the previous status quo. Secondly, Knowles tends to treat Benedictine monastic life as the equivalent of fervent community life and so necessarily sees the communities it replaced as more primitive, corrupt and certainly spiritually insignificant. So the monastic reformation, which may, in fact, have swept aside not merely corruption but a native canonical version of conventual life, is presented unequivocally as the triumph of progressive forces.[21]

The previous example illustrates that a frequent result of cultural clashes was that the traditions which became predominant were gradually assumed to be *inherently* superior and other spiritual cultures to be more primitive. This may indicate either the degree of exposure obtained by a particular tradition, with its consequent popularity, or the greater ability of one group to control its environment and to subordinate other groups or traditions. The history of political and economic colonialism offers a striking parallel to this process, thus it may not be too extreme to view the dominance of certain spiritual traditions over others as, in some cases, examples of 'imperialism'. Nowadays, reflections on clashes of spiritual cultures, and the attitudes of predominant and subordinate groups to each other, will inevitably include an ecumenical perspective. Neither the Roman Catholic nor Reformed tradition is free from the accusation that, in countries where either tradition predominated, it tended to write the other out of the history book and to disparage its spirituality as inadequate, deviant, misconceived or unorthodox.

'Spiritual colonialism' may be an appropriate concept within which to reassess the fate of the Celtic tradition (or, indeed, the Syriac one in the East) in the more distant past. It is an even more powerful notion when we consider the history of European missions in Africa, Asia and North and South America from the sixteenth century onwards and their rejection of local religious symbols and practices. From its origins in the pages of the New Testament, the underlying history of Christian spirituality has been culturally plural. However, because, within a fairly short period of time, Graeco-Roman culture became dominant in Christianity other traditions were usually treated, if at all, only in relationship to, and from the point of view of this culture and not in their own right. As Christendom expanded so this tendency eventually broadened to become eurocentric in relation to other worlds.

Finally, when we think about groups in the history of spirituality that did not fit, one of the unavoidable questions is: where are the women? The priorities of *clerical élites* and *uniformity* made lay people in general an 'under class' but, as we focus on women in particular, these priorities are expressed primarily by the dominance of male experience over female. It is not simply a question of noting that, with some exceptions (for example, Julian of Norwich), feminine imagery for God and God's way of relating to the human condition does not play a significant part in what are considered as the great spiritual classics.[22] Common spiritual stereotypes, as well as theories about spiritual development, tend to echo the assumptions of a male, clerical establishment. To what extent, and in what circumstances, did women contribute to the development of spiritual theory and practice? For example is Teresa of Avila, as a doctor of the Church, the token female, an honorary male or what? If we reflect on those women, such as Teresa, who have achieved a place in history as significant spiritual figures, it is possible to see their *public* presentation as offering to women merely conventional roles as 'daughters of the Church'. In other words, their lives were recorded selectively for institutional purposes in such a way as not to disturb time-honoured patterns of attitude and behaviour. It is important, of course, to distinguish between these edited models of women's holiness (for example, in terms of humility, hidden service of God and a somewhat disengaged ministry to the weak) and the fulness of human (and specifically feminine) experience which was the hidden reality of these women's lives.[23]

The numerical significance of women in the history of spirituality is rarely reflected in standard accounts. Some historians object to contemporary attempts to retrieve the forgotten women in history by arguing that *significant* women find a place in history as readily as men. Presumably there just happen to have been fewer significant women in history than men! However, this begs the question. The problem with traditional history is that it tends to work within preconceived notions of 'importance' and so to highlight what can be defined, in these terms, as *necessary* to the progress of a spiritual tradition. Thus, our traditional historical sources are themselves products of a culture where the psychological, moral or social inferiority of women is taken for granted. Even the 'big' women who cannot be ignored in the institutional version of events are presented, as has already been noted, within accepted cultural frameworks. Even if women wrote about themselves in history, they often spoke in conventional ways. For example, Julian of Norwich seems to suggest that her theological creativity is in spite of her gender (*The Showings*, Short Text, Chapter 6). It is interesting to note that until fairly recently there has been an assumption, rather than any concrete proof, that Julian was a nun. Apart from the influence of the monastic editors who promoted her work, there may have been a subtle presumption that no woman could think for herself in a creative and theological way and that Julian must therefore have had formal instruction and guided reading from a male cleric! In the end, the problem is not simply one of rediscovering more significant women, in the sense of adding women to our histories, because the stage on which significant historical figures act out their lives continues to be the one that has been defined by a male-dominated world. Women still have to qualify as historical according to norms that are predetermined.[24]

It is a sobering fact that, over the last ten centuries, relatively few woman have been accorded the status of saints. A high proportion of those who were, date from a time when popular cultus was of greater importance in the process of formal recognition and canonisation. One survey suggests that between 1000–1900 about 87 per cent of saints were men and only 13 per cent were women. This both reveals the historically inferior position of women and continues to reinforce this view in the present. The improvement since 1900 has been only marginal: about 75 per cent men and 25 per cent women.[25] I suspect that this reflects a close association between traditional understandings of holiness and a dualist emphasis on liberation from that embodiment of which women were potent symbols. Men, in order to reach spiritual transformation, needed to escape from their bodies while women really had to escape from *themselves* which was a much more difficult matter! So, in summary, we may ask whether traditional spiritual theory made of women as a whole a group that did not fit – even if individuals were able to transcend the limitations.

It may be argued that there are periods when the evidence for the visibility and influence of women appears, at first glance, to be more positive. For example, in the Beguines of the thirteenth century we have what has been described as probably the first women's movement in western religious history. Here, undoubtedly, women did create a new religious role opposed to the complex and male-dominated institutional structures and exercised spiritual leadership. The same century also saw a substantial increase in the number of women attracted to religious life in new reformed convents as well as large numbers who joined bands of wandering preachers. Equally, in the same period, women made a distinctive contribution to piety. While devotion to the Virgin Mary seems to have been more prominent in male writing, certain aspects of the new interest in Christ's humanity (including the infant Jesus) were more characteristic of women. The increasing devotional emphasis on the Eucharist and the institution of the liturgical feast of Corpus Christi were largely inspired by women mystics. Lastly, what has been called the 'feminization of religious language' in this period has also been adduced by some scholars as evidence that there was an increasingly positive attitude towards women in the later Middle Ages.

However, this evidence, on more careful scrutiny, is less encouraging. Those wandering preachers who remained within the bounds of the institutional Church had no desire to establish bands of itinerant female evangelists. On the contrary, their response to the enthusiasm of women was to found traditional monasteries for them. The increase in female language about God did not originate with women and at least as many men used it as women. The presence of maternal and even erotic imagery in spiritual writing does not necessarily point to a greater theological openness to the feminine dimensions of human experience, but may partly reflect the fact that from the twelfth century onwards the new orders tended to recruit a higher proportion of adults who had been married or who had sexual experience. Finally, by the twelfth century and on into the thirteenth, women were losing their occasional power to preach; in the general context of the age the political and legal status of women deteriorated; and the effect of growing numbers of religious women and female followers of preachers seems to have been to increase, rather than decrease, the articulation and enforcement of prohibitions against the clerical status of women and their exercise of spiritual leadership. Thus, while on a certain level women had developed greater opportunities to fill recognised religious roles in society by the late thirteenth century, they were also more effectively excluded from the exercise of authority or active ministry than had been the case a hundred years before.[26]

Oppression, victims and dissent

In reflecting along these lines, it becomes apparent that spirituality as a historical phenomenon has its victims as well as its heroes. 'Victims' is a weak word and there is no doubt that many people in marginalized groups succumbed to the pressures of the dominant spiritual culture by accepting a subordinate place and whatever supports they could find within a clerically dominated spiritual ethos – for example, by association with religious communities in Third Orders.

Some medievalists have noticed a kind of compensation among groups that were excluded from the mainstream. Thus women, while excluded from Holy Orders and unable to consecrate, could at least have an extraordinarily close relationship to the Eucharist in visions and even through miraculous contacts with the Host.[27] Many people channelled their unfulfilled spiritual energies into pilgrimages and unsanctioned devotions associated with the cult of local saints. There were also examples of substitutes for official spiritual structures. Popular devotion was often imitative so, for example, the rosary, meditations on the Passion and Books of Hours were effectively lay imitations of monastic rhythms. If the social or clerical élites apparently made the greater commitment, devotions were often the substitutes for the spiritually poor. The growth of devotional spirituality was one of the most significant developments in late medieval Christianity. The monastic-contemplative approach was marked by an effort to transcend the particularity of time and place. Devotional religion, in contrast, pointed to the popular need for the specific – for sacred places and objects. As a way of going beyond public religion, devotional religion had an ambiguous effect. It could provide a link between Church and home but it could also make people increasingly independent of the first. Germany as a whole was notable for its prolific devotions in the Middle Ages and yet anticlericalism was common and a substantial proportion of the country readily accepted the Reformation.

Marginalization, however, did not merely produce victims,

compensation or substitutes. A minority of people, of course, dramatically transcended limitations. But the demand for social and religious conformity also provoked the development of a substratum of apocalyptic and spiritual poverty movements among the disadvantaged classes – and even, at times, active dissent. This certainly existed in the early Middle Ages (for example the role of the poor in the early crusades) but the important period of literary, artistic and spiritual creativity, known as the twelfth-century Renaissance, undoubtedly reinforced in a striking way the divide between a theologically sophisticated mainstream and popular fervour. There were some people, such as the extraordinary woman Hildegard of Bingen, who to some extent bridged the divide between the two. Despite her apocalyptic preaching Hildegard defended classical monasticism, continued to support aristocratic privilege among her nuns, was not particularly sympathetic to newer spiritual currents such as the poverty movements, and was a 'Gregorian' reformer rather than a proponent of radical social or ecclesiastical change. On the popular level there were the flagellant movements and others concerned with spiritual simplicity, in contrast to the this-worldliness of the official Church, such as the Humiliati in Italy or Peter Waldo and the Poor of Lyons who in many ways anticipated the Spirituals within the Franciscan movement. In an essay on the clergy during this period of 'ecclesiastical proliferation', Gabriel le Bras shrewdly comments:

> By a curious chance, the multiplication of clerical modes in no way corresponded to the needs of the century: rather did it correspond to the needs of the rich for salvation (or for pomp) and to the (sometimes excessive) comforts of the canons and priests.[28]

No doubt there are psychological and social reasons why certain individuals or groups became victims and others dissenters. It cannot be denied, too, that sometimes an inherent unorthodoxy preceded and caused suppression and that such weakness within dissenting movements, as much as the actions of authority, led to their gradual marginalization from the Christian mainstream. The Manichean inspiration of the Cathars who viewed all matter as evil would be a case in point although we may ask why this movement was so widely attractive to laypeople in twelfth-century southern France. The presence of women among the Cathar élite, the rejection of a sacramental system and the challenge to the wealth

81

of the Church may well reflect a wider lay dissatisfaction with the patriarchal and clerical dominance of Church life. However, the fate of Waldo's followers (like the later Franciscan Spirituals) points us to the way in which prior marginalization is often the cause of eventual dissent. Waldo condemned the Cathars and had no difficulty in making an orthodox profession of faith. It seems that the role accorded to lay people in preaching (including some women) and the espousal of poverty and spiritual simplicity were the main reasons for the gradual marginalization of the movement. The Archdeacon of Oxford, Walter Map, was very revealing in his protest against new lay movements. It was their effrontery in preaching, thus usurping a clerical monopoly, that scandalized him: 'Like a pearl cast before swine, shall the Word be given to ignorant people whom we know to be incapable of receiving it, let alone of giving back what they have received?'[29] It was only when a formal ban was imposed in 1184 on Cathars, Humiliati and Waldensians, in one indiscriminate decree, that the Waldensians began to move towards separatism and gradually to develop distinct beliefs.

Dissent became endemic in the Middle Ages largely because there was an increasing emphasis on orthodoxy and orthopraxis, defined by the institutional Church and socially enforced by the secular powers. In seeking to interpret this phenomenon, we need to be careful how we understand 'heresy'. Sometimes there were identifiable doctrinal deviations but equally the accusation of heresy often reflected merely a refusal to conform to prevailing disciplines. Dissent, from the twelfth century onwards, tended to share the common characteristic of a desire to emulate the precepts of the gospel through a life of strict poverty and preaching. The key to marginalization was a failure to gain recognition and sanction. The shift towards heretical beliefs and overt anticlericalism was provoked, in part at least, by the need to stabilize the identity of the group against active rejection by the official Church and so to emphasize the divinely 'chosen' or 'gathered' nature of dissenting groups.

Finally, while it is fair to emphasize social causes for dissent, it would be anachronistic to describe it as 'class struggle'. Fundamentally, the increasing emphasis in radical spirituality on untramelled poverty, reading the Bible, preaching and individual experience ran counter to the concentration of the institutional Church, from the eleventh century onwards, on developing itself as a corporation independent of secular control. It would be simplistic and unfair to characterize the Gregorian reforms as purely structural and institutional. There was certainly a moral and spiritual content – especially a concern for the quality of clerical life and, by extension, of pastoral care. However, the problem in the end was that, apart from new monastic or quasi-monastic foundations up to about 1250, the Church as institution could not cope adequately with the radical fervour inevitably produced by any movement of reform. Its main emphasis instead tended to be on a higher pitch of law, finance and government.

As a footnote, it is questionable whether we ought to view the radical nature of dissent in this or any other age (whether, strictly speaking, heretical or not) as progressive and the institutional structures as conservative. A reasonable argument can be made for the suggestion that dissent (and heresy) is fundamentally conservative in the sense that it seeks to preserve, or return to, values or structures which seem threatened by developments within the institution. Thus, the *vita apostolica* movements sought a *return* to what were seen as gospel values partly in the face of what were, from another standpoint, progressive movements in the institutional Church towards better organization. Equally, to move forward several centuries, the more radical the dissenting groups in the period of the Reformation, the more they tended to appeal *backwards* to the purity of the Apostolic Church and the early Christian centuries.

The development of spiritual traditions

In seeking to highlight some of the questions which may lead us to revise our perceptions about the process of spirituality in history, the concentration has been on how some groups become predominant and others subordinate or marginalized. However, it is also revealing if we turn to some further questions concerning those spiritual traditions which ultimately become well-established in history. These traditions continue to develop beyond their initial phase and in this process we need to analyse how they adapt, or fail to adapt, to changing circumstances (not to mention the motives involved). The development of traditions is no more a matter simply of divine guidance, detached from contextual factors, than was their original emergence.

For ease of analysis it may be helpful to conceive of development in terms of certain stages.[30] The first stage is that of *emergence* which may be further divided into *origins* and *expansion*. This period is characterized by the greatest flexibility because, at this point, the specific structures or expressions which later become associated with a particular spiritual tradition will not be firmly defined. The point of origin is when the initiator or founding group senses a need in society and Church which is then interpreted in the light of the gospel. It is a time of vitality, strong sense of purpose, idealism and fluidity. The point of expansion arrives when the vision of an emerging spirituality is somehow recognised by society as answering its needs. Many people join the original group or become associated in other ways with the spiritual vision. Internally, the core group begin to concentrate resources and to consolidate their vision into some coherent pattern. New groups who want to share the vision emerge beyond the place of origin – or, in the case of an embryonic religious order, new foundations proliferate.

At the heart of an emerging spirituality lies its original constituency, that is to say, the initiators whether individuals or a group. To interpret how these arrived at a given spiritual theory or praxis, the historian must examine the constraints that influenced the initiators. These constraints are both internal (that is, the theological-spiritual tradition within which they worked) and external (that is, the surrounding social or cultural realities). Thus some key questions would be: Who were the initiators and what were their motivating values? How did they understand the contemporary world in which they lived? And how did this world view influence their interaction with existing theological and spiritual theory?

A subsequent stage of development in spiritual traditions will be that of *maintenance* or *stability*. Here, the flexibility of the period of emergence gives way to a more detailed formulation of principles (for example the creation of a Rule) and a formalization of appropriate structures. The tradition has reached a point where it has a certain momentum of its own which makes it increasingly difficult to change its chosen direction. This inevitably means that certain options are chosen and others closed off. The danger then consists in reading back these later choices into the original process of emergence so as to justify their inevitability. A tradition has by now become socialized and respectable. A kind of protectiveness emerges whereby those who benefit from the tradition (whether within it or helped by it) seek to defend it against whatever seems to threaten it. An interesting example would be the development of the Society of Jesus in the sixteenth century from an originally informal group of companions gathered around Ignatius Loyola in the Paris of the late 1520s and early 1530s into one of the major institutions of the post-Reformation Roman Catholic Church.

A failure to distinguish the *emergence* stage from the *maintenance* one will tend to imply that everything of significance was established in the first stage. In the case of the Society of Jesus, just cited, the danger has sometimes been to assume that the essential lines of development were fully anticipated and dealt with in the various deliberations of the first companions in 1537 and in the formal papal approval of the Society of Jesus in 1540.[31] However, there is, in fact, a great deal of evidence (for all that it still needs to be systematically interpreted) that the years from 1540–56, when Ignatius Loyola was the first superior-general, and even those from 1565–1615 during the generalates of Francis Borgia, Everard Mercurian and Claudio Aquaviva, saw substantial changes of emphasis and the emergence of a significantly revised tradition of custom and practice which was to last for several centuries. More controversially, there seems to have been a move towards a greater rigidity, both with regard to life-style and specifically with regard to the interpretation of *The Spiritual Exercises* and approaches to prayer, which departs substantially from what seems to have been Ignatius's original intention and insight.[32] While the original *Constitutions* of Ignatius Loyola presuppose that Jesuit communities will look very different, depending on work and context, a recognisably Jesuit style soon emerged in practice which meant that people travelling from country to country, and even continent to continent, existed within a fairly uniform framework of life.[33]

The motivation for these changes is as yet unclear but it seems likely that two factors played a role – both of which are associated with the need to appear more acceptable to authority. Firstly there may have been a desire to avoid any accusation of the heresy of Illuminism and this would fit with the tendency to forbid the kind of prayer which would appear contemplative or even mystical. Secondly, there may well have been a need to bring the radical form of religious life in the Society of Jesus more into line, in some respects, with more traditional ways. Of course, people other than the Jesuits themselves became dependent upon and were influenced by this spiritual tradition (for example, certain European rulers, popes, reforming bishops, former alumni of Jesuit colleges). Thus, important questions would be: Who were the people or institutions who profited from this spiritual tradition in the longer term? How did they preclude developments that threatened the tradition?

How was their world view affected by their investment in the formalization of the tradition?

As a human creation, every spiritual tradition reflects a limited set of values and so, inevitably, its life-cycle eventually reaches a third stage of development which may be termed *senility* or *breakdown*. This may not be terminal although there is an increasing 'hardening of the arteries' which usually leads to a substantial disconnection of the inherited values of a spiritual tradition from the contemporary culture. The original vision no longer appears to work. Structures have become more important than meaning. Rules fail to supply needs and are increasingly ignored or bypassed. The wider community begins to look on the tradition as anachronistic and consequently membership declines.

This decline points in two possible directions which may be seen as a process of transition. The spiritual tradition may find its way back to the radical flexibility that characterized the phase of emergence so that a new synthesis between the tradition and its context may emerge. In other words, the tradition rediscovers meaning, renews itself and takes the risk of opening itself up anew to the concrete demands of the gospel in the present. This should not be confused with an option for survival, whereby a tradition is tinkered with but no new vision emerges. At the other extreme, the inbuilt rigidities of the tradition may lead to resistance and a rejection of the need for flexibility. There will then be an attempt to force the contemporary context or culture back into line with the inherited theory! The result, eventually, will be death.

A recent illustration may be the crisis which overtook the Roman Catholic Church as a whole and, within it, religious life in the aftermath of the Second Vatican Council. The Council Fathers recognized the disconnection that had arisen between the long-standing and predominant theological-spiritual framework within the Church and a world that was in a process of rapid change and, within a wider reinterpretation of the Church's call to holiness, invited religious communities to return to their origins (or 'original charisms'). This, implicitly at least, meant a recovery of a state of renewed flexibility. The willingness and ability of particular spiritual traditions (not to mention religious life as a whole) to carry out this task and so to break free from the constraints of 'senility' is, arguably, still in the balance. Thus, a coherent evaluation is not yet possible. However it is possible to move backwards in the history of spirituality and observe, for example, the sobering fact that, while the Middle Ages in the West saw a phenomenal growth in the number of new religious orders or individual monasteries, only a small minority survived the Reformation and some of those that did died out in the changing world of the next century and a half. Here we may usefully enquire how those dependent on a particular spiritual tradition viewed the new cultural context and the questions that it raised for the continued functioning of established frameworks. How open to radical change were they? What strategies did they employ in order either to preserve or to transform their tradition?

The directions that traditions take are not absolutely predetermined for there is a continuous dialogue between them and changing contexts, whether specifically religious or social and cultural. Neither the origins nor the unfolding story of spiritual traditions are value-free for there are, within both, implicit values at work which tend to enhance the status of certain groups or practices at the cost of others.

Conclusion

The pages of Christian history are strewn with marginalized people and traditions as well as forgotten or disparaged ideas. Allowing for an inner weakness in some of them, it seems nonetheless fair to say that many have been left behind or actively repressed in the name of progress, institutional development or orthodoxy. Equally, dominant traditions have usually developed from early flexibility and fluidity to a greater institutionalization, characterized by structures and clear formulations of the spiritual vision. The proponents of dominant forms of spirituality would claim that ultimately both processes were in the name of truth. However, in our own century such cataclysmic events as the Holocaust have caused much heart-searching about Christian history and have heightened our consciousness of its ambiguity. More recently our sensitivities have been finely tuned by the awareness of the effects of patriarchy and other forms of exploitation to which feminist and liberationist movements draw our attention. It seems that we can no longer avoid the need to approach even our cherished spiritual traditions and their history in a much more critical fashion.

Notes
1. André Brink, *Looking on Darkness* (London 1982), p. 35.
2. ibid., p. 48.

3. See essay on Franciscan spirituality in Jill Raitt et al., eds, *Christian Spirituality: High Middle Ages and Reformation*, (London/New York 1987) espec. pp. 31–3; Jacques le Goff, 'Francis of Assisi Between the Renewals and Restraints of Feudal Society', *Concilium* 149 (1981), '*Francis of Assisi today*', pp. 3ff; Hester Goodenough Gelber, 'A Theater of Virtue: the Exemplary World of St Francis of Assisi', in John Stratton Hawley, *Saints and Virtues*, (Berkeley 1987) pp. 15ff. The quotation from the *Later Rule* is from ch. 6, 2. See *Francis and Clare: The Complete Works*, trs. Regis Armstrong and Ignatius Brady, London/New York 1982.

4. See Ewert Cousins, ed., *Bonaventure: Life of St Francis etc.*, Classics of Western Spirituality (London/New Jersey 1978), p. 199.

5. In formulating these priorities and questions I have been greatly helped by reading Giuseppe Alberigo, 'New Frontiers in Church History', *Concilium* 7:6 (1970), pp. 68–84 and also John Staudenmaier, *Technology's Storytellers: Reweaving the Human Fabric* (The Society for the History of Technology/MIT, Cambridge, Mass., 1985), introduction and chs 1 and 5.

6. The interpretation of medieval spirituality is complex. The article by John Van Engen, 'The Christian Middle Ages as an historiographical problem', *American Historical Review* 91 (1986), pp. 519–52, offers a helpful and critical summary of contemporary interpretations of the medieval religious world. Some of his points have relevance to spirituality in particular. By suggesting that our élitist view of medieval spirituality needs critical assessment, I do not mean to adopt the questionable division between two radically different religious cultures (a 'high' clerical one and 'low' popular folklore) which Van Engen rightly criticises.

7. See Jacques Fontaine, 'The Practice of the Christian Life: the Birth of the Laity' in Bernard McGinn and John Meyendorff, eds, *Christian Spirituality: Origins to the Twelfth Century*, (London/New York 1986), pp. 453ff.

8. See Claudio Leonardi, 'From "Monastic" Holiness to "Political" Holiness', *Concilium* 129 (1979) 'Models of Holiness', pp. 46ff.

9. For example, St Peter of Verona or Peter Martyr, a former Cathar who, it appears, turned from poacher to gamekeeper as a Dominican.

10. See Michael Goodich, 'Ancilla Dei: the servant as saint in the late Middle Ages', in J. Kirshner and S. Wemple, *Women of the Medieval World* (Oxford 1987) eds, pp. 119ff. For a more general survey of saints in relation to social class, see D. Weinstein and R. Bell, *Saints and Society: the Two Worlds of Western Christendom, 1000–1700* (Chicago 1982), ch. 7, 'Class'.

11. Pieris, Aloysius, 'Spirituality and liberation', *The Month* (April 1983), p. 120.

12. See, for example, Gustavo Gutiérrez, *We Drink From Our Own Wells: The Spiritual Journey of a People*, London 1984.

13. The most definitive text is Phyllis Hodgson, ed., *The Cloud of Unknowing and Related Treatises*, Analecta Cartusiana 3, Salzburg 1982.

A good modern English version is that edited by James Walsh in the series The Classics of Western Spirituality (London/New York 1981).

14. See Caroline Walker Bynum, *Jesus as Mother: Studies in the Spirituality of the High Middle Ages* (Berkeley 1982), pp. 3–4 and 9–21, Robert Lerner, *The Heresy of the Free Spirit in the Later Middle Ages* (Berkeley 1972), pp. 44–54.

15. On understandings of holiness, see, Richard Kieckhefer, *Unquiet Souls: Fourteenth Century Saints and Their Religious Milieu* (Chicago 1984), pp. 14–15, 87ff. and 194ff. C.H. Lawrence in *Medieval Monasticism* (London/New York 1984), pp. 149–52, rightly suggests that to *reduce* the co-option of lay-brethren to the exploitation of the illiterate by a clerical aristocracy would be a simplification as it would ignore the importance of genuine religious motivation among the peasantry. Like David Knowles in *The Monastic Order in England* (Cambridge, reprinted 1976), pp. 214–15, Lawrence also points out that the 'illiterate classes' had traditionally been neglected by religious orders for centuries. However, neither of these points, it seems to me, detracts from the force of my three questions. A more critical assessment of the position of lay-brethren among the Cistercians is offered by R.W. Southern in *Western Society and the Church in the Middle Ages* (Harmondsworth 1970), pp. 257–9.

16. See Pierre Delooz, 'The Social Function of the Canonisation of Saints', *Concilium* 129 (1979), pp. 14–24; and 'Towards a Sociological Study of Canonised Sainthood in the Catholic Church' in Stephen Wilson, ed., *Saints and Their Cults* (Cambridge 1983), pp. 189ff. Also Weinstein and Bell, *Saints and Society*, ch. 5 'Who Was a Saint?'.

17. See Lerner, *Free Spirit*, introduction and ch. 2. For a general survey of the Beguine movement, see Southern, *The Church in the Middle Ages*, pp. 319ff.

18. The full story of Mary Ward's struggles and condemnation has yet to be told with any clarity or historical exactness. Some reference is made to these events in Lavinia Byrne IBVM, *Mary Ward: a Pilgrim Finds Her Way* (Dublin 1984), pp. 22–5 and ch. 1.

19. See Timothy George, 'The Spirituality of the Radical Reformation', in Raitt, *Christian Spirituality*, pp. 334ff.

20. See Knowles, *The Monastic Order in England*, pp. 21–25 and ch. 3, 'The Monastic Revival under Dunstan and King Edgar: the *Regularis Concordia*'.

21. Knowles relies largely on the *Vita S. Aethelwoldi* 260, by Aelfric for the corruption in the older communities and Ministers. Aelfric, be it noted, was a disciple of Ethelwold who was the most intransigent of the reformers. For the *Regularis Concordia* see the edition by Thomas Symons in the series, Nelson's Medieval Texts (London/New York 1953).

22. On the use of feminine imagery for God, see Bynum, *Jesus as Mother*, ch. 4.

23. See Mary Collins OSB, 'Daughters of the Church: the Four Theresas',

Concilium 182, (1985), 'Women–Invisible in Theology and Church', p. 17–26.

24. On the problem of women writing in conventional ways in the context of the Middle Ages, see Bynum, *Jesus as Mother*, p. 136 and n. 86. On the monasticisation of Julian, see Benedicta Ward, 'Julian the Solitary', in *Julian Rediscovered* (Oxford 1988), pp. 11–29 and endnotes. On adding women to traditional conceptions of history, see Gerda Lerner, *The Creation of Patriarchy*, Women and History 1, (New York/Oxford 1986), pp. 12–13. For a critical edition of Julian's text, see Edmund Colledge and James Walsh, eds, *The Book of Showings to the Anchoress Julian of Norwich*, Toronto 1978. The same editors have produced a modern English version in The Classics of Western Spirituality series (London/New York 1978).

25. See Delooz, 'The Canonisation of Saints'.

26. See Bynum, *Jesus as Mother*, chs. 4 and 5.

27. On this point, see Bynum, *Jesus as Mother*, pp. 256–8.

28. Quoted in English in le Goff, 'Francis of Assisi', p. 8. For a good general survey of twelfth century developments in spirituality, see George Tavard, 'Apostolic life and Church reform' in Raitt, *Christian Spirituality*, pp. 1–11. For a recent scholarly appreciation of the role of Hildegard of Bingen, see Barbara Newman's Introduction to Columba Hart and Jane Bishop, trans., *Hildegard of Bingen: Scivias* (New York 1990), esp. pp. 19–20. Newman has a fuller study, *Sister of Wisdom: St Hildegard's theology of the feminine*, Berkeley 1987.

29. Quoted in le Goff, 'Francis of Assisi', p. 8.

30. See Staudenmaier, *Technology's Storytellers*, pp. 192–8, whose stimulating reflections on the history of technology helped me to formulate some of what follows. See also the classic account of stages of development in religious life, Raymond Hostie, *Vie et Mort des Ordres Religieux: Approches Psychosociologiques* (Paris 1972), ch. 9, pt 2, 'Le cycle de vie'. Also Joan Chittister, *Women, Ministry and the Church* (New Jersey 1983), ch. 4, 'The future of religious life'.

31. For details of the deliberations of the first companions which led to the decision to formalize as a religious order, see Javier Osuna, *Friends in the Lord*, tr. Nicholas King, The Way Series 3 (London 1974), pp. 69–82. Important questions of interpretation for early Jesuit history are raised by Philip Endean, 'Who Do You Say Ignatius Is? Jesuit Fundamentalism and Beyond', *Studies in the spirituality of Jesuits* 19:5 (1987), pp. 12–36.

32. For a helpful introduction to some of the issues, see Joseph Veale, 'Ignatian Prayer or Jesuit Spirituality' in *The Way Supplement* 27 (1976), pp. 3–14.

33. The *Constitutions of the Society of Jesus* are available in English translation, edited with an introduction and commentary by George E. Ganss (The Institute of Jesuit Sources, St Louis, 1970). See especially [136], p. 121.

CHAPTER FOUR

How We Use Our Spiritual History

The introductory chapter discussed briefly some of the basic questions associated with the study of history, particularly concerning how we define and value it, and in the last chapter it was further suggested that our Christian spiritual tradition is a flawed reality that demands careful reinterpretation. At this point it will be helpful to reflect more specifically about the ways in which we choose to use our spiritual history. Our contemporary awareness of the different understandings of history which determine what we seek from the past, what we highlight as significant, and how we give 'meaning' to events, personalities or patterns of change, has considerable relevance to traditional accounts of spirituality. For example, what is called the 'Whig' view of history, which interprets it in terms of the inexorable progress of modernizing forces, has particular weaknesses. This is closely associated with, and is to a degree a secularized version of, certain questionable understandings of how Divine Providence works in history which have played a significant role in how we have framed our histories of spirituality.[1]

All specialist histories involve two competences: historical and 'technical' and, in spirituality, until fairly recently the assumptions of the second, that is to say spiritual theology, tended, in an unbalanced way, to determine our approach. In the light of this, it is possible to identify some approaches to history that seem to have predominated and which now need to be questioned. My choices do not cover all the possibilities, and to some extent at least these approaches overlap, but an understanding of them may help us to appreciate how history has been used to reinforce limited perceptions of 'life in the Spirit'. In particular, these approaches tend to do two things. Firstly, in different ways, they work within the old-fashioned narrative structure which reinforces a sense that history is simple rather than complex, universal and monolithic rather than varied, plural and particular. Secondly, they tend to operate from the standpoint of a particular ideology, or of apologetics, and subordinate truly historical considerations to non-historical needs.

Instances of enduring truths

The first approach to history may be characterized as the study of particular, and almost accidental, instances of *enduring truths*. In fact, as has already been suggested, spirituality is neither disincarnate nor on some ideal plane beyond the limitations of history but rather reflects both theological and social or cultural values. In short, particular spiritual traditions are limited and conditioned. So, for example, 'St Ignatius [Loyola] was not, and could not be, a stained-glass figure abstracted from his environment and its influences'.[2] While there continue to be differences of viewpoint concerning the precise influences on Ignatius Loyola and his spirituality, no historian could agree with an attempt to place Ignatius outside *any* significant historical conditioning.

The theologian Karl Rahner accepted that Ignatius's spirituality occurred 'in accord with historical circumstances'. Yet, having said that, he appears to place Ignatius essentially outside the limitations of history. His spirituality was 'not really an event in the history of ideas that could be inserted, if we were so to choose, in the 'Tridentine' or 'Baroque' period . . . It is something of exemplary value in a quite fundamental way, for an age that is only just starting'. In a footnote, Rahner developed this thought further by suggesting that 'Ignatius has something almost of the archaic and archetypal about him . . . He has nothing that really belongs to the Baroque or the Renaissance about him'.[3] The danger here is that Ignatius may be radically detached from the assumptions of his age and his spiritual horizons may be placed beyond criticism. Hugo Rahner, the brother of Karl, in arguing for a radical distinction between Ignatius and the *devotio moderna* tradition (which may, historically, be accurate) appeared to suggest that the formulation of *The Spiritual Exercises* was associated *essentially* with 'the mystical transformation [of Ignatius] which took place at Manresa'.[4] The writings of the Rahner brothers have led such British historians as Outram Evenett and John Bossy to point out the danger of making spiritual experience 'a region of certainty transcending any historical or psychological conditions'.[5] To suggest that a particular spirituality, like a good wine, may in some sense travel

across centuries is not the same as to seek to place it in a realm
beyond or above history.

A transcultural phenomenon

A second approach to history also presents Christian spirituality
as essentially one and universal by treating it as a *transcultural
phenomenon*. For example, holiness was for a long time assumed
to be an absolute type that could be transcribed into different
social categories, cultures or ages. The individual saint 'instantiates
and thus clarifies general principles of morality and qualities of
character that can be articulated as meaningful and understood as
possible for all participants in a society or community of faith'.[6]
This conception of sanctity, therefore, was *deductive* as it moved
from universal norms to specific examples. Such a viewpoint has
obvious dangers. Nowadays we are much more aware of the fact
that saints belong to, and reflect, the societies which produce or
honour them. Notions of sanctity change and so do the preferred
types of saint. Equally, from a theological standpoint, all models
of sanctity are relative and can never exhaust the possible forms
of Christian holiness. Saints and models of holiness may be guides
but they may also be obstacles if, by stereotyping holiness, they
overvalue the forms of the past and discourage the innovating force
of the gospel or lead us to forget Jesus's own refusal to conform to
predetermined criteria for holiness.

These perceptions have been reinforced by the development of
what may be loosely thought of as a new school of historical
study concerned with saints and sanctity. Thus a Belgian Catholic
sociologist, Pierre Delooz, has helped to elucidate the underlying
criteria for canonized sainthood in the history of the Church and,
by implication at least, has highlighted the differences between
official perceptions of sanctity and the criteria for popular cults.[7]
Other historians have concentrated their attention on analysing the
specific characteristics of sanctity in particular periods or among
distinct groups.[8] Finally, social historians are examining the *vitae* of
medieval saints as evidence for the relationship between perceptions
of sanctity and changing values in society. The premiss here is that
the ways in which we conceive of holiness mirror social values rather
than reflect an autonomous category of experience. So the study
of saints, individually and collectively, may lead us to a better
understanding of ideals of holiness and through this to a fuller
appreciation of the societies which produced them.[9]

The treatment of spirituality as a single, transcultural phenomenon may also produce a historically reinforced mind-set which
unconsciously views mainline spirituality in terms of the values
or presuppositions of a dominant western culture. Sadly, some
contemporary studies continue to suffer from this bias. Universalist
models of holiness are oppressive because they fail to acknowledge
their own relativity and cultural rootedness and effectively impose
the values of one culture on others. For example, Christians in
Latin America, Asia and Africa are forced to become 'consumers
of spiritualities that are doubtless valid but that nonetheless reflect
other experiences and other goals'.[10]

Affirming what must have been the case

Thirdly, history may be understood as an affirmation of *what must
have been the case* within a purposeful and reassuring framework
and based on a 'true' understanding of the meaning of history. To
take a general historical example, nineteenth-century Catholics and
Protestants in England openly used the issue of the Reformation to
support contemporary positions. The latter might be political (for
example, whether Catholics should be allowed any political voice)
or religious (for example, whether the Roman Catholic community
or the Church of England was the legitimate successor to the pre-
Reformation Church). While it would be unfair to write off such
Catholics as Lingard or Cardinal Gasquet as essentially polemicists
rather than historians, it is undoubtedly the case that they began
their researches with sectarian presuppositions: that the destruction
of the Catholic Church in England was disastrous and that the
Protestant Reformation was essentially political and unambiguously
wrong. Leading reformers could not be considered saintly and the
spirituality of the Reform, if it could be thought of as such, was
something that should be attacked and if possible demolished.[11]

This general approach filters out what does not fit the established
thesis. While all attempts at historical interpretation necessarily
highlight particular evidence, there is a distinction to be made
between this unavoidable process and a kind of censorship which
ignores some of the relevant material, or a polemical stance
which subordinates historical considerations to extrinsic ones.
Such illegitimate historical approaches will often result in a quite
anachronistic perspective. The historian, whatever his or her own
interests, must first attempt to reach as broad an appreciation as
possible of the period or tradition under examination on its own

terms. A good example would be the way that the spirituality of the seventeenth-century Caroline Divines has often been viewed through the preconceptions of the nineteenth-century Catholic revival in the Church of England. This movement was, in a sense, conducting a polemic about the nature of the Church against those people whose views and actions were felt to undermine sound doctrine and practice. The Tractarians claimed to know what the Church was and consequently exalted a one-sided portrayal of the theological position of the first generation of Anglicans after the period of the Elizabethan Settlement. If the English Church was part of the Church Catholic, then the first generation of its theologians and spiritual writers must have been unambiguously Catholic.

Two facts stand out that are relevant to the interpretation of seventeenth-century Anglican spirituality. Firstly, it arose within and fed upon the formularies and liturgies of the Church. The Book of Common Prayer is fundamental to any understanding of the period. All seventeenth- and eighteenth-century devotional literature (for example the poetry of George Herbert in *The Temple*) was influenced both by its language and content. Secondly, the Carolines manifest a confusing mixture of what is traditionally thought of as Protestant and as Catholic. For example, John Cosin, Bishop of Durham (died 1672) was a friend of the Huguenots, tried to reconcile Anglicans and Presbyterians and directed his polemical works mostly against Roman Catholicism, whose influence at the court of Charles I he deplored. In his attitude to grace and salvation he was a Calvinist. Yet his *A collection of Private Devotions* (1627) was an attempt to fill the devotional gap that was attracting some courtiers towards Rome. Thus it contained a defence of Saints Days, fasts, ritual (including vestments and candles), confession (the book contained a form of preparation for this) and frequent communion.

The first of these factors, the obvious dependence of Caroline spirituality on liturgy and sacraments, encouraged nineteenth-century Tractarians to over-emphasize the Catholicity of the Carolines, which they *needed* to find in order to ground their presuppositions about the nature of the Church of England, and to pass over the Reformed, and particularly Calvinist, elements of Caroline thought. For example, critical readers of George Herbert's poetry cannot but become aware as much of his Protestant emphasis on justification and assurance of salvation (for example in his poems: 'Justice, II', 'Aaron' and 'Conscience') as of his eucharistic piety and even references to medieval Catholic liturgy. While there are indications that the poem 'Sacrifice' is based structurally on the old Good Friday Reproaches of the Sarum Rite it also manifests a Calvinist conception of the sacrifice of Calvary.

Until recently, the Catholic, as opposed to a Calvinist, model for interpreting seventeenth-century Anglican spirituality has held sway. In contrast, contemporary revisionism emphasizes that Anglicanism, while 'eccentric', has to be seen within the overall Reformation movement rather than simply as in continuity with the medieval past. Seventeenth-century Anglicans would undoubtedly have called themselves Protestant and, in the context of the time, this would not have prevented them from being conscious of medieval roots. Secondly, Anglican doctrine was compatible with a Protestant standpoint. Thus its eucharistic doctrine was within legitimate Reformation bounds and was usually expounded explicitly against what was understood to be Roman Catholic doctrine. Anglican Church order, and its traditional three-fold ministry, was also one valid Protestant position among others (for example Presbyterian or Congregational). Equally, all the Carolines would have accepted, though to differing degrees, the classical Protestant positions on Scripture and salvation.[12]

Progress and the triumph of sophistication and orthodoxy

Finally a significant model of history presents a record of the triumph of *the sophisticated over the primitive* and *the orthodox over the deviant*, which concentrates on dominant groups or 'spiritual cultures', is intimately bound up with the western ideology of autonomous progress and is thus a version of what is popularly known as the 'Whig' version of history which I referred to earlier. In terms of overall conceptions of 'history', this results, in part, from a disjunction between method and context, a sense of value-free knowledge, a rejection of the subjective and consequently of the contextual nature of experience. The problem is that, if we accept uncritically the liberal Enlightenment 'progress' model of history, which arranges events into a pattern of crescendo, we will tend towards determinism. The model makes too many assumptions – particularly that situations were as they were simply because that is 'how matters fell out', that what we have inherited was inevitable and the directions taken fully appropriate. In specifically Christian approaches to history, this deviation has often been related to a sense that Divine Providence directly controls all aspects of human history, ultimately guiding it towards its proper conclusion.

The temptation, therefore, to present Christian history in *visibly* providential terms is obviously considerable.[13]

A vision of progress, linked to Divine Providence, means that sometimes assumptions about meaning originate entirely outside history and then are brought into play within historical interpretation as such. Thus, it could be argued that the history of Christianity begins with the coming of the Spirit at Pentecost and will end with the parousia. In other words, 'history' loses its integrity by being placed absolutely under the umbrella of theology and thus the story, in its essential features, is moved beyond the scope of strictly historical description or analysis. History then becomes the inexorable, inevitable and necessarily visible unfolding of the growing Kingdom of God. Associated with this was the tendency to see theology less as a process of development within cultural and historical conditioning than as 'a series of formulations of that one content of faith diversifying and finding expression in different cultural contexts'.[14]

Now from a theological standpoint, we may quite validly understand Providence to be a reality. This is one level of truth. However it is a fact that the Christian community, and its spiritual traditions, are also human realities and dependent on the contingent factors of the human condition. Christianity, in its growth or development, has sought to influence human history and has also adapted to historical circumstances. When, therefore, we seek to interpret our past there is a legitimately committed standpoint which will include an overall sense of what history means in the light of Christian revelation and tradition. We are not bound to believe that history has no meaning or is entirely arbitrary. However, one of the great advances in historical study has been a realization of the dangers of teleology, that is, of presenting history selectively in the light of our sense of meaning and final purpose. We must retain a proper respect for the demands of history as a human discipline by seeking always to reach out for as complete and authentic encounter with the past as possible, even if we know that it is inevitable that, as individual historians, our sense of the past will be imperfect. The history of spirituality, in the past, has all too frequently adopted an apologetic approach to particular questions, or even imposed what may be called a non-historical orthodoxy on earlier development, in order to show up the present reality in the best possible light or to prove that the movement of history accords with an orthodox theological perspective.

Models and the histories of spirituality

The historical models of spirituality as particular instances of enduring truths and as a transcultural phenomenon are very apparent in some of the older textbooks. P. Pourrat, writing shortly after the First World War, has been described by some as the first historian of spirituality for his four volume *La Spiritualité Chrétienne*. However, his theological presuppositions, reflecting a unified and systematic approach to spiritual doctrine, force him to view Christian spirituality as essentially a unity. At the end of the first volume, he suggests that in all the various manifestations of the life of the Spirit there could be found the same basic doctrine regarding prayer, virtue, mysticism or the theory of spiritual growth. In the Preface to the second volume, he describes the different 'schools' of spirituality as fundamentally the same (*tout en étant la même dans son fond*). Finally, in the Preface to the third volume he asserts, concerning national types of spirituality, that they are really one and the same in so far as they are Catholic, differing only in presentation.[15] This approach also means that, inevitably, Pourrat's cultural perspective is one-dimensional. The Graeco-Latin dominance is accepted without question – indeed the presence of other spiritual cultures is effectively ignored.

While Louis Bouyer is critical of Pourrat in his Preface to the multi-volume *A History of Christian Spirituality*, published in the 1960s, he also stresses the essential oneness of Christian spirituality. While particular circumstances and the unique personality of each major figure lead to variations in the application of the gospel to human life, 'we must be very reserved about speaking of spiritualities in the plural'. The volumes' preoccupation with the essential unity of spirituality rather than with concrete diversity, means that they often lack a nuanced awareness of the differences between 'schools' and, indeed, of the plurality within them. The cultural perspective is broader than Pourrat's; the Syriac tradition receives an occasional mention and there is a brief chapter on Celtic spirituality. However, on the whole, Christian spirituality is presented as a fairly unified culture.[16] Jean Leclercq, who shared in part of one of Bouyer's volumes, has provided the Introduction to two collections of essays in the Cistercian Publications' occasional series 'The Spirituality of Western Christendom'. While at times acknowledging the intimate links between spirituality and social context, he also emphasizes an essential unity. Christian experience has 'a universal echo far beyond the individual himself and his social milieu'.[17]

The two most substantial attempts recently to provide a broad historical treatment of Christian spirituality, *The Study of Spirituality*[18] and the three Christian volumes published in the series, World Spirituality: an Encyclopedic History of the Religious Quest, contrast with Pourrat and Bouyer in several ways.[19] Both are collections of specialist essays by international and ecumenical teams of scholars rather than continuous narratives by one author. In neither case has a determining definition of spirituality, let alone a unified, systematic theological framework, been imposed on the writers. Both publications provide a good balance between East and West and make other attempts to express the cultural plurality of Christian spirituality beyond a Graeco-Latin hegemony.

The third and fourth models of history, which affirm what must have been the case and record the triumph of sophistication and orthodoxy are, like the first two, closely related to each other. Both tend to assume that development moves in straight lines and that this is progress under the guidance of Providence. Historical development has frequently been interpreted in terms of a kind of spiritual theory of evolution, based on principles of supernatural selection. As an example of this, we may consider the way in which histories of spirituality, without any attempt at critical interpretation, chart the development and dominant role in the Church of particular spiritualities. Thus, traditional histories move smoothly from the apostolic period through the patristic to the development of structured monasticism. They then present the history of spirituality in terms of the changes within particular monastic traditions, or the development of new ones, without any attempt either to analyse why monasticism as a whole became of such overwhelming importance or to evaluate this process. The implication seems to be that, while monasticism in fact came to dominate the spirituality of the West, this was because it was inevitable and a good thing. Furthermore, as one writer has noted recently, the emphasis on a monastic matrix for change or development in religious life (and, by implication, in spirituality in general) forces us to interpret spiritual history in terms primarily of asceticism or personal perfection and to exclude the themes of ministry and pastoral practice from studies of spirituality.[20] Equally, if the history of spirituality describes the processes whereby certain theological standpoints came to be interpreted as orthodox and others as deviant, the assumption was that this was for the best and that the concepts of 'orthodoxy' and 'deviance' need no further justification.

This sense of progress and providential history means that we tend to interpret origins in terms of consequences. In other words, our sense of what came to be leads us to a sense of 'what must have been the case' to start with. If a particular theological standpoint carries the day then the contrary tendencies are assumed to have been deviant. If one spiritual trend emerges as predominant, then what it replaced must have been less effective or fruitful.

The volumes of Pourrat concentrated firmly on the development of monasticism and on mystics and gave no attention to lay or popular spirituality, except indirectly in a chapter on medieval 'devotions' and briefly in reference to Ozanam (the founder of the charitable St Vincent de Paul Society) in the nineteenth century. Dissenting spiritualities are hardly touched upon, except in reference to the triumph of orthodoxy. Louis Bouyer is healthier. His second volume, on the medieval period, has fully three chapters on lay spirituality. However, the scholarship is dated and contemporary historians would undoubtedly question the rather negative assessment of such dissenting movements as the Waldensians and the Beguines. In the third volume, on Orthodox and Protestant spiritualities, the proponents of the radical reformation, such as the Anabaptists are characterized as 'sectarian' in relation to the orthodoxy of mainline Protestantism.

Sadly, one of the recent volumes, *The Study of Spirituality*, has missed the opportunity to take into account a more critical approach in this regard. Even important dissenting traditions receive little or no serious attention and significant lay movements such as the Beguines are not mentioned at all. Indeed, lay spirituality as a whole is notable only by its absence. As for women, the two great mystical Catherines receive four pages between them and Teresa of Avila shares a chapter with John of the Cross. Apart from that, all is effectively silence. In general, this volume shows a lack of awareness of revisionism in historical circles. In contrast, the second and third volumes in the series, 'World Spirituality' show signs of a broader perspective as well as up-to-date scholarship. Lay spirituality and women are given explicit attention (although I feel that some opportunities to give greater exposure to the latter may have been missed and the balance of scholars is still heavily male). Dissenting traditions are still relatively under-exposed although, when they are mentioned, there is a greater willingness to recognize that official interpretations (for example of the 'heretical' nature of

Peter Waldo and his followers in the twelfth century) need some revision. Unfortunately, the first volume, which deals with the period up to the twelfth century, is more traditional. Mainline traditions still predominate and, although there is a provocative essay on lay Christians, women are almost entirely invisible.

The age of the grand, general historical survey of spirituality is now over. One reason is because at heart it reflected a transcultural and perennial theology of the spiritual life. As theology has shifted towards a more experiential and, therefore, culturally plural starting point (even if in dialogue with inherited tradition), so too the history of spiritual traditions is increasingly linked to specific contexts and has in consequence, become a specialist discipline in which we can no longer expect a single person to have the detailed knowledge to write a multi-volume history. The second reason is, as was suggested in the summary of historical models, that such approaches to spirituality concentrate largely on history as narrative. This moves easily from one period to another in well-ordered sequence, while the variety and irreducible complexity of history tends to be replaced by a certain sameness and simplicity. Narrative history lends itself easily to the 'Whig' version of the history of spirituality, conceived of as progressive evolution and inexorable progress, 'a necessary sequence unfolding easily to a predetermined conclusion'.[21] This has been effectively undermined by the impact of revisionism in historical study. As a consequence of these factors, the major proportion of new historical works in spirituality are either collections of specialist essays or detailed scholarly studies of particular traditions or groups, within their specific social, cultural and theological contexts.[22]

History and choices

All historical studies, not least of spirituality, involve choices. Firstly, we choose specific *temporal limits*. The boundaries for understanding spiritual movements are partly shaped by the evidence we discover. However, at some point we decide on the proper limits which will enclose a specific interpretation. For example, if we adopt a classical 'popes and cloister' view of history, we will tend to treat the Reformation as beginning about 1517, with a peak sometime in the middle of the sixteenth century and effectively complete by about 1600 (with a few loose ends remaining until the Thirty Years War). This is to interpret history from the point of view of religious and political élites. A concentration on the high politics of history also tends to produce a simplified and universal picture with a consequent underestimation of local differences. The variation of time-scales and plurality of experiences is sacrificed to a synthetic portrait. An alternative standpoint might see that the Reformation, as a movement affecting the 'person in the pew', was only just beginning to take effect by 1600 and was hardly complete before 1700. In other words a decision on the proper limits also depends on what evidence we deem to be *relevant*.

There have also been different points of view regarding the relationship of both Catholic and Reformed tendencies to the medieval past. Should we refer to the Catholic Reformation or the Counter-Reformation? The first seeks to emphasize that new developments in Catholic thinking and behaviour in the sixteenth century, and not least spirituality, have their roots prior to the Protestant challenge to the Church and therefore cannot be seen as purely a reaction to and defence against the threat of the Reformation. To call this renewal *Counter*-Reformation may therefore give a false impression. Such a revisionist approach was synthesized in the works of such historians as the Frenchman Pierre Janelle and the Englishman Outram Evenett which began to become standard textbooks for students in the early 1970s. A similar revision, with regard to the continuity between the Middle Ages and the Protestant Reformation, has begun to achieve respectability and plays a significant role in the decision about how to divide the treatment of Christian spirituality in the new series 'World Spirituality: an Encyclopedic History of the Religious Quest'. The treatment of the leading reformers, such as Luther, Calvin and Zwingli (not to mention the Anabaptists and the radical Reformation), is included in the same volume as the High Middle Ages. The temporal limits for the whole volume therefore stretch from the twelfth century to approximately 1550 thus emphasizing continuities rather than simply new beginnings.[23]

We also choose *geographical* limits. In traditional approaches to Church history, it is possible to note a fairly strong geographical bias in much of its interpretation. Once again, the role of a classical, narrative approach to history is evident. The overall criterion is 'significance' and if the historical process is associated mainly with rulers, popes and power-structures, the tendency will be to adopt a geographical framework which reflects the significant orbits of national, 'high European', or more broadly, world politics (wherever the 'world' is deemed to be centred). The local and specific gives way to the central and general as an organizing idea. So traditional geographical limits often reflect perceptions of power.

There has also been a cultural bias which is partly associated with the issue of power but is also distinct. While accepting that the Church is a world-wide phenomenon, even prior to the sixteenth-century colonial expansion, interest has usually been confined to *western* Europe or its missionary activities (or, at best to Eastern Orthodoxy as well) and ancient Christian communities in the Middle East, Ethiopia or South India, for example, are ignored or accorded a footnote as they came into contact with the religion of Europe. Standard histories usually accorded a little space to Eastern Europe, Scandinavia and Scotland but the proportions made it clear where cultural priorities lay. Histories of the spirituality of western Christianity usually showed the same cultural bias when it came to establishing geographical limits for the treatment of particular movements or periods. Western Europe was the centre of operation with details becoming more sparce as we move outwards to the fringes (whether eastwards or northwards) except in those few cases where significant movements were actually focused there (for example a fourteenth-century mystical trend in England).

Cultural bias is closely associated, in practice, with a preference for a universalist understanding of the Church (that is, from the centre outwards, or all the parts in reference to the centre). This inherently prevents appropriate attention being given to the Christian experience as a communion of local communities and therefore to a more balanced spatial or geographical perspective. The notion of variation is excluded.[24]

Some recent studies in the history of spirituality have shown a greater awareness of the need to attend to geographical variations. For example, an essay by Jean Leclercq on the development of monasticism in the West, up to the twelfth century, is regional in approach and the study of holiness in the Middle Ages by Donald Weinstein and Rudolph Bell gives serious attention to regional variations in 'types' of holiness. An even more fascinating approach is to consider the way in which specific geography, or landscape, is both moulded by religious imagination and, at the same time, moulds us. Someone such as Belden Lane has written an ambitious and highly original study of North American spirituality in terms of 'sacred places' and how they function.[25] A few Church historians have begun to write more critically of the eurocentrism present in Church history. For example the celebrations planned for 1992 to mark the five-hundredth anniversary of the arrival of Christopher

Columbus in the Americas has already provoked negative reactions in Latin America. Involved with eurocentric triumphalism, which conceives of invasion and genocide as 'discovery', is another kind of arrogance which sees these questionable events as the glorious expansion of Christianity. Spiritually, therefore, as well as culturally the indigenous peoples acquire meaning only insofar as they enter the world of the Europeans. Their own traditions were largely discounted and they became merely objects of that missionary zeal that for so long has been understood as a vital dimension of the spirituality of reformed Catholicism in the sixteenth and seventeenth centuries. With Hegel, such a historical perspective identifies western Christianity simplistically with civilization.[26]

Another choice which operates in the history of spirituality has to do with viewing *certain kinds of evidence as significant*. This relates to an evaluation of what history *is*. Is it merely 'ideas' or is it more? The contemporary approach to the history of spirituality is increasingly influenced by developments in the discipline of history since the Second World War, particularly by the *annales* school of French historians. Two elements of the approach of this school are central. Firstly, a kind of religious sociology has emerged which aims to know the 'average Christian' from the past through paying attention to the broadest range of evidence available rather than by relying on traditional sources alone. Secondly, the history of spirituality is viewed as a discipline which, while interested in people's explicitly religious life, must consider their beliefs and spiritual practices within the context of all the dimensions of their existence. Despite its increasing influence, some dangers in this new approach to religious history have been noted by historians from Britain and North America, even when they do not reject it entirely and are themselves influenced by it. A striking danger that has been noted is the tendency to be unnecessarily impatient with traditional approaches to religious history, to reduce everything to economic or demographic factors, to ignore the specifically religious or theological dimensions, and then, based on this reductionism, to indulge in hasty judgements.[27]

Most serious scholars of the history of spirituality now accept the general thesis that basic religious attitudes are conditioned by society and share the desire to study the spiritual aspirations of popular religion. But the more perceptive among them would also reject a total abandonment of traditional sources, such as mystical treatises, saints' lives or chronicles, in favour of an exclusive attention to artifacts, wills or charters, architecture and rituals.

The point is that these new sources for the history of spirituality are in practice more difficult to handle. A more balanced approach falls somewhere between the two poles of an exclusive concentration on theories of contemplation and the newer concentration on the social context of religious movements. On the one hand, it is possible to address new questions to old material and thus to determine how the differences between people (e.g. gender or socio-ecclesiastical status) are reflected in their approach to topics even within the constraints of conventional language. On the other hand, a substantial body of popular devotional literature (which has often been neglected in the past) does in fact survive and, by attention to other kinds of evidence, whether art, wills, or the vitae of popular saints, it is possible to recover a surprising amount of detail about popular spirituality.[28]

On the question of choices, finally, we cannot ignore the exclusion of women. The fact is that women, like men, have always been agents in history. However, history-making has tended to record what men do, or at least what a theory of history, created in a male-dominated world, finds significant. In terms of mainstream spirituality, women have been conceived as generally marginal to its creation. Alongside other marginalized groups, their absence distorts our historical mentality and causes conceptual errors. Because the process of giving meaning to the past is vital for the development of the Christian tradition, women's marginalization effectively structures them as 'a minority'. They are effectively excluded from the formation of theory which determines not only what history is but what spirituality is. This has had an effect on the way in which women have understood the Self in relationship to God, other people and spiritual growth. Exclusion from the account of history not only reinforces subordination but, more damagingly, may create a sense of being *essentially* insignificant.[29]

Hagiography as deviation

In the past, the treatment of spirituality has been susceptible to a striking historical deviation that I would call the *hagiographical*. 'Hagiography', whether in the technical sense of saints' lives or, more broadly, as a general approach to the history of personalities and movements, is essentially a form of popular story-telling – a narrative discourse built around the classical structures of folk-tale and myth. Every group finds a way to reaffirm its mythical conceptions of history which offer a collective sense of

105

destiny. This is usually organized within a framework of a plot –
clearly delineated heroes and villains as well as ultimately helpful
endings. Such 'history' presents a purposeful framework that leaves
us reassured about the ordered nature of the world. Because of this,
it too is likely to manifest the tendency to universalize and to ignore
the particularities of time and place. The world of hagiography is an
idealized one, which is constructed in terms of those values that are
presumed to be pre-eminent. The tone of hagiography is moralistic
in that it presents only what the writer wants the reader to believe
and to value and what, at the time of writing, is in need of reform.
The hagiographical approach frequently adopts a narrative form of
history.

On one level, myths have a value in that they point beyond event
to meaning and remind us that the human story involves more
than purely recorded history. However, unless we take care, myth
can easily become a reassurance about the 'rightness of things as
they are'. We might even argue that the hagiographical tendency
is inherently élitist precisely because it focuses on special or
outstanding people as summing up a period, region or group. Both
of these aspects may involve a social judgement because, so often in
spirituality, mythical stories of 'spiritual nobility' have been linked
quite clearly to particular socio-economic values. A cautionary and
true story illustrates the dangers. An elderly nun had been deeply
impressed by a book concerning the short, and undoubtedly
beautiful, life of a little French boy called Guy de Fontgallant.
He was apparently so good and noble (not only spiritually, but also
socially as it happened) that after making his First Communion he
died in the odour of sanctity. In conversation with other sisters the
nun said that she had afterwards looked in the library for another
book with the same admirable sentiments and values and had the
good fortune to find one. It was the story of *Little Lord Fauntleroy*!

Because it is so often associated with social as well as religious
values, the hagiographical deviation is one expression of *ideology*
– in other words, the ways in which what we believe connects
with power-structures. Ideology involves those ways of feeling,
valuing and perceiving which have some kind of relationship to the
maintenance and reproduction of power, whether social or religious.
Indeed, religion is one aspect of human life that is particularly
susceptible to ideology. One of its strongest features in this regard
is its mythology by which it can intertwine with deep, unconscious
a-rational fears and needs. In its ideological aspect, closely linked to
the hagiographical, religion provides a social cement which not only

keeps the community united against the outside but, within, staves off the frightening spectre of fragmentation or conflict. In this way, we might say, hagiography pacifies!

The reassurance provided by the hagiographical deviation is expressed in histories of spirituality in other ways. The last chapter suggested that those women who are permitted a place in history are effectively edited so that they may be presented as examples of acceptable attitudes, virtues and behaviour. Any possible challenge they may have provided is ignored. Another context for reassurance is the way in which founders of religious orders (and therefore, presumably, important elements of the orders' contemporary myths of origin) have their complexities or foibles edited out. Their human and spiritual development is simplified, or even pre-empted entirely, by questionable stories of precocious childhood saintliness which indicate that their 'chosen' quality and spiritual maturity were evident from the beginning. Thus the holiness of founders became a static quality and one that was also quite unambiguous. Any clashes between founders and Church authority were passed over in silence or reduced to the anodyne and insignificant. Such people were rarely portrayed as advocates of questionable views – their orthodoxy must remain unstained.

Traditional thinking about holiness began with a fixed ideal rather than with an individual's concrete situation. And yet, as we have seen, the values implied in the popular promotion of saints differed from age to age. However, either way, saints were often presented in such a way as, consciously or unconsciously, to reflect quite specific values. This, once again, links with the hagiographical tendency to remove holiness from the ups and downs of normal life, to smooth out the rough edges of people thought of as holy. The traditional genre of 'Lives of the Saints' on which I was brought up frequently eliminated weakness or reduced it to amiable eccentricity and painted a picture of consistency for its subject. Holiness was also used as a way of removing particular people from the realm of criticism. In general, therefore, the model of holiness presented by the hagiographical deviation was at base a defence of the institution and its values. Institutional holiness demands conformity. This was the acceptable face of the Church, untouched by conflict.

The problem of interpreting history

The presentation of the history of spirituality is not merely a scholarly issue but is of general concern. This is partly because many of us belong within living spiritual traditions which have a long history, and partly because many people today are turning to the wisdom of the past, often through the medium of spiritual classics. The issue of historical interpretation is therefore a live one. We know that value-free history is not possible. As we have seen, historical investigation and interpretation always start from somewhere and have some assumptions about history and, at the same time, about the process of interpreting it. Present values in spirituality demand that we seek to retrieve or revise because we believe that history has subordinated certain groups and advanced others and that it is important for our present identity and desire to live more complete Christian lives, to recover their story. Equally, the belief that this group or the other are, in fact, the victims in history, depends on my contemporary perceptions.

Facts and values are intimately linked together. So we have to acknowledge that we cannot avoid value judgement. Yet, I do not believe that historical agnosticism or total scepticism is the necessary corollary. Once again, we need to distinguish between a total lack of awareness of our conditioning by contemporary horizons and a conscious *committed* standpoint on history, which is nevertheless open to revision in the light of new facts as they present themselves and which seeks to expose as fully as possible the horizons of another age before entering into dialogue with it. Here, I would suggest that some contemporary critics of traditional approaches to Church history, such as Professor John Kent, appear not to distinguish clearly enough between an apologetic-confessional approach and commitment. Kent seems to assume that commitment of any kind in the context of Church history, inevitably leads to distortion although he does admit that complete neutrality in historical study may be impossible. He under-estimates the degree to which Church historians are nowadays self-conscious about the delicate balance between falling into unacceptable distortions and nevertheless offering some value judgement.[30]

While the amount of evidence available about spiritual traditions, as well as its quality, varies from age to age there is usually enough to be able to judge that certain assertions are valid and others not. With a proper attention to the widest range of available evidence, it is therefore possible to construct an image of a period or movement with reasonable accuracy even if we must acknowledge that this is always incomplete and therefore open to future revision. The process of interpretation is, for the historian, the meeting of *two* horizons, consciously acknowledged, rather than the uncritical imposition of one on another. Arguably, there is a fine line between the inevitable and valid selection of evidence in history and a kind of censorship which deliberately seeks to screen out the inconsistent and inconvenient to force facts into predetermined conclusions. Yet this line must be maintained. For historians, or those seeking a deeper understanding of a spiritual tradition, not all facts are equally relevant but no fact should be seen as an *enemy*.

The misgivings by some historians concerning the unbalanced effect of present-day issues on our historical perspective (or what is called 'presentism') really means that our interpretations must first of all seek to do full justice to the personalities or spiritual cultures of other ages. We must not be excessively influenced by what we find unattractive or peculiar from a contemporary perspective – and there is plenty of such material in the history of spirituality. 'Presentism' essentially collapses the past into the present. This has two aspects. Negatively, it will blame the past for not being the present. Augustine's attitudes in all respects are culturally conditioned and cannot be adopted uncritically in the present. However that is different from accusing him of the moral fault of being, for example, a male chauvinist (implicitly, he *should* have known better). Secondly, positively, it will turn some past traditions, uncritically and anachronistically, into images of the present (for example, the Beguines become a 'feminist' movement or popular religious poverty movements in the twelfth century become examples of 'class struggle') or it will adopt certain people as heroes and honorary members of another century and its concerns (for example, Thomas More was a martyr for an ultramontane understanding of the Church or Meister Eckhart wrote 'creation-centred spirituality'). No historian can present the absolute truth and so we must settle for offering, as honestly as possible, what we believe to be as near to the truth as we can reach, after detailed and rigorous research and reflection.[31]

A committed standpoint on history certainly means that we all have some sense of what history, in an overall sense, *means*. It has already been noted that theological considerations must not prevent us from paying proper attention to historical ones so that point does not need to be laboured again. However, a religious view of history will inevitably see, behind the historical, social and cultural 'facts', the revelation of God's action in and through human processes. The 'theologian' (and, by this, I mean anyone who is consciously engaged in their own spiritual journey, within a community of faith) is inevitably engaged with the material in a different way from a person who has a more agnostic standpoint. More specifically, a commitment to the belief that the unfolding of the Kingdom of God is intimately linked to issues of human justice will lead us to retrieve the underside of history as we ask ourselves who is left out of establishment history. Because the past acts as a mirror for our present, a revision of our historical perspectives and an attempt to reach as full a picture as possible, is vital if our establishment of a contemporary spiritual identity is not to repeat the oppressions of the past in new ways by preventing others from having a history and, therefore, a proper identity at all.

Notes

1. See my general remarks on the meaning of 'history' and on problems of historical enquiry in chapter 1. I am not aware of detailed historiography in English in the area of spirituality. However, I have been stimulated by work in Church history as a whole. While at times flawed by precisely the kind of ideological reading of history which he stigmatizes, the volume by John Kent, *The Unacceptable Face: The Modern Church in the Eyes of the Historian* (London 1987), nevertheless makes a number of telling and provocative points. The historiography of the Reformation in particular, for example, Rosemary O'Day, *The Debate on the English Reformation* (London 1986), and Christopher Haigh, ed., *The English Reformation Revised* (Cambridge 1987), introduction and ch. 1, have some fruitful lessons for our reading of the history of spirituality. More specifically, John Van Engen's 'The Christian Middle Ages as an Historiographical Problem', *American Historical Review* 91 (1988), pp. 519–52, touches directly on some issues in the interpretation of spirituality. There is also a recent, and very helpful essay by the American historian John O'Malley on certain historiographical issues in the history of religious life which has obvious applications to spirituality as a whole. See 'Priesthood, Ministry, and Religious Life: Some Historical and Historiographical Considerations', *Theological Studies* 49 (1988), pp. 223–57.

2. H. Outram Evennett, *The Spirit of the Counter-Reformation* (Cambridge 1968), p. 55.

3. Karl Rahner, *The Dynamic Element in the Church* (ET, London 1964), pp. 85–7 and footnote 1.

4. Hugo Rahner, *The Spirituality of St Ignatius Loyola* (ET, Chicago, 1953), p. 55.

5. See Evennett, *The Counter-Reformation* pp. 55–6 and the editor's postscript, pp. 126–32 by John Bossy.

6. John Stratton Hawley, ed., *Saints and Virtues* (Berkeley 1987), introduction, p. xvi.

7. See, Pierre Delooz, 'Towards a Sociological Study of Canonized Sainthood in the Catholic Church', in Stephen Wilson, ed., *Saints and*

Their Cults (Cambridge 1983), pp. 189–216; and 'The Social Function of the Canonisation of saints', *Concilium* 'Models of Holiness' 129 (1979), pp. 14–24.

8. See Richard Kieckhefer, *Unquiet Souls: Fourteenth Century Saints and Their Religious Milieu*, Chicago 1984; Elizabeth Petroff, *Consolation of the Blessed*, New York 1979, which deals with women saints in Italy in the thirteenth century.

9. See Donald Weinstein and Rudolph Bell, *Saints and Society: the Two Worlds of Western Christendom, 1000–1700*, Chicago 1982.

10. Gustavo Gutiérrez, *We Drink from our Own Wells* (London 1984), p. 28.

11. For some further background, see O'Dea, *The English Reformation*, ch. 3, 'Historians and contemporary politics: 1780–1850'.

12. See P.E. Moore and F.L. Cross, *Anglicanism: The Thought and Practice of the Church of England, Illustrated from the Religious Literature of the Seventeenth Century*, London 1935; Gene Veith, *Reformation Spirituality: the Religion of George Herbert* London 1985, introduction and ch. 1. There is a modern edition of John Cosin, *A Collection of Private Devotions* edited by P. Stanwood, Oxford 1967. For George Herbert's poems see the volume in The Classics of Western Spirituality series, *George Herbert: The Country Parson, The Temple*, John Wall, ed. (London/New York 1981).

13. See remarks about providence and progress in Church history in Kent, *The Unacceptable Face*, pp. 4–7.

14. Yves Congar, 'Church History as a Branch of Theology', *Concilium* 7: 6 (1970), p. 87.

15. P. Pourrat, *La Spiritualité Chrétienne*, 4 vols, Paris 1918. For some critical remarks on Pourrat's approach to history, see Kent, *The Unacceptable Face*, p. 22 and p. 223 n. 18; also Owen Chadwick, 'Indifference and Morality' in Peter Brooks, ed., *Christian Spirituality: Essays in Honour of Gordon Rupp* (London 1975), pp. 206–07.

16. Louis Bouyer et al., *A History of Christian Spirituality*, 3 volumes, ET, London, 1968. For a brief critique of Bouyer, see Thomas Gannon and George Traub, *The Desert and the City* (Chicago rd 1984), p. 5 and p. 294 n. 7.

17. See the Introduction in E. Rozanne Elder, ed., *The Spirituality of Western Christendom*, Cistercian Studies 30, Kalamazoo 1976; also the introduction in *The Roots of the Modern Christian Tradition*, Cistercian Studies 55, Kalamazoo 1984.

18. Cheslyn Jones, Geoffrey Wainwright and Edward Yarnold, eds, *The Study of Spirituality*, London/New York 1986.

19. See, Bernard McGinn and John Meyendorff, eds, *Christian Spirituality: Origins to the Twelfth Century* London 1986; Jill Raitt and John Meyendorff, eds, *Christian Spirituality: High Middle Ages and Reformation*, London 1987; and Louis Dupré and Don E. Saliers, eds, *Christian Spirituality: Post-Reformation Modern*, New York 1989; London 1990.

20. See O'Malley, 'Priesthood, Ministry and Religious Life', pp. 226–7.

21. Haigh *The English Reformation*, p. 30.
22. Rowan Williams's recent study, *The Wound of Knowledge: Christian Spirituality from the New Testament to St John of the Cross* (London 1979), makes no pretensions to being a comprehensive narrative history even of the period up to the sixteenth century where it ends. While the framework is broadly chronological, it is not history on the model of Pourrat or Bouyer but a stimulating reflection on the ways in which theology and some central themes in the history of spirituality interrelate.
23. See Pierre Janelle, *The Catholic Reformation*, Milwaukee 1963; Evennett, *The Spirit of the Counter-Reformation*, ch. 1; Raitt, *Christian Spirituality*, introduction. On the dating of 'the Reformation', see the Introduction by John Bossy to Jean Delumeau, *Catholicism between Luther and Voltaire*, London/Philadelphia 1977.
24. For some observations on this phenomenon, see Giuseppe Alberigo, 'The Local Church in the West (1500–1945)', *The Heythrop Journal*, 28: 2 (1987), pp. 125–43.
25. See Jean Leclercq, 'Monasticism and Asceticism 2: Western Christianity' in McGinn, *Christian Spirituality*; and Weinstein and Bell, *Saints and Society*, ch. 6, 'Place'. On geography and 'Sacred Place' see Belden C. Lane, *Landscapes of the Sacred: Geography and Narrative in American Spirituality*, New York 1989.
26. See for example the article by the Mexican Church historian, Enrique Dussel, 'Was America Discovered or Invaded?', *Concilium* 200 (1988), 'Truth and its Victims', pp. 126–34.
27. See John Bossy, 'Introduction' to Jean Delumeau, *Catholicism Between Luther and Voltaire* (ET, London 1977), pp. xiii–xiv. A good description of the *annales* approach is contained in Delumeau's Part II, chapter 2.
28. For a balanced critique of this approach see Caroline Walker Bynum, *Jesus as Mother* (Berkeley 1982), introduction, pp. 3–8. For her own approach see this work *passim* and also her essay 'Religious Women in the Later Middle Ages' in Raitt, *Christian Spirituality*, pp. 121ff. See also Richard Kieckhefer, 'Major Currents in Late Medieval Devotion', in Raitt, who pays attention both to devotional literature and to art, relics, liturgical practice, pilgrimages and popular cults.
29. For some analysis of women in relation to the interpreted past, see Gerda Lerner, *The Creation of Patriarchy*, Women and History 1 (New York/Oxford 1986), introduction and chs 2 and 11.
30. See Kent, *The Unacceptable Face*, pp. 26–7.
31. See Bynum, 'Religious Women in the Later Middle Ages', pp. 136–7 on methodological observations.

PART TWO

Two Case Studies

CHAPTER FIVE

A Question of Development: Religious Life

This chapter, and the following one, illustrate some of the questions of historical interpretation that have been raised, with reference to two case studies. Traditional interpretations of the history of religious life illustrate the problems of an old-fashioned narrative structure which reinforces a sense that history is simple and monolithic rather than complex and plural. Indeed, religious life is not so much a single spiritual tradition as a variety of movements and Christian life-styles which, because they interrelate, are generally viewed as a single phenomenon. A particular problem with religious life is that it has often been viewed from a rather 'Whig' perspective. When the development of religious life is presented as a single line, what emerges tends to appear as the inevitable consequence of progress. 'What emerged' is read back into the process of development in such a way as to edit this in the light of the results.

The example of religious life seems important because, despite always being a numerical minority in the Church, it developed into a dominant force in western spirituality to a remarkable degree. This makes it of interest well beyond the Catholic tradition even if certain aspects of the influence of religious life on spirituality seem to be primarily a Roman Catholic problem subsequent to the Reformation. The identity of lay Christians was effectively obscured for centuries because religious life became a kind of normative framework for Christian life. Throughout its history, religious life has often related in an uncomfortable way to the institutional Church which has therefore sought to define and control it. As a consequence, its nature, history and relationship to the Christian community as a whole have come to be understood in ways that demand critical re-evaluation. This chapter highlights a few important questions and then suggests how assumptions about the nature of religious life and its history may be challenged.

Where did religious life begin?

Traditional histories tended to situate the origins of religious life in Egyptian desert monasticism at the end of the third century. However, such a starting point is questionable because a great deal occured, before the desert experience, which has often been ignored. It is difficult to disentangle all the strands of embryonic religious life, how they arose and what relationship they had with the Christian community as a whole. Two examples stand out as symptomatic in several respects. These are the early autonomous virgins and the tradition of Syriac asceticism.

The free commitment of virgins and widows, and the creation of a distinct life-style within the Christian community from the apostolic period onwards, is the starting point for all later developments.[1] New Testament evidence (e.g. Acts 6. 1–6; 1 Tim. 5. 3–16) seems to indicate that the category of widows developed at an early stage, that they were supported by the Church and helped the local community by prayers and visiting. It is possible that virgins emerged initially as an element within this group.[2] By *c.* 270, virgins and widows were described, in the 'Apostolic Church Order', as distinct groups alongside deaconesses.

Because virginity really becomes the distinguishing feature of life-styles that were ultimately described as 'religious life', the question of the origins of such an ideal is important. It is difficult to distinguish in an absolute way the theological and wider social and human origins of the ideal of virginity. The inspiration for its importance cannot be said to be directly evangelical in the sense that the gospels do not centre their attention on virginity as an *indispensable* means of proclaiming the Kingdom of God. Some commentators have concluded that the original inspiration for the ideal arose from a Greco-Roman culture whose sexual licentiousness may have provoked a cult of virginity as an antidote. In addition, there was, in the early Church, a strong sense that the end time would soon replace the corruptions of society and that virginity was an anticipation of this. There may be some truth in this, although it would seem less likely that the original inspiration for virginity was universally and exclusively the result of sexual puritanism.

There were other, more 'social' factors. Thus celibacy was particularly important for women as it made them equal participants, with men, in a common search for perfection. It also created a space for them other than that alloted to wife, mother or courtesan.

Equally sexual relations and marriage were essentially *social* facts and so, therefore, was virginity. Because marriage was the accepted framework for the unity and the continuity of the human race, the choice of virginity had radical social implications. It has been suggested that the ideal of living 'like the angels' originated not so much in a concern for physical purity as in a conception of the perfect society which, like the angels around God's throne, would be voluntary and completely harmonious rather than simply conventional relationships.[3]

Virgines sacrae appear at an early date in Rome, perhaps inspired in part by the tradition of virgin martyrs and even the Vestal Virgins. By the time of St Ambrose in the fourth century, many virgins were consecrated annually in Italy, Constantinople, Alexandria and North Africa. Some lived with their parents, or in their own houses, and others with clergy around a Church. They were under the care of the local bishop and were frequently well-educated. As well as engaging in prayer and fasting, virgins frequently gave hospitality to the needy and undertook various forms of charity. Some offered spiritual counsel and studied Scripture with other virgins. There is evidence that a number of virgins travelled as pilgrims, especially to the Holy Land, as an expression of a perfect imitation of Christ. One well-known pilgrim is generally called Egeria. The evidence indicates that she wrote her diary for the members of a community over which she presided. She was accorded great respect by the authorities and seems to have had surprisingly open relationships with male ascetics. She was given hospitality by them, ate with them and even conducted discussions in their cells.[4]

The emergence of celibate *community* life cannot be dated with certainty. However, the indications are that it first emerged among the virgins. Certainly, by the fourth century, there were communities of virgins in Palestine and others existed in the main cities of the Empire. It is recorded that Antony of the Desert sent his sister into a community before he retired as a hermit at the end of the third century. Female-directed communities offered further security for women and it may be that the more affluent virgins began the process by supporting poorer virgins in their households. The growing number of virgins, the emergence of community life, and the increasing concern of Church authorities to regulate this phenomenon, probably contributed to the beginnings of enclosure. By the fifth century the process had begun and the fate of this initially autonomous and informal way of life was to merge with the growing cenobitic-monastic movement. By the eighth century

117

the order of widows had disappeared and consecrated virginity had become associated with monastic profession in convents following a rule.[5]

In the history of *organised monasticism* the position of Egypt is powerfully etched in popular imagination and has only been challenged recently by Syriac scholars. The tradition that Syriac monasticism was an Egyptian export, inspired by Pachomius, originated only in the ninth century when the prestige of Egypt was well-established. Syrian monks appear to have forgotten their native heritage. Part of this amnesia may be explained by the fact that the original Syriac tradition differed considerably from the values of the dominant Egyptian movement. The Syriac ascetical movement involved both men and women and seems, like the virgins, to have been predominantly autonomous in its early stages. Of course, the Egyptian desert, too, had once been full of solitaries, but there had eventually developed a strong cenobitic movement and so Egypt became the 'story of origin' of cenobitism as the latter developed into the paradigm of religious life in general.

What is important about the 'priority' of the Syriac tradition is that it may reflect (albeit at times subject to exaggeration) the original understanding of *discipleship* as a literal imitation of the poor, homeless and celibate Jesus. Thus asceticism was a model, for all members of the Church, of costly discipleship. The particular influence of Luke's Gospel on Syrian Christianity may have triggered this radical asceticism. Certainly, it was characteristic to emphasize the Lucan theme of total abandonment of possessions and homes in order to become wanderers with nowhere to lay their heads.

The general Syrian term for consecrated ascetics was *ihidaya*. While the Greek word *monachos* may be a translation, it would be misleading to express this in English simply as 'monk' or 'hermit'. Rather, it means the 'single one' or the one who adopts 'singleness'. Fundamentally it referred to those who obey Jesus's command to leave the dead to bury their dead (Luke 9. 60). So the ascetic, or single one, was separated from what is dead and linked with the one who gives life, Jesus the Lifegiver. So *ihidaya* implies three elements: to leave family ties, to be singleminded, and to become 'one' by putting on 'The One' in a special relationship with Christ. This way was not conceived as a gratuitous commitment analogous to vows. It was understood simply as the fulfilment of baptismal promises to the extent that, in some places, those who were married remained catechumens.

The holy men and women in Egypt did not impinge on society around them to the same degree as the Syriac ascetics, despite the latter's often wandering life in imitation of Jesus's homelessness. Several authors have suggested that the differences may be partly geographical. The traditional agrarian culture of the Nile, which valued a regulated life, as well as the nature of the deep desert, led to some co-operation for survival (hence the gradual growth of monastic villages). The Syrian wilderness was never deep desert and was not so starkly separated from village communities. Consequently the 'single ones' remained a visible challenge near human habitation. Paradoxically, in their greater geographical seclusion, the Egyptian ascetics tended to recreate the habits of normal village community while the Syrians, closer to ordinary villages, adopted a life-style which contrasted more strongly with 'the world'.

Many Syrian ascetics lived in villages. Some may even have remained at home judging by Cassian's strictures against those who called their homes 'monasteries'. We shall encounter this phenomenon later in present-day Ethiopian religious life. There is evidence that, in the villages, the 'single ones' emerged into leadership roles. These were both religious, in the absence of clergy who inhabited the towns, and secular, as a result of the growing reluctance of landowners to leave suburban villas. This free-floating, autonomous life was fiercely criticised by Cassian who tried to promote a more organized monasticism. However these 'single ones' leave us with an interesting model. A radical gospel life-style made them wanderers, strangers and outsiders and yet, by standing outside the normal ties of family, property and ambition, the 'single one' could be accepted as guide, arbitrator and supporter. Dissociation, strangely, made the Syrian ascetic socially significant.[6]

Does religious life have a single line of development?

We need to question the assumption, not only that the original model for religious life was cenobitic-monastic, but that development moved in a single line. The 'Pachomius to Ignatius' approach made popular by David Knowles suggests that all forms of religious life are merely variations on the basic theme of monastic asceticism and indeed, implicitly, that monasticism itself was essentially a unified concept. In fact, historians today are more cautious about such terms as 'the Benedictine centuries' than they were because they are more aware of a variety of competing, rather than unified, monastic enterprises.[7] This approach has recently been questioned by such scholars as Professor John O'Malley.[8] His thesis is that a framework of 'ministry' and its development in the Church may provide a fruitful alternative to 'asceticism' as a way to re-read the history of religious life. To interpret the friars of the thirteenth century, the Jesuits of the sixteenth and subsequent 'apostolic' life for men and women, simply as developments within an overall monastic framework is inadequate. They were radical institutional innovations for whom ministry was not a secondary addition but part of their identity.

The fact that 'apostolic' religious communities (perhaps, more frequently the women than the men) retained some 'monastic' features does not undermine the point. Such practices merely highlighted a tension with what was primary in their charism. The monastic goals of personal perfection through withdrawal and the salvation of society through prayer, were not so much adapted as abandoned. For example, the option by Francis of Assisi for radical poverty was not primarily an *ascetical* choice. Spiritually, it was christological (imitation of the poor Christ) and evangelical (costly discipleship as evidenced by the gospels). It also reflected a practical sense that the Church needed not only the example of poor preachers but also the mobility and freedom for mission that such poverty brought.[9]

Whatever the degree of institutional innovation represented by friars and clerks regular, the non-monastic stream of religious life in the West is as ancient as cenobitic monasticism. The roots, I believe, lie in the regular clerical life which eventually became known as 'canonical'. Its non-monastic nature has often been misunderstood partly, I suspect, because of a tendency to view all *conventual* life-styles as the same, and partly because cenobitic monasticism became more universal and more dominant. By tradition, it was St Augustine who gathered the first canonical community around him at Hippo in North Africa. The Rule which bears his name was subsequently to have considerable influence. It is not simply because the Rule was originally intended for clergy that makes it appropriate to see it in ministerial terms. Its emphasis on community and charity (thus, by implication, on external relationships) contrasts, in significant ways, with the central spirit of monasticism. The Rule of St Benedict, for example, discusses the external framework for cenobitic life, but its spirituality remains that of the individual journey. The Rule of St Augustine says little concerning communal structures but emphasizes the creation of community *relationships*.

Scholars such as Jean Leclercq and Caroline Walker Bynum have criticized the neglect of canonical life by historians because it reinforces distortions in our understanding of religious life and its development. Both agree, too, that canonical life has been treated as a sub-species of monasticism, but while monastic and canonical life influenced each other at points in history they are in important ways quite distinct.[10] Unfortunately the most recent English-language edition of *The Rule of St Augustine* continues to refer to it as the 'oldest monastic rule in the West'. Yet the editors are not monks but friars and the list of Augustinian communities they provide includes every variety of religious life *except* monastic![11]

Ministry to others was an integral part of canonical life. Originally most canonical houses were involved directly in pastoral care. Although, for a time, canonical life was overtaken in the enthusiasm for new monastic rules, many new houses emerged by the eighth century in the Rhineland. Bishop Chrodegang of Metz in *c.*755 compiled a rule of life which was particularly influential and spread to several countries including England. Parallel to the Gregorian reforms, the period from 1050 to the early thirteenth century saw a fundamental change in people's conception of the Christian life. Central to this was the importance of love and service of neighbour. Thus canonical life received a new impetus as a means of raising the life of the clergy and as an expression of this renewed spirituality. It became common to give the care of large urban churches, or groups of rural churches, to canons. A certain lack of definition, and the challenge of new monastic reforms, seem to have provoked canonical communities to seek a distinguished founder and to find a common way of life in the Third Rule of St Augustine. The almost universal adoption of this Rule is also contemporary with the great spiritual ferment, known as the *vita apostolica*, which emphasized a return to the early Church, especially as evidenced in the Acts of the Apostles. The Rule of St Augustine may therefore have been attractive because its central ideals corresponded so well with the spiritual values of the age. By 1100, the canons were much more identifiably a religious order (though not centralized). While important elements of their spirituality meant that the canons remained an alternative to monastic life, some houses or federations, like Premontré, took on a monastic appearance.[12]

Professor Bynum has helped to recover canonical spirituality from its omission from the pages of history, or at least relegation to an insignificant footnote. She suggests that it is difficult to produce evidence for consistent contrasts between the activities of medieval canonical and monastic communities. However, from an examination of spiritual treatises, she has been able to discover significant differences concerning the purpose of religious life. Edification by word and example is central to canonical self-understanding. The canon is teacher as well as learner. In some treatises, edification is linked explicitly to preaching but this is not to suggest that all canons preached and that no monks did so. Rather, it is that conduct, for the canon, is understood to have an effect on others while the monastic stress is essentially ascetical. Silence in canonical spirituality is not merely a matter of self-discipline but is a preparation for fruitful discourse between people, for 'useful speech'. Secondly, while the concept of a mixed life of action and contemplation is not a canonical invention, it appears in their writings, in contrast to monastic treatises, as part of *their own* responsibility.

Because canonical authors thought in ministerial terms, they drew upon written traditions (such as descriptions of the preacher) that pointed beyond a narrowly monastic focus. This sense of moral responsibility and education also pointed forwards to the appearance of the friars in the thirteenth century. Canons claimed that their life was stricter and more 'apostolic' precisely because they were more subject to the temptations of the world than were monks. For the canon, and later for the friar, religious life consisted of conforming oneself to a Christ who ministered to others. Thus the more one became available as an instrument of conversion, the more one became a better canon or friar.[13]

By recovering the tradition of the canonical life we establish clearly that cenobitic religious life did not develop in a single straight line but was plural from its earliest stages with both a monastic and a non-monastic stream. There was not, and is not, a common ascetical-monastic root for religious life as a whole. The plurality of religious life extends further. The autonomous way of discipleship, which predates the cenobitic, reminds us that common life or conventual models for religious life have a limited value. It is now appropriate to turn in more detail to the question of the place that personal values, and especially individual forms of consecrated life, had in history once the mainstream had become cenobitic.

Is a common life model adequate?

It is worth noting, to begin with, that even cenobitic monasticism was not the monolithic edifice which it has sometimes been portrayed. It has already been suggested that the Rule of St Benedict was not unambiguously cenobitic but retained an underlying understanding of the monk as *solus* or alone. Consequently, the upheavals of the eleventh and twelfth centuries, which produced a variety of new religious orders, were perhaps less the crisis of cenobitism that has traditionally been described. Within this revised perspective, the Carthusian life does not diverge radically from the mainstream of monasticism in its explicit emphasis on solitude-in-community. Rather, it was the Cistercians who emphasized something new by working out an articulate approach to the possibilities of *community* and making room for brotherly love as part of growth towards God.[14] If Professor Bynum is correct, the original singleness of consecrated life was absorbed into cenobitic structures. Solitude-in-community replaced full autonomy. However, it remains true that the perceived norm for religious life in the West became common life. Yet it is possible to trace a fully autonomous tradition in the West which is rarely considered in terms of the history of religious life. There were anchorites, other kinds of hermits or solitaries, wanderers and members of groups such as Third Orders or Beguines who did not necessarily live in common.

Originally, the 'anchorite' and the 'hermit' were synonymous and sought simply 'to be solitary', to 'withdraw to the desert (*eremos*)'. This could imply total seclusion and stability or allow freedom of movement and social contacts. Even in its Syriac or Egyptian origins, the solitary life did not always imply an absence of contact with the world. While the Egyptian form was geographically distant from towns, and explicitly emphasized withdrawal and distance, there was a degree of interchange with outsiders.[15] In reading the lives of the desert ascetics it is striking that charity and hospitality, whether to fellow solitaries or to local people, is deemed to have priority over the strict observance of a rule. As one *abba* commented, 'My rule is to refresh you and to send you away in peace.' While continuous service would have been seen as infringing the desert principle of non-interference, there are many instances where solitaries provided food or clothes to villagers during times of famine. Solitaries also visited towns and cities on

Church business or to sell their work in the markets. Some even returned to the city because they found the life hard and unattractive and yet were subsequently received back with relatively little fuss.

It was in the Middle Ages that the terms 'hermit' and 'anchorite' became more distinct. 'Hermit' continued to express the more general meaning of 'the one alone'. 'Anchorite' became restricted to those who had the more specialized vocation of recluse, enclosed and stable.[16] The anchorite vocation continued to attract adherents throughout the Middle Ages and indeed up to the present day, when there has been a striking revival. Many of those who felt called to this way of life were already members of religious communities. Equally, such groups as the Carthusians or Camaldolese revived, to a limited degree, the ancient tradition of the *lavra* or collection of hermits around a common teacher. From time to time, members of other monastic orders felt themselves called to a life of greater solitude and many monasteries in England, for example, had responsibility for recluses. Sometimes these were close to the parent community but the cathedral priory of Durham is one example of a monastery that maintained a hermitage at a distance on the islands of Farne off the Northumbrian coast. Even in semi-eremitical orders, such as the Carthusians, there may have been the opportunity for greater isolation. On the edge of the moors above the Carthusian ruins of Mount Grace in Yorkshire there are the remains of an isolated hermitage where, it is thought, monks from the priory below retired from time to time.

There were many individual recluses as well and in England this life, without any previous connection with a monastery, was especially popular. The chronicles and romances describe such recluses as familiar people who were often consulted. Three of the best-known English recluses, Godric of Finchdale, Wulfric of Haselbury and Christina of Markyate had never been monastics (although Christina eventually became a nun). Julian of Norwich is famous for her great mystical text, *The Showings* or *Revelations of Divine Love*. However, little is known of her life. She lived in an anchorhold attached to the Church of St Julian in the last decades of the fourteenth century and perhaps well into the fifteenth. Perhaps because her writings were rediscovered and promoted by monastic editors it was often assumed that she had once been a member of a Benedictine convent. The monastic scholar, Benedicta Ward, has recently argued cogently against this monasticization and speculates that Julian may have had children and been widowed. Finally the best-known rule for the anchorite life, the *Ancrene Wisse* of the twelfth century, was written explicitly for three women living outside traditional monastic structures.[17]

There were other kinds of autonomous solitaries. In fact most medieval solitaries were not secluded anchorites. Many lived in towns or on the edge of villages. Even if they were predominantly contemplative in style, this did not necessarily prevent fairly close contact with the world around them. Richard Rolle of Hampole in Yorkshire called at local houses to eat and drink. For him, as for many such solitaries, what essentially distinguished their life was personal liberty and freedom of action. The true solitary is the one who vows obedience to God alone. This liberty meant that there was no uniformity amongst solitaries with regard to life-style or religious observance. Not all solitaries were given over solely to a life of prayer. Some engaged in works of charity. In France it was fairly common for them to act as guides to travellers. Some used their cells as hostels offering frugal hospitality. Others acted as bridge or toll-keepers and a few, particularly in England, looked after coastal beacons. The remains of the chapel-hermitage on St Alban's (or Aldhelm's) Head in Dorset seem to offer evidence of this. The main point is that many medieval solitaries were accessible rather than isolated.

Some solitaries belonged to more identifiable groups. The mendicant orders and others, such as the Humiliati, who came into being in the thirteenth century as part of the *vita apostolica* movement, were of their nature more in contact with ordinary people than monastic orders. These new orders founded branches, known as Tertiaries, for those unable or unwilling to take on the full life-style of the parent body. Some members lived in community but others continued to live at home and to undertake a life of prayer and good works compatible with their everyday commitments. A number of these were single or solitary and probably merit comparison with earlier forms of autonomous consecrated life. The Beguines (and their male counterpart, the Beghards), who emerged towards the end of the twelfth century in Germany, the Low Countries and France, offered another alternative to traditional structures of fully conventual religious life. Although, later in their development, the Beguines became more institutional they began as single women living with parents or separately in tenements. There were common features to their piety, but no rule of life, and initially only the most informal association between individuals.

The final kind of solitary life was that of the wanderers. Such individuals can be dated to an early period and seem to have survived cenobitical opposition (as in the Rule of St Benedict) fairly well. As has been noted, some early virgins became famous as pilgrims to the Holy Land. The Celtic monastic tradition produced an above average number of such wanderers. Throughout the Middle Ages the wandering tradition continued in different forms. Undoubtedly some wanderers were simply beggars or eccentrics but there were others who led a celibate wandering life for devotional and ascetical reasons. Many became pilgrims to the Holy Land or other great shrines of Christendom, and sometimes the distinction between hermits and everyday pilgrims is rather blurred. Pilgrimage was, of course, a striking phenomenon in the Middle Ages and involved people of both sexes, all classes and every category of life. Not all were 'single ones'. Some, like Margery Kempe who at different times went to Rome, Compostela and the Holy Land, were married with families and their wandering was only a temporary break in an otherwise ordinary life-style. However, there do seem to have been pilgrims who made the wandering style of dedicated Christian life a more or less permanent occupation.[18]

Although the Society of Jesus, founded in the sixteenth century, was a religious order, and not a movement of autonomous people, the wandering tradition found a place even within its relatively structured framework. The wandering theme in Ignatian spirituality played a role in modifying the common life of Jesuits and was institutionalized in their fourth vow to travel on missions to any part of the world. It may be argued that 'apostolic' religious life in general, dedicated *primarily* to mission, should not be interpreted within a 'common-life' model even if, historically, it has at times adopted (or been forced to adopt) a more structured and stable community life-style.[19] Jerome Nadal, the assistant to Ignatius Loyola, highlighted the vital importance of mobility and journeying in his 1554 exhortation to Spanish Jesuits. There are four kinds of Jesuit community: houses of probation, colleges, professed houses and 'the journey', 'and by this last the whole world becomes our home'. In his 1557 annotations to part of the Jesuit Constitutions, known as the General Examen, he developed this idea further. 'The principal and most characteristic dwelling for Jesuits is not the professed houses but in journeyings.'[20]

Is a woman's proper place in the cloister?

A revision of the history of religious life must attend to the limitations experienced by women. Their relative freedom at the heart of Church life, and spiritual equality with men in the Early Church, contrasts with their seclusion and consequent marginalization in later centuries. I am not positing some Golden Age, to which we may return, but simply that restrictions on women are an *historical* phenomenon. That is, they had origins in history, and for contingent reasons. They are not, therefore, some divine given, and the historical process involves the possibility of change. Enclosure became the most effective limitation on the roles of women. Originally the motives were to safeguard 'spiritual space' and to protect people against the social anarchy that attended the demise of the Roman Empire. The strict sixth-century rule for women by Caesarius of Arles was particularly influential in the various attempts at legislation after the seventh century. These increased the authority of bishops, monasticized many houses and resulted in gender-specific canons on enclosure which created a double standard. As early as the ninth century, the *Regula monachorum* talked in very ascetical terms of women's seclusion. The vanity of the world (a female problem?) was contrasted with nuns who were dead and buried in Christ and with convents which were described as 'tombs'.

Restrictive legislation for women was not quite universal. Canonesses remained distinct from 'nuns' (or *moniales*) in that their enclosure remained less rigid. Even in English monastic houses, during the Anglo-Saxon period, nuns appear to have retained an unusual degree of collective freedom, at least in terms of the authority of abbesses over the regulation of enclosure. The constant repetition by local councils of regulations aimed at women suggests that uniformally strict enclosure was difficult to enforce. Most historians agree on two things. Firstly, inflexible seclusion was not enforced until relatively late on and, secondly, the move from protection of 'spiritual space' to uniform legal sanction beyond the control of women themselves was largely imposed.[21]

After the twelfth century, the canonical limitations on women's religious life were most strongly expressed by the decree of Pope Boniface VIII in 1298 which stated that all religious women should henceforth remain in perpetual enclosure. However, the rigidity which remained familiar to Roman Catholic nuns until the reforms of Vatican II arose only in the sixteenth century. Enclosed medieval nuns continued to leave the cloister for necessary business or even to preach. According to the statute of 1242, Cistercian nuns normally had to speak through a thick window with bars. However they could still go out on business and a room was provided in convents where they could meet 'honest persons' quite freely. Clearly some discretion was left to the nuns.[22] However, in general, women's houses found themselves 'hemmed in on all sides by the old traditional forms of monastic life that held sway from before the twelfth century and that became more austere, more rigid, and in all cases more uniform'.[23] Formal enclosure for women meant that convents became predominantly contemplative and 'nuns' became a single category.[24] The Beguine movement, from the late twelfth century, avoided this process by remaining outside the canonical definition of 'religious', despite attempts to control it and the growth of some common structures in its later stages.

Stricter enclosure paralleled a decrease in women's roles in the Church. This was part of a wider process of change in the aftermath of the Gregorian reforms. Clerical celibacy, the greater freedom of Church government from secular interference and greater definition of the sacraments created a clergy who were more radically 'set apart' with the exclusive right to preach and exercise the cure of souls.[25] It cannot seriously be doubted that women had exercised clerical roles within religious houses prior to the Gregorian reforms. This included preaching, hearing the confessions of fellow religious and bestowing blessings. Some of the evidence for this is indirect, through the medium of criticism and attempts to suppress such practices even as late as the thirteenth century. In 1210, Pope Innocent III noted with astonishment the continued exercise of clerical powers by nuns. The thirteenth-century canonist, Bernard of Parma, argued that even if such practices had been current in the past, women could no longer teach, touch sacred vessels, absolve nuns or exercise judgement. Yet, women continued to preach and teach for a time even outside the cloister. The great spiritual movement, the *vita apostolica*, which swept Europe in the twelfth century gave a new impulse to preaching and women who were attracted to the movement were initially involved. When St Dominic founded the Prouille convent in 1206, the nuns helped the friars not only with preaching but with education.

Apart from the development of clerical theory, negative stereotypes of women also affected the limitations placed upon them. Jean Gerson, the fourteenth-century theologian and canonist, wrote that the female sex was forbidden to teach in public, even through writing. 'All women's teaching . . . is to be held suspect unless it has been diligently examined, and much more fully than men's.' Women are more easily seduced and are determined seducers and 'it is not proved that they are witnesses of divine grace.'[26] One might add that a lack of theological formation was often an operative, if unexpressed, motive behind the reluctance to allow women to minister. However, such a lack was substantially the result of the male clerical monopoly of centres of theological learning.

Women religious were severely limited for longer than men. Even after the emergence of active and mobile religious life in the sixteenth century, attempts to form female groups largely foundered. Angela Merici (1474–1540), inspired by the image of Ursula and her virgin missionaries, sought to found a similar group in Italy but, in the aftermath of the Council of Trent, they, like all who wished to be considered as 'nuns', were forced to adopt a more traditional enclosed life, at least in modified form. The radical vision of the Englishwoman, Mary Ward, in the early seventeenth century, was condemned by the Church (not least because her sisters dared to teach even men about faith) and her Institute of the Blessed Virgin Mary was, until modern times, unable to live the fully mobile and uncloistered life envisaged by the foundress. A group such as the Daughters of Charity, founded by Louise de Marillac and Vincent de Paul, managed to remain relatively free to work amongst the poor by avoiding permanent vows and the legal status of 'nun'.[27]

The limitation of roles is associated with a growing separation of female from male religious. Initially, in the early centuries, some actually lived with male celibates as 'sisters and brothers in Christ' in a kind of spiritual marriage (*agapatae, gyne syneisaktos,* or *virgines subintroductae*). The underlying conviction was that oneness in Christ could eliminate the barriers of gender so as to allow for close relationships within a commitment to consecrated virginity.[28] A more common phenomenon was the double monastery. In the Celtic and Anglo-Saxon traditions such houses appear to have been especially prevalent. Archeological excavations at Whitby in England indicate that there was no rigid division between the areas of the enclosure occupied by men and those by women.

Apart from some women who lived in houses of the Canons of Premontré in the early years of the order, three double orders were founded in the High Middle Ages: Fontevrault, the Gilbertines and the Bridgettines. Fontevrault was founded by Robert of Arbrissel in 1100 and, following the spiritual maxims of the *vita apostolica* movement, its members sought to live according to the model of the apostolic Church. Robert explicitly chose not to perpetuate male leadership and so the abbess was not merely the juridical head of the

monks but also their spiritual leader. The second of three versions
of the Rule which survive stipulates:

> They [i.e. brothers as well as sisters] are to revere her as their
> spiritual mother, and all the affairs of the Church [i.e. the com-
> munity], spiritual as well as secular, are to remain in her hands,
> or to be given to whomever she assigns, just as she decides.[29]

Fontevrault was unique in this respect. However, the phenomenon
of double houses had important features apart from the leadership
of women. There was a symbiotic relationship between men and
women on both spiritual and material planes. Both were equals in
a co-ordinated effort. Finally, double houses mitigated the effect of
enclosure by enabling women to maintain autonomy from outside
authority. With the decline of such houses in the later Middle
Ages, something very favourable to women on a practical level was
removed. On a deeper level, the suspicion which confronted double
houses was symbolic of a widening gap between men and women.
Their decline underlined the fact that distinction and separation had
largely won the day.[30]

Are our cultural limits adequate?

If the story of women's consecrated life reminds us that there are
dangers in a one-sided view of history, we need to remind ourselves
that our histories and identities exist within limited cultural
horizons. Thus western perceptions of religious life have largely
ignored the eastern tradition and some western spiritual cultures,
such as the Celtic, are now merely distant memories. Attention to
unfamiliar cultural perspectives questions our assumptions.

In the East, divisions into distinct 'Orders' are unknown. A
variety of patterns exist within a single, all-embracing tradition.
John Climacus (died *c.* 649) highlighted three main types of religious
life: solitude, a few companions and the cenobitic. These remain
broadly the same today.[31] In the monastic 'republic' of Mount
Athos the twenty ruling monasteries are cenobitic, though varying
in intensity. There are a significant number of smaller, semi-
eremitical groupings which preserve the ancient desert tradition
of *lavra*, or hermits around a teacher. These are called *kellia*,
usually with between two and six members. Some are isolated,
others are grouped in monastic villages or *sketes*. Finally, there

are the true hermits. A few are closely dependent on monasteries but others live in extreme solitude.[32]

Individuals may move from one style to another, usually but not exclusively from the cenobitic to the eremitical. This flexibility enables religious to follow a personal spiritual path within the wider monastic journey towards God. Unlike St Benedict in the West who carried the cenobitic ideal further, St Basil in the East saw cenobitism, while having a value in itself, as also a school for future hermits. The cenobitic way never became the norm in the East that it did in the West. It is this factor, probably more than others, which enabled eastern religious life to retain a unity-in-diversity rather than to develop the western diversity-in-separation encapsulated in different Orders with particular vocations.

Within Orthodox cenobitic life there is also some diversity. Some houses are what are called 'idiorhythmic' where each member adopts a personal rhythm, within a flexible common life. Although more reformist cenobitical religious do not approve of this way, a case can be made for viewing it as a legitimate spiritual emphasis rather than the breakdown of community life. It certainly accords with the general principle of Orthodox religious life which is to give the individual more personal freedom than has traditionally been the case in the West. This has led one commentator to describe the idiorhythmic way as, in some sense, 'archetypal'.[33]

Ethiopian models of religious life are even less familiar in the West than the Orthodox tradition because for centuries the country was cut off from the rest of the Christian world by the expansion of Islam. It retains a living connection with early forms of consecrated life. Firstly there are widow-nuns and lay-nuns. These more or less correspond to the orders of widow and virgin in the Early Church. They mainly live at home in the midst of the local community and occupy their time with Church work such as making vestments or flour for the communion bread. Then there are couples who become celibate, sometimes temporarily, as married religious at home. They are answerable to the archpriest but their life is informal. A third category who live, to a degree, among ordinary people are the city hermits. Some are extremely ascetic, communicating by signs or living on the road-side. Others carry a heavy staff in literal imitation of the injunction to take up the cross daily. Their life is primarily one of prayer. While some hermits preach, all avoid involvement in normal social relationships.

In formal monasteries of men or women there may be up to 600 religious. The organization appears remarkably informal compared to the West or even Eastern Orthodox communities. Initially, men or women arrive as guests at the monastery or convent and, if they can keep silence and join in the work, they may eventually stay as long as they like. Spiritual formation is informal as they learn how to pray and to serve the older religious. Joyful and humble service is one of the important signs of a vocation. Apart from those monks who are to be ordained, and who therefore study theology, the life of silence and prayer itself is deemed to be the main teacher. Individuals are assisted by a *komas* or spiritual guide. Abbots or abbesses have no temporal authority but are purely spiritual fathers or mothers. There is a strong antipathy to the accumulation of power in a few hands. Because monastic commitment is to *a way of life* rather than to a place, individual religious may move freely from one monastery or convent to another.

Monasteries are semi-eremitical and look like ordinary villages. Each religious has a hut and a garden. In the middle there is a church and a hall for the weekly common meal. There is daily worship but apart from this, each person develops his or her own rhythm of prayer. Religious meet casually during the day, as in any village, and in the evenings groups may gather for conversation. A simple framework of common life provides a context for an otherwise personal search for God. As no plants or animals are killed within the monastery, the environment is fairly untamed and even wild animals may be found living peacefully around monasteries.

A number of monks and nuns go out from their monasteries to become hermits in the forests and mountains. Like the city hermits, they live a very ascetic life sometimes dressed in animal skins in literal imitation of Hebrews 11. 37–38. Some eat only leaves with the even more stringent asceticism of blindly picking these behind their backs! The older hermits generally live near a monastery but the younger ones go further afield and are rarely, if ever, seen.[34]

A similar 'village' model mingled with native Irish culture and the nature of the land to give Celtic religious life a character all of its own. It was eventually superseded by Latin, mainly Benedictine, monasticism and caricatured as too extreme, primitive and eccentric. This has led some historians of religious life seriously to underestimate the positive features of Celtic monasticism. Certainly, Celtic religious life was idiosyncratic, if by that we mean that its rugged individualism contrasted with the more hierarchical, and urbane Latin tradition. Celtic monasticism was very varied because it accorded great value to the individual even within the monastery. Monks or nuns could always move freely from one monastery to another or go off in search of greater solitude even without the agreement of the head of the monastery. Individual hermits played a major role in this tradition. New monastic settlements often arose as the result of groups forming around a hermit who had originally sought solitude but who developed a reputation for guidance. Spiritual guidance by a 'soul friend', or 'the one who shares the cell', was considered a necessity rather than an option.

Celtic spirituality was undoubtedly ascetical and sometimes extreme. However the motivation was strongly evangelical. A literal imitation of the poor and homeless Christ invites comparison with the Syriac tradition. Equally, Celtic spirituality did not reject the material world. Ascetical principles were balanced by a closeness to nature and a great sympathy with the land and the sea. Monastic settlements were often like pioneer communities civilizing the wastelands. This pioneering element also characterized the approach of Celtic ascetics to society around them. Irish and later Scottish and Northumbrian monasticism arose in territories still largely unchristian. Monastic settlements were also, therefore, centres of evangelisation.

The interplay with the surrounding culture sometimes involved a blending of traditional elements with Christian forms. In fact, Celtic monasticism became interwoven with society to a remarkable degree. Often the frontiers between monastic settlements and normal places of habitation were blurred. Some settlements eventually became the seat of local kings and a form of family monasticism developed. Perhaps it is this blend of monastic life with wide society which led to the peculiar form of Church government whereby bishops had their functions but were firmly subordinated to abbots and abbesses.

Finally, one feature of Celtic monasticism is of particular interest. This is what was known as *peregrinatio*, voluntary exile or 'green martyrdom'. This wandering, which in some ways recalls the ascetics of Syria, was in part a logical consequence of the search for greater solitude and in part a reflection of evangelising zeal. However, it also reflects the ideal of imitation of the homeless Christ. The exile voluntarily left the security of home and native roots for the unknown, in faith and trust.[35]

Conclusions

Historical precedent is a complex matter. The examples that have been chosen to illustrate my questions cannot simply widen the range of possible models for contemporary imitation, but they do raise some important issues about the definition of religious life and its relationship to the wider Christian community. First and foremost, a recognizable yet, initially, relatively undefined pursuit of gospel values developed into a structured, separate and regulated category, 'religious life'. This process of definition led to three paradoxically related features. Firstly, there was an expansion of normative characteristics beyond the primary emphasis on gospel living associated with consecrated virginity. Secondly a limitation of the variety of religious life to common conventual structures took place. Thirdly particular 'charisms' were formalized into rigid divisions.

There were other by-products of this process. The original fluidity was lost as the personal and autonomous was subordinated to common life. Indeed, if I may adopt a concept from recent Soviet history, a more generous understanding of community gave way to 'collectivization'. Religious life, through greater definition, was increasingly separated from the discipleship of all the baptised. While adherents of autonomous or communal forms of 'consecrated' Christian life in the early Church thought of themselves as laypeople, greater institutionalization created a hierarchical mentality whereby even those religious who were not ordained understood themselves to be a distinct class or level of Christian.

Secondly, religious life has historically been a diverse phenomenon and cannot be reduced to a predetermined or universal pattern. Because new communities, whether reforms of previously existing patterns or institutional innovations, appear most frequently at points in history where the Church and society are in crisis, they always respond to specific situations and embody specific values. The originators were able to identify specific needs and sought to respond to these in the light of the gospel in a fresh and immediate way. It is also the case that geographical location caused the emergence of different patterns of religious life.

Least of all can religious life be limited to what is recognized institutionally within a particular culture (for example, the West) or at a given point in history. Consecrated virgins existed long before Church order recognized them, autonomous forms of life have been formally recognized at certain times and not at others, and certain groups with temporary commitment, such as the Beguines, existed in a kind of twilight zone. Canon law is too blunt an instrument to be the final arbiter of limits and definition.

Thirdly, the issue of development has been present implicitly at several points. I have emphasized that it is questionable to understand this in terms of a single line, with a common normative root. It may also be added that the very concept of 'development' is ambiguous. There have been many changes but these have not always been improvements. Change has brought loss as well as gain. Women's status and opportunities were greater in the Early Church than in the High Middle Ages. The progressive exclusion of particular spiritual cultures (the Celtic or the whole of the East) meant the loss of certain fruitful emphases. Any 'Whig' view of history as the inevitable triumph of progressive forces is dubious.

Arguably the need conclusively to *define* religious life graphically illustrates the process of limitation and separation I have described. To reduce meaning to definitions is the product of a religious culture which has valued law, distinctions and the objective. The subtle discernment of 'charisms', at the service of community, has been progressively subordinated to an institutional model of the Church which demands free-standing structures as a precondition for recognition. Consecrated life undoubtedly began as distinctive. Its common feature, chastity, was a powerful symbol of dissociation from established family, social, economic and religious structures. This costly discipleship did not so much invite a literal imitation of *the powerful ascetic* as of the powerless Christ. Consequently, the stranger had a religious role within the community not as an exact role-model but as a prophetic challenge to all who were tempted to adopt material values uncritically. However, dissociation gradually progressed towards separation. Structures, dress and practices eventually changed the state of 'being other' *within* the Christian community into ritual behaviour as an élitist way. Withdrawal came to imply a special context for perfection apart from the common herd. Religious life ceased to be a symbol and became a substitute for what most people could not achieve.

It was a short step from this to a hierarchy of Christian life – a more perfect (spiritual) path and a less perfect (material) one. This division between classes of Christians had several consequences. It reinforced the priority of religious over lay, a belief that the 'spiritual' was above the 'material', and withdrawal superior to engagement. This hierarchy of values, expressed by a hierarchy of life-styles, meant that only a small minority of Christians could have access to those contexts where a higher way was possible. The resulting sense of spiritual inadequacy meant that those gospel values which the Christian community believed were central were projected on to religious life. And these values were often visibly ascetical ones that most Christians were not attracted to imitate because they denied activities and aspirations which necessarily formed part of ordinary human life. In other words, by dividing religious from ordinary life, the latter was effectively secularized and the former was expected not to be concerned with the everyday.

Even as sophisticated a thinker as St Thomas More, who seems to have made a deliberate option for lay life and who could be bitterly critical of the ignorance and presumption of some religious, shared the belief that religious life was inherently superior to ordinary Christian living rather than primarily exemplary:

> It would help me and others in the same condition, tossed as we are on the waves of an unhappy world, to look up to you religious and to marvel at your orders as models of angelic life, so that, while we admire the virtue in others, our own way of life may seem all the more worthless.[36]

The phenomenon of structured religious life presents us with a paradox. On the one hand, Christian faith and a committed life-style is for everyone. Yet, historically speaking, the most successful religious movements in the West have been those which make the spiritual journey more complex, more difficult and somehow separate from the everyday. Undoubtedly radical challenge is attractive. Yet, if that challenge becomes more than the simple gospel there is a danger, present at times in the history of religious life, that the hidden attraction is for something that offers a kind of gnosticism – a secret knowledge or way that is progressively revealed to a spiritual élite. Apart from the sense of status which this may provide, the additional danger is that such a special way appears to offer a kind of short-cut, admittedly involving considerable sacrifice, to salvation and union with God. Equally, religious life becomes a measure of Christian life as a whole, instead of the baptismal vocation of all being the measure of any particular form of Christian living.

It seems that we are, once again, in a situation of fluidity and flexibility where theoretical and visible distinctions between religious life, as we have conceived it for so long, and other Christian ways have blurred. This reminds us, perhaps, that while it is possible to discern those groups that are distinctive, and their prophetic or culturally-critical gifts, at particular points in history, it may not be possible to arrive at abstract definitions of religious life with universal or permanent application.

Notes

1. Jean Leclercq, *Aspects of Monasticism* (Michigan 1978), pp. 72ff.
2. See Ignatius of Antioch, *Letter to the Smyrneans*, 13, 1 in William R. Schoedel, *Ignatius of Antioch* (Philadelphia 1985), p. 247.
3. See Rosemary Rader, 'Early Christian Forms of Communal Spirituality: Women's Communities', in William Skudlarek, ed., *The Continuing Quest for God* (Collegeville 1982), pp. 88–99. See also Aloysius Pieris, 'The Religious Vows and the Reign of God', *The Way Supplement* 65 (1989), pp. 10–11. Peter Brown has cogently presented the wider social and human implications of the ideal of virginity. See 'The Notion of Virginity in the Early Church', in Bernard McGinn and John Meyendorff, eds, *Christian Spirituality: Origins of the Twelfth Century* (London New York 1986), pp. 427–43. Brown has developed his ideas more fully in a recently published book, *The Body and Society: Men, Women and Sexual Renunciation in Early Christianity*, (New York 1988; London 1989).
4. See Egeria's *Travels* London 1971.
5. On widows and virgins as well as early forms of communal life, see Rader, 'Early Forms of Communal Spirituality'; Elisabeth Schüssler Fiorenza, 'Word, Spirit and Power: Women in Early Christian Communities', in Rosemary Radford Ruether and Eleanor McLaughlin, eds, *Women of Spirit*, New York 1979; Jo Ann McNamara, 'Muffled Voices: the Lives of Consecrated Women in the Fourth Century' in John Nichols and Lillian Thomas Shank, eds, *Distant Echoes: Medieval Religious Women* 1 (Kalamazoo 1984), pp. 11–30. I am grateful to Elizabeth Rees, a contemporary consecrated virgin working in London, for drawing my attention to some of these essays and for providing me with copies of her own writing on consecrated virginity.
6. On the Syriac ascetical tradition, see Robert Murray, 'The Features of the Earliest Christian Asceticism', in Peter Brooks ed. *Christian Spirituality: Essays in Honour of Gordon Rupp*, London 1975; Gabriele Winkler, 'The Origins and Idiosyncracies of the Earliest Form of Asceticism', Skudlarek, *The Continuing Quest for God*, pp. 9–43; Peter Brown, 'The Rise and Function of the Holy Man in Late Antiquity', in his *Society and the Holy in Late Antiquity*, London 1982.
7. David Knowles, *From Pachomius to Ignatius* Oxford 1966.
8. John O'Malley, 'Priesthood, Ministry and Religious Life: Some Historical and Historiographical Considerations', *Theological Studies* 49 (1988) pp. 223–57.
9. See Caroline Walker Bynum, *Jesus as Mother: Studies in the Spirituality of the High Middle Ages* (Berkeley 1982), p. 10 and pp. 12–14. On the motivation for poverty see Regis Armstrong and Ignatius Brady, eds., *Francis and Clare: The Complete Works* (London/New York 1982), for example, pp. 46, 48, 117, 140, 141, 145, 154–55.
10. See Jean Leclercq, *Contemplative Life* (Kalamazoo 1978), chapter 1,

espec. pp. 4–5; Bynum, *Jesus as Mother* ch. 1; also Grover Zinn provides a brief general introduction in 'The Regular Canons', in McGinn, *Christian Spirituality*, pp. 218–28.

11. See the Introduction by Tarcisius van Bavel in Raymond Canning tr., *The Rule of St Augustine – with Introduction and Commentary*, London 1984. Contrast the communitarian spirituality of mutual love, responsibility and service in The Rule of St Augustine with the chapter headings of The Rule of St Benedict. See Timothy Fry, ed., *The Rule of St Benedict in Latin and English with Notes* (Collegeville 1981), thematic index, pp. 560–61.

12. See David Knowles, *The Monastic Order in England* (Cambridge 1950), pp. 139–42.

13. See Bynum, *Jesus as Mother*, ch. 1.

14. Bynum, ch. 2. See also Aelred of Rievaulx, *The Mirror of Charity* and *On Spiritual Friendship* which appear in a number of editions, the most recent of which are in the Cistercian Fathers series, Kalamazoo, Michigan.

15. For a selection of extracts from the lives and sayings of the desert fathers and mothers, see Benedicta Ward, tr. *The Wisdom of the Desert Fathers*, Oxford 1986. On the priority of charity, see for example, nos. 149, 151 and 155. On visits to the towns and cities, see nos. 30 and 47. On solitaries who returned to city life and even married and yet were ultimately received back into the desert, see nos. 44, 47 and 54.

16. On the vocabulary of the solitary life, see Ann Warren, 'The Nun as Anchoress: England 1000–1500', in Nichols, *Distant Echoes*, pp. 197–212.

17. Benedicta Ward, 'Julian the Solitary', in *Julian Reconsidered*, Oxford 1988. Ward's essay also contains some general material on the eremitical life in England. For more detailed background on English solitaries, see, for example, Jonathan Hughes, *Pastors and Visionaries: Religion and Secular Life in Late Medieval Yorkshire* (Woodbridge, Suffolk/New Hampshire 1988), ch. 2 'The Eremitic Movement in the Diocese of York; Also Sharon K. Elkins, *Holy Woman of Twelfth-Century England* (Chapel Hill/London 1988), ch. 7, 'The Eremitic Life', and pp. 150–60. For the traditional monastic view of Julian, see Edmund Colledge and James Walsh, eds, *Julian of Norwich: Showings* (New York/London 1978), pp. 20–1. An excellent modern study of Julian is Grace Jantzen, *Julian of Norwich: Mystic and Theologian*, New York/London 1987. Another recent study is Brant Pelphrey, *Christ is Our Mother: Julian of Norwich*, Wilmington/London 1989. The Latin and English texts of the *Ancrene Wisse* or *Ancrene Riwle* have been published by the Early English Text Society (EETS) as volumes 216 (ed. Charlotte D'Evelyn, London 1944) and 252 (ed. Frances Mack, London 1963) of the EETS series. A modern English version appeared as *The Ancrene Riwle*, M. B. Salu, ed., London 1955.

18. On forms of the solitary life, see the general survey by Peter Anson, *The Call of the Desert* (London 1964), ch. 15. A modern version of Margery Kempe's spiritual autobiography has appeared as *The Book*

of Margery Kempe, B. A. Windeath, tr., London 1985.

19. Gerald Arbuckle, in 'Suffocating Religious Life: A New Type Emerges', *The Way Supplement* 65 (1989), notes three different models of community of which the third, 'mission', is not to be associated essentially with conventual structures.

20. For the 1554 exhortation, see *Epistolae et Monumenta P. Hieronymi Nadal* 15: 54, *Monumenta Historica Societatis Iesu*. For the 1557 annotations, see ibid., 5; 195–6. For comments on these and other relevant texts of Nadal with regard to 'journeying' see John O'Malley, 'To Travel to Any Part of the World: Jeronimo Nadal and the Jesuit Vocation', *Studies in the Spirituality of Jesuits* 16: 2 (1984).

21. For the enclosure of women up to the twelfth century, see Jane Tibbets Schulenberg, 'Strict Active Enclosure and its Effects on the Female Monastic Experience (500–1100)', in Nichols, *Distant Echoes*, pp. 51–86. Chapter 27 of the *Regula Monachorum* on enclosure appears in *Patrologiae, Series Latina*, J.-P. Migne, ed., volume 30 (Paris 1865), columns 427–8. Cited subsequently as *PL*.

22. On enclosure from the twelfth century onwards, see Jean Leclercq, 'The Spirituality of Medieval Feminine Monasticism' in Skudlarek, *The Continuing Quest for God*, pp. 129–31. The Cistercian statutes appear in *Statua Capitulorum Generalium Ordinis Cisterciensis*, J. M. Canivez, ed., (Louvain 1934) 2: 248, 2.

23. Skudlarek., p. 122.

24. See Barnabas Sandeman, 'Nuns and Monks: A Thousand years of Change' in *The Way Supplement* 40 (1981).

25. See Bynum, p. 11.

26. Quoted in Bynum, pp. 135–6.

27. For example, see Ruth P. Liebowitz, 'Virgins in the Service of Christ: the Dispute Over an Active Apostolate for Women During the Counter Reformation', in Ruether, *Women of Spirit*, pp. 132–52.

28. See Rosemary Rader, 'Christian Pre-Monastic Forms of Asceticism: *Syneisaktism* or Spiritual Marriage', Skudlarek, *The Continuing Quest for God*, pp. 80–5.

29. Quoted in Penny Schine Gold, 'Male/Female Cooperation: The Example of Fontevrault,', in Nichols, *Distant Echoes*, p. 154. The article as a whole, pp. 151–68, provides a useful summary of the organization of the monastery. The Rule appears in *PL*, volume 162 (Paris 1889), columns 1083–4.

30. Schulenberg, 'Strict Active Enclosure', p. 76. On the appropriateness of the term 'double monastery', and on monasteries for women and men in England, see Elkins, *Holy Women*, pp. xviii, and chs 3, 6, and 7.

31. John Climacus, *The Ladder of Divine Ascent*, step 1, in the edition by Colm Luibheid and Norman Russell, London 1982.

32. For a very general overview, see David Knowles, *Christian Monasticism* (London 1969), ch 9 and 13.

33. See Raimundo Panikkar, 'The Archetype of the Monk', in *Blessed Simplicity*, New York 1982.

34. This information is drawn largely from 'Ethiopian Orthodox Models of Religious Life', a privately circulated document made available courtesy of Elizabeth Rees.

35. For a general introduction to Celtic spirituality and monasticism see for example, Pierre Riché, 'Spirituality in Celtic and Germanic society', in McGinn, *Christian spirituality*, pp. 163–76, and Diarmuid O Laoghiare, 'Celtic Spirituality' in Cheslyn Jones et al., eds., *The study of Spirituality* (London/New York 1986), pp. 216–25.

36. *St Thomas More: Selected Letters*, E. F. Rogers, ed., (New Haven/London, 1976), Letter 26 'To a Monk', p. 140.

CHAPTER SIX

Context and Conflicts: The Beguines

The second case study to be examined is the Beguines. Although what follows may be viewed as a useful overview by readers interested in but not particularly familiar with the Beguines, this is not my primary aim in this chapter. My point, as in the previous chapter, is to use a more detailed example to ground some of the questions of analysis and interpretation raised in the first four chapters. As such, this examination of the Beguines does not claim to be original in its detail. However, it may be said in passing that, while Beguine texts and information about their life have been readily available in the Low Countries, Germany and, to a lesser extent, France where they predominantly flourished, these have not been particularly accessible until recently to a purely English-speaking readership. The appearance of scholarly essays and more popular studies in English has both reflected and provoked an increase of interest. A fair range of these are cited in footnotes for those readers who desire to pursue the subject in greater depth. What I hope may be new and provocative, apart from some questions raised directly in this chapter, is the invitation to situate the Beguines within the critical framework provided by the opening chapters. This may enable us to reconsider the *significance* of the Beguines within a wider historical framework and within the overall picture of western spirituality, how it developed and how it has subsequently been interpreted and used.

KEY

The Beguines emerged as a spiritual movement of women towards the end of the twelfth century in northern Europe and have already been cited in chapter three as one of the examples of groups *1.* that did not fit. In the present chapter this example will be developed further in terms of two of my basic contentions: that *2.* spiritualities necessarily reflect particular historical contexts and that certain fundamental priorities have to a great extent controlled *3.* the development of spirituality, how it was viewed and therefore recorded. This, we saw, was particularly striking when there was

141

a culture clash between the dominant spiritual culture and a group that represented different values. In the light of what has been said about religious life, it is worth noting at the outset that the Beguines deliberately sought a form of lay commitment and yet were always in danger of being subsumed into religious life.

The Beguines existed in a kind of twilight zone which, depending on your standpoint, was defined as lay spirituality or semi-religious life. The problem of definition seems to have played an important role in the mixed reactions to this spiritual movement of women when it first emerged around the end of the twelfth century. Were the Beguines truly a movement? Many contemporaries treated them as one and viewed it either as heretical, and thus a danger to the Church, or as a bulwark against the attractions of heresy, and therefore full of potential for it. Indeed, those who took the more positive view sought to institutionalize the Beguines and to give them greater coherence. Other questions have been posed by historians and others. Was the 'movement' essentially spiritual or were its causes primarily socio-economic? Were the Beguines a women's movement in the modern sense? The Beguines have in fact been interpreted variously, and sometimes simplistically, as a movement of heretics, of lay spirituality, of semi-religious life, of quasi-feminists or of social radicals. The interpetations have been various, not least today when there has been a remarkable revival of interest in the Beguines, and their spirituality, among Christians of different persuasions.

In fact we know surprisingly little about the origins of the Beguines. The first evidence of the use of the term was in 1199, in the *Dialogus Miraculorum* of Caesar of Heisterbach, and was already pejorative.[1] There was no single founder, no original rule of life and, in the early days at least, the Beguines are difficult to distinguish from a multitude of individuals or groups who sought a radical Christian life-style outside the canonical constraints of religious life. The Beguines, and their spirituality, clearly reflect the realities of a particular age, yet the relationship of the Beguines to the predominant spiritual culture is ambiguous. They expressed the values of the powerful and diverse spiritual movement known as the *vita apostolica*, which advocated imitation of the primitive Church; evangelisation and service; gospel poverty, frequently associated with some form of manual labour, in imitation of the poor Christ; and chastity. However, like the movement as a whole, the Beguines came into conflict with the priorities of the institutional Church: greater structural organization, centralism, control and the

142

increasing powers of the clergy. The Beguines provided an effective outlet for much religious fervour, hitherto untapped, and yet their values appeared to challenge those in authority. It is not surprising, therefore, that they were received with enthusiasm by many lay people, cautious approval by spiritual reformers and suspicion by many in authority. *Spectrum of acceptance.*

First of all, it is important to examine the emergence of the Beguines in the late twelfth century and whether this should be interpreted in primarily religious or socio-economic terms. The second consideration will be to examine, in more detail, how their values and their organization reflected contemporary needs. Then, some reassessment of their difficulties with Church authorities, as well as their gradual institutionalization, will be attempted. Finally, it seems helpful to outline an overall evaluation of the Beguines. Were they totally original or were their ideals and structures derivative? Were they essentially a radical or a conservative movement? Can they be said to have succeeded or failed?

The general religious process

It may be argued that by the thirteenth century, in the context of medieval religious and social realities, all possible forms of organised religious life had been explored. The emergence of the mendicants who, while freeing themselves from a properly monastic spirituality, retained some conventual structures pushed the adaptation of cenobitic life to its institutional limits. The maximum degree of freedom and mobility that was attained applied, in the main, to men rather than women. Although some important elements of the new religious fervour, such as radical poverty, were expressed institutionally by women's communities such as the Poor Clares, freedom from cloister was not one of the options available to women seeking formal religious life at this time.

Only one further step was possible for both men and women and this was to seek greater freedom from institutional pressures by exploring more informal ways of life. The broader context, therefore, for the emergence of the Beguines was a period of fluidity where there was a movement away from the structured pattern of religious life and towards the small, the simple and the less well-defined. If the 'monastic centuries', in the period up to the twelfth century, had tended to produce outstanding and memorable individuals *within* the cloister, the subsequent centuries witnessed an increase of significant individuals, whether mystics (such as Julian of Norwich), reformers or critics who stood a little apart from formal organizations. 'The spiritual warrior was out; the critic and contemplative came in.'[2]

A growing gulf between religious fervour and institutional structures emerged during the eleventh and twelfth centuries which reflects a dissatisfaction with the official reform movement within the Church in the period from about 1050–1300. This was a reform both of general Church structure and of religious orders. The tendency, prevalent until recently, was to see this reform period in entirely positive terms. However there was a gulf between its dominant values of order and organization and a more inchoate religious fervour which paralleled it and which was, to an extent, set in train by the expectations created by official reform. This indicates that, in important respects, official reforms failed. That is to say, they helped to raise expectations, but ultimately failed to capture the minds and hearts of many lay people and outstanding religious spirits of the age. As a result of the important spiritual and institutional shifts in the Church, religious experience developed three notable elements. Firstly there was widespread disquiet with, and even at times active dissent from, the institutional Church. Secondly, a new spiritual temper emerged which favoured quiet, evangelical piety and simplicity. Thirdly, there was a growth of individualism, a movement outwards from the privileged context of the cloister and a suspicion of attempts to force the spiritual life into organised systems of observance, designed for a specialized religious 'class'.

The inevitable disappointment created a number of fringe movements, such as the Waldensians, Humiliati and Cathars, some of which became doctrinally unorthodox. Even among some religious, particularly the friars, there were apocalyptic expectations. The vision of the Abbot Joachim of Fiore was outstandingly influential. The Franciscans produced such exponents of radical poverty as the Spirituals and the Dominicans, individuals like Eckhart who taught that union with God was open to all the Godly but, in a way characteristic of the spiritual values of the time, particularly to those free from possessiveness, both spiritual and material. Of course, the majority of people remained firmly attached to the religion of the institutional Church, whatever their degree of private dissatisfaction. Yet the laity were never completely at home with their role as observers or outsiders, and it is this which, perhaps more than anything else, explains the emergence of such groups as the Beguines who attempted, initially, to create a kind of lay fringe around the established structures and religious communities.[3]

The emergence of the Beguines and religious factors

The immediate religious context for the emergence of the Beguines was the *vita apostolica* whose motivating force was the enrichment of people's spirituality which had been sapped by formalism. The values of the movement were generated by an invigorating interpretation of discipleship which was noted earlier. In its early stages, the appeal of the *vita apostolica* was largely to laypeople and it coincides with the more lively participation, in matters of faith, by townsfolk who were often untouched by the ministrations of a poorly educated clergy and were less in contact with traditional monastic life. Devotion was also travelling outwards from the cloister into the world and especially into the family. It should be noted that, in families, women played a valued role and consequently were drawn into this spiritual movement which, in so many ways, suited their needs. As a result, laypeople sought to implement the programme of the *vita apostolica*, by teaching and preaching and thus usurped a role which the Church hierarchy claimed as its sole prerogative. They also created associations for prayer and good works outside a liturgical framework, began to read the Bible in the vernacular and, even in orthodox groups, rather disliked the excesses of sacerdotal religion.[4]

The groups which came into being as a result of the *vita apostolica* were varied. As well as some new religious orders, there were leper-houses and other charitable hospitals, recluses, contemplative stigmatists and a variety of groups who occupied a twilight zone between formal religious life and everyday Christian existence. It should be noted that the Beguines were an urban phenomenon. The rapid growth of towns in this period seems to have left a large number of women in a particularly insecure position. Some women began to live singly within their family homes or in small groups in houses inherited by one of their number or bought by pooling their resources. There is statistical evidence in Cologne, especially for the years 1250–1310, of property transactions as Beguines bought and sold small tenements in order to obtain some security for their life-style.[5]

The only major study of the Beguines in English remains that of Ernest McDonnell, originally published over thirty years ago. McDonnell provides an unrivalled guide to the huge bibliography on the Beguines, especially in Flemish, which is inaccessible to most English-speaking students. Most of the modern essays or short studies continue to rely on this work because of its prodigious detail, even though in many respects its perspective is dated. McDonnell suggests that the movement for spiritual reform divided clearly into two: those who preached submission to the hierarchy and acceptance of the sacraments, and those who openly revolted against the established order. This, I believe, oversimplifies the issue but it fits with McDonnell's general concern to portray the Beguines not only as orthodox but also as part of the mainstream of the Church. This leads him to place great emphasis on the institutional development of Beguine life and not to question the process by which the Church authorities sought to bring the Beguines under control. In fact, lay spirituality (or semi-regular as McDonnell terms much of it) existed on a spectrum, from undivided obedience to canonical prescriptions to rejection of their validity, combined with doctrinal unorthodoxy. However all the lay groups that emerged shared, to some extent, in an *implicit* criticism of traditional forms of committed Christian life. McDonnell tends to view the atmosphere of religious fervour, including the Beguines, as a direct byproduct of the Gregorian reforms, a view now overtaken, as we have seen, by a sharper distinction between the values and direction of institutional changes in the Church and the various movements of spirituality.[6]

virginity The Beguines expressed two key religious motivations, the cult of chastity and a desire for voluntary poverty, which relate to the general spiritual fervour of their age. The reputation of one of the best-known and significant figures in the Beguine movement, Mary of Oignies (born 1176), made the Nivelles area near Liège a centre of lay piety and inspired Jacques de Vitry to become one of the most influential supporters and noted chroniclers of Beguine life. He was a reformist priest who later became Bishop of Acre and a papal advisor. De Vitry was also a friend of the Poor Clare movement in Italy. Mary became a kind of symbol of the motivation of the Beguines as a whole in her mortification, dedication to chastity, ardent pursuit of gospel poverty, lively interest in the poor and devotion to the Eucharist.[7] McDonnell correctly notes the strong religious motivations expressed in Beguine statutes. For example, in the oldest rule of the beguinage (or community of Beguines) at Bruges (*c.* 1300), the externals of life are firmly subordinated to a meticulous attention to religious exercises. The primary motivation seems to be contemplative, and what he calls 'mystical excitement' led to a voluntary withdrawal from social privilege in order to pursue an evangelical ideal.[8]

The emergence of the Beguines and social factors

The Beguines have been interpreted by historians in a variety of ways, including as a socio-economic phenomenon, that either provided a corporate life for the poor and socially maladjusted or was a radical form of social protest.[9] It is difficult to distinguish, in an absolute way, the social and religious roots of a spiritual tradition yet it is vital to remember that, as we have seen, the Beguines themselves appear to have understood their values in primarily, if not exclusively, religious terms. We stand at a distance and so may be aware of more complex factors but it would be reductionist to ignore the explicit religious values and to concentrate exclusively on implicit social or cultural ones.

In what sense were the Beguines a social phenomenon? Demographic causes play a role in any religious movement, even if this can never tell the whole story. Within limits, it is possible to trace demographic factors for the emergence of the Beguines in that by about 1200 the population of parts of Western Europe showed an inbalance of the sexes. This had two principal causes. Firstly, there was a natural female longevity in comparison to men and a higher survival rate for female babies. However, male mortality was aggravated by a specific factor of the age: many men died violently in battle. Secondly, relatively high numbers of men also became unavailable as spouses in this period. This was due to a number of factors, including absence on crusade for long periods of time, the recent imposition of celibacy on all clerics, the increased access to religious life, brought about by the new orders and the creation of a class of *conversi*, or lay-brothers, which broadened the social and educational base of religious communities (although there are questions about the significance of *conversi* as I have mentioned in chapter 3). Given the socially anomalous position of single adult women at this time, any decrease in the possibilities of marriage would almost certainly encourage a movement towards the socially acceptable status of 'nun', if convents were available, or other forms of religiously dedicated singleness.

The problems of women were further stimulated by their disadvantageous social position. Primogeniture became more usual in this period and this depressed the independent means and status of some women of the richer classes. Equally, it seems that an increasing number of nobles could no longer afford the large dowries needed either for the marriage of daughters or for their entry into the traditionally aristocratic convents.[10]

It is now widely accepted that the early Beguines came largely from the aristocratic or the urban bourgeois classes. Apart from financial factors, it seems likely that these were the social groups most affected by new ideas and to whom the ideal of radical poverty was most striking. Beguines were often touched by limitations of attitude characteristic of their social origins. For example, radical poverty was expressed in ways appropriate to their social status. Even the amazingly ascetical Mary of Oignies was always attended by a maid and her work clothes, though simple, were carefully groomed![11] For example, Liège housed what was reputedly the first beguinage, inspired by a priest Lambert le Bègue. Despite the fact that he was working class, and addressed his radical preaching to the weavers, the women whom he gathered together included not only prosperous burghers but also the children of the nobility. Again, the evidence provided by Jacques de Vitry supports the view that the Beguines often came from affluent families yet chose to live simply by the work of their hands or in imitation of apostolic poverty. Most of the leading names of the movement, such as Mary of Oignies, were of noble or bourgeois extraction and were often well-educated. In Germany too, where the Beguines have often been portrayed as a movement of the poor, the surviving references to the family names of members in Cologne between 1223–1450 indicate that all the patrician families were represented.[12] In general, the Mainz and Cologne archives suggest that very few came from the artisan classes and that many were aristocrats or urban upper classes.[13]

In general, the interpretation of the Beguines has changed because the former belief that the *vita apostolica* movement, as a whole, was one of social protest by the new urban lower classes has been discounted. On the contrary, like many of the new communities of nuns (for example, the Cistercians), the Beguines seem to have come from *rising* rather than repressed social groups. Bishop John of Durbheim, in his investigations during the early 1300s, recorded that Beguines came from all classes, *aliquas clari, aliquas nobilis, alias mediocris, et alias humilis status.* Indeed the attraction of a life of poverty may have reflected some anxiety about their new wealth and status.[14]

The fact that a significant proportion of the Beguines came from the prosperous classes accords with a general impression that a voluntary reversal of social and economic status was particularly powerful in models of holiness in the Middle Ages. The *vita apostolica* movement was not primarily a radical movement for the overthrow of the monied classes. The emphasis was on apostolic poverty rather than on apocalyptic reversals of the traditional social order. Even a heretical tract such as *Daz ist Swester Katrei Meister Eckhart Tohter von Strasburc*, which found some favour in orthodox Beguine circles in the early fourteenth century, has a distinctly upper-class feel. Christ was described as 'the most noble man who was ever born' and it was suggested that 'one tests people by nobility'. There is some evidence that the assertion by hostile witnesses that Beguines (and others accused of heresy) were 'rustics' or 'idiots' originated not in a social judgement but in the suspicion by Church authorities of lay theological speculation, particularly when based on the study of Scripture in the vernacular.[15]

The specific problems of women

While heretical groups were attractive, spiritual fervour was not limited to them. The response of male enthusiasts included the foundation of a number of new religious orders. With women, the situation was more complex. It has been suggested that the particular attachment of women to the *vita apostolica* may have been caused partly by the scarcity of legitimate vocations open to women and the fact that relatively fewer women could gain entrance to religious life in comparison to men. Some were attracted to radical mysticism, which on occasions might be heretical, because spiritually, as well as socially, women were relegated to an inferior status. They could not be priests but mystical doctrines offered something as good or better – a close union with God. Traditional convents continued to be proportionately fewer in number and were usually socially exclusive. While Fontevrault was founded as a double monastery specifically for adherents of the *vita apostolica*, it soon became exclusively aristocratic in recruitment. Norbert of Xanten, one of the leading 'poor preachers', founded double houses for the new order of Premontré but by the end of the twelfth century these were being closed down. Women founded Cistercian-inspired houses for themselves, but the monks viewed this with considerable suspicion and retained a very ambivalent attitude towards women associates.

In general, the fervour of women provoked opposition, or at least vacillation, on the part of Church authorities. The prevalent, negative stereotypes of women meant that their vocations were not necessarily seen in a serious light. It was thought that women were particularly receptive to devotional extremism and that, on the whole, they contributed to indiscipline in religious life. What was to be done about the large numbers of women seeking some kind of committed Christian life? The instinct was to control the trend in some way but the problem was that the male orders were fearful of providing pastoral care.[16]

Apart from the problem of sheer numbers, an additional dilemma faced the Church. The life-style which women were creating for themselves outside established orders was active as well as contemplative and this was something which, in the case of women, the Church had not supported for centuries. The new religious orders which emerged in the twelfth and thirteenth centuries made some attempt to meet the needs of women but, of course, no uncloistered order emerged to match the friars and so the apostolic dimension of the new religious spirit was not addressed institutionally. The popes sought to protect the rights of women but by giving adequate maintenance to those who were already members of orders. There was also a fairly crude anti-feminine polemic which depressed the status of women.[17]

Although there were generic differences between the groups that emerged, there were some common features in the 'women's movement'. Devout women found it difficult to remain at home, surrounded by secular and materialistic attitudes. Groups such as the Poor Clares and Beguines placed an emphasis on poverty which reflected a sense that competition to achieve social status was incompatible with the gospel. In this way poverty, for early Poor Clares and Beguines alike, went against the natural order of society and involved a deliberate denial of their background and an acceptance of a way of life that was socially distasteful. Thus, poverty was a personal and social renewal by means of adopting a new and alien life-style.[18] Chastity was also an important emphasis. Unmarried women and widows presented a problem in a culture where to be unmarried was anomalous. There was also, without doubt, some dislike of marriage when it involved such unequal relationships. This combined with an intense interest in virginity in twelfth-century devotional literature.

We should not see the Beguines purely as a response to negative features of religious or social life. It is now accepted that the period from the late twelfth to the early fourteenth century was not merely a difficult time for women but also, paradoxically, saw a significant increase in religious roles despite negative institutional reactions. The *vita apostolica* had produced a taste among women for a wandering, free and active life alongside the early reforming preachers. Despite the limitations on the life-style of new female religious communities, there was some increase in variety in that the female versions of the Franciscans and Dominicans, while eventually cloistered, espoused values that were significantly different from more traditional monastic houses. There were also new forms of life outside convents. The Beguines were among these and if their development reflects a sense of frustration with traditional structures it also suggests that certain values of the new spiritual climate appealed especially to women, and indeed may be said to have been significantly generated by them.

The Beguines provided a positive and attractive alternative to convents. It gave women a greater role in reflecting and creating piety, especially of a lay variety. In a period when quasi-clerical roles were increasingly closed to women, beguinages offered both the possibility of women shaping their own religious experience and a clear alternative to male religious roles based on the power of office in which religious women, such as Benedictine abbesses, had previously shared. The attraction of the Beguine life also reflects a shift in female spirituality away from the emphasis on structures in male religiosity towards looser affiliations for mutual and equal support. It is fascinating to note that male observers wrote of beguinages in traditional language, associated with religious life, emphasizing their rules and authority structures thereby suggesting that their more informal arrangements, to give religious significance to ordinary life, were difficult to grasp and may have seemed dangerous.[19]

The influence of locality

The Beguines took two basic forms: autonomous individuals or groups who bought tenements and built beguinages. However there were considerable regional variations. Broadly, in Flanders the Beguines tended to create fairly sizeable buildings which eventually became independent parishes. They might resemble a miniature town with a large church at its hub, or a convent enclosure behind a high wall, or sometimes a tree-covered square hardly distinguishable from others in the town. In contrast, in Germany there were very few large units (Strasburg was something of an exception). In fact it is inappropriate to talk of German 'beguinages'; and parishes never developed. German Beguines usually resided in small houses ranging from three to no more than twenty people. The three sites in the English city of Norwich, which are now known to have housed Beguines briefly during the fifteenth century, were all small. Two were in tenements and one was in a parish churchyard. Although Flemish influence was considerable in Norwich, because of strong trading connections, the style of the 'beguinages' bears no resemblance to those of Flanders and may in fact reflect a purely local development based on the custom in that part of England for recluses on occasion to live together.[20]

These variations reflect the strong influence of locality on the development of the Beguines. The traditional religious orders had striven to subordinate local conditions to the requirements of a universal system. The new groups resisted centralism and sought to preserve local pecularities in the face of attempts to impose common legislation. Thus, there is a danger in making too many generalizations about the Beguines. Insofar as they constituted a movement, it was not international even though it crossed frontiers. There was no common, corporate framework. For this reason they do not stand out in history in the same way as the monastic orders. It has proved easy, until relatively recently, to underestimate or even overlook the Beguines as they left a relatively small literary corpus compared to other spiritual traditions that arose from within traditional religious life (for example, the Cistercians) and this output was generally not available to English-speaking readers, not least because much of it was in an unfamiliar medieval vernacular rather than Latin. Equally, Beguine architecture (when it developed in those areas where separate beguinages were built) may be said to be 'domestic' rather than grand or distinctive as was the case with traditional monastic architecture. The Beguines were not a single movement, if by that we understand something comparable to the Franciscans or Cistercians who emerged at much the same time. Rather, they constituted a series of similar responses to conditions of urban life, combined with a reaction against the elaborate governmental structures or systems of perfection in monastic communities.[21]

The religious values of the Beguines

Professor Bynum has noted that there were common religious values in all the new movements that appeared around the twelfth and thirteenth centuries, whether orthodox or heretical. She reduces these to five: a concern for an affective religious response; penitential asceticism; an emphasis on Christ's humanity; an emphasis on the inspiration of the Holy Spirit; finally, the bypassing, to different degrees, of clerical authority. Undoubtedly we can see these values expressed in Beguine life.[22]

Poverty was one of the central ideals of the Beguines, even if its mendicant expression was generally modified to mean simply the voluntary renunciation of social status and support by the 'labour of hands'. This led some commentators to speak of *la contagion beguinale*, an 'infectious desire' to give up riches.[23] There was a desire to be self-sufficient, to base one's life not on family property but on personal responsibility. This desire for poverty places the Beguines firmly within the spiritual atmosphere of the time. Whether they worked or begged the Beguines were part of the same religious fervour that inspired St Francis of Assisi.

The Beguines became famous for their weaving and spinning partly because of economic necessity. However, spiritual motivations were never entirely lost because they sought to imitate the renunciation of Christ. The Beguines shared in the growing devotion to the humanity of Christ, whose roots lay in the spirituality of the Franciscans and Cistercians, and, in the face of social and ecclesiastical materialism, they aspired to the radical purity of the Early Church.[24] Jacques de Vitry's biography of Mary of Oignies notes that she hardly maintained the necessities of life (though 'necessities' is relative when you have a maid!) and often meditated on the poverty of Christ. She saw work as both self-support and as penance.[25]

The ideal of poverty was not austerity purely for its own sake. Apart from being a social renunciation, poverty was also 'apostolic' in the sense both that it increased the ability to 'save souls' and that it imitated the life-style of the apostolic Church. The emphasis on poverty was often threatening because it was so strongly idealistic and tended, implicitly at least, to criticise the wealth of the Church. While many Beguines are recorded as practising a fierce asceticism, it is nowadays accepted that medieval attitudes to penance were not purely, or even predominantly, associated with a rejection of the flesh but were inspired to a great degree by a desire to imitate as closely as possible the human life of Christ and his sufferings. The mendicant orders, and especially the Franciscans, had a profound influence on penitential movements in the later Middle Ages with their emphasis on the imitation of Christ – an emphasis which predisposed people towards penitential exercises.[26]

Devotion to the human Christ, while a general characteristic of spirituality at this time, was particularly strong among the Beguines. This manifested itself both in a concentration on the Eucharist and in a strongly emotional mysticism among some Beguines. The Passion of Christ and the Eucharist seem to have been the main stimuli for visions and revelations. Because of their close relations with the Cistercians it would seem that the Beguines owed their eucharistic piety especially to the influence of that order. The Beguines were noted among contemporary commentators for their love of the Eucharist not merely in the celebration of Mass and reception of Communion but also in extra-liturgical devotions. Mary of Oignies, for example, experienced visions of Christ when she gazed on the reserved sacrament.[27]

The practice of Beguines with regard to Mass and Communion varied. There is some evidence that lay reception in general was rather infrequent. Thus, the Fourth Lateran Council in 1215 felt bound to prescribe a *minimum* of once a year. The Beguines surpassed common practice and for many this was the precise attraction of the life. There is some evidence for weekly reception of Communion, within a pattern of daily attendance at Mass. However, the surviving Beguine statutes mainly date from a later period of their development when increasing institutionalization had led to a decline in spontaneity. For example, at Bruges daily attendance at Mass continued, but reception of communion ranged from a minimum of four times a year to seven times without specific permission.

The mystical trend in the Beguines, inspired by devotion to Christ and the Eucharist, frequently expressed itself in the language of spiritual marriage. Thus, Jacques de Vitry wrote of the experiences of the Beguines at Nivelles, 'The cheeks of one were seen to waste away, while her soul was melted with the greatness of her love,' and, 'I saw another whom for thirty years her Spouse had so zealously guarded in her cell, that she could not leave it herself, nor could the hands of others drag her out.' The deep emotion of their spiritual life may, in part, mean that a fulfilment lacking in medieval marriage was found in a free relationship with the divine, reinforced by living and working in a supportive feminine environment. However, the mystical way was also provoked by an understanding of imitation of Christ that involved not purely becoming *like* Christ but becoming one with him. The Beguines shared this vision with the cloistered Cistercian nuns. Thus Beatrice of Nazareth was trained by the Beguines as a young girl but subsequently spent the rest of her life in various Cistercian convents. The Beguine Hadewijch probably knew of Beatrice's work. Mechtild of Magdeburg began as a German Beguine but ended her days living at the convent at Helfta the precise status of which is unclear but which seems to have had Cistercian aspirations. The ecstatic mystical poetry of Hadewijch and Mechtild expressed a *Minnemystik*, or 'bride-mysticism', comparing the union of the soul with Christ with that of the bride and bridegroom.[28]

Although conventual life was never central to the Beguines, and came about only in a later stage of development, predominantly in Flanders, mutual support was a vital part of their way of being. A contemporary described this objective as, broadly, 'to encourage each other in virtue by means of mutual exhortation' (*ut in sese invicem mutuis exhortationibus ad bonum invitent*).[29] They sought an appropriate daily pattern and an opportunity to discuss spiritual ideas in all-female communities. They studied the Scriptures together in the vernacular and their mistresses or supervisors of beguinages occasionally preached. This was a measure both of their concern for as full a development of a personal spiritual life as possible and of the emphasis, in the *vita apostolica*, on instruction and conversion. The search for mutual support and instruction and the often vocal and critical responses to visiting preachers also indicate that, even in thoroughly orthodox beguinages, there was a certain suspicion of clerical prerogatives. The flexible life-style, including the very relative value given to common life, reflects the desire of the Beguines for the freedom to undertake active and charitable work. Indeed the Beguines have been represented as an attempt to harmonize the individual and the communal: united but freely so; living in common with a degree of autonomy; with a balance of personal and collective work; with independent budgets but strong collective authority.[30]

Organization as expression of values

If the values of the Beguines reflected many of the contemporary religious themes and needs, their forms of organization also effectively expressed these values. The *vita apostolica* had in its early stages supported the equality of women with men in the search for spiritual perfection and the life of the gospels. Despite a certain wariness of clerical control, the Beguines from an early stage maintained close relationships with men. In 1207 Mary of Oignies went to the Augustinian community of St Nicholas of Oignies near Namur as a kind of lay sister or associate. What seems to have attracted her was the practice of the values of the *vita apostolica*, especially a balance of contemplation with intense pastoral activity. So many women joined Mary to live next to the Canons that by 1213 a beguinage was built.[31] Throughout their history, the Beguines had continuous interchange with, and support from, sympathetic male religious, particularly the Cistercians and the mendicant orders. A notable example would be the work of the Dominican mystic, John Tauler, among the Beguines in the Rhineland. The relationships between Beguines and men was also reciprocal as evidenced by the influence of Beguine spirituality on the fourteenth century Flemish reformer and mystic Jan Ruusbroec.[32]

The structures common to the Beguines were relatively few even in the more structured atmosphere of Flemish beguinages. Part of each day was dedicated to prayer. Promises were made to live a life of simplicity, to undertake certain religious duties, to observe chastity during residence in the beguinage and to obey the statutes. Provision was made for spiritual guidance and public confession to fellow Beguines seems to have been practised. There was a period of probation which normally lasted for two years during which the aspirant was guided by a senior whether she lived in a beguinage or autonomously. Beguinages were supervised by a 'grand mistress' who was usually elected and each group was entirely self-governing. The mistress regulated the members fairly closely although they were not strictly enclosed. If a Beguine lapsed she was usually given a series of admonitions and only if she persisted in breaking the statutes was she expelled.

The relative informality of the Beguines in comparison to members of religious orders was most effectively symbolized by their attitude to personal possessions. In some beguinages the members were expected to have independent means but most worked for their livelihood. This also applied to autonomous Beguines although some, especially in Germany, begged for their living. If a Beguine left the community she had to renounce her house and either gave up her possessions or paid all the expenses incurred during her residence. If a group dissolved itself the members kept their own possessions and divided up the common property among them. Even as late as the end of the thirteenth century, municipal records indicate that Beguines had rights over their individual houses and could bequeath them to other Beguines. Despite a degree of common life (which often but not always included common meals), the retention of at least some degree of personal property seems to have been usual.[33] This was logical in a life which was always voluntary and temporary, in principle if not in fact.

The contemporary needs and aspirations of women were central to the organization as well as the values of the Beguines. They sought to create new ways of giving religious significance to women's ordinary lives. Hence the relative simplicity and flexibility of the arrangements and, despite some restrictions, the lack of separation between Beguines and the surrounding world. This may also explain why some Beguines practised certain sacramental functions among themselves, for example confessing to each other or to the mistress, although it is difficult to judge how general this practice was.[34]

It was inevitable that once the Beguines began to develop communities of some size they became gradually more institutional. Some beguinages adopted a public vow which, while general in form ('to follow our Lord Jesus Christ' for example), approximated to the practice of religious. Some individual Beguines affiliated themselves to the Franciscans through the Third Rule. However irrevocable vows were never prescribed and those communities which eventually adopted them ceased to be Beguines and became convents in the formal sense. A distinctive dress eventually evolved but uniformity between houses was never characteristic. On the whole, they wore 'modest clothes' (usually grey-brown undyed wool) and the emphasis was on avoiding bright colours or *curioso habitu et pomposo*. In general the Beguines continued to resemble simple townswomen. The movement remained largely anonymous and ill-defined and never developed into a religious order nor adopted a uniform rule. Insofar as rules did appear in the fourteenth century, these simply codified traditional customs in order to forestall criticism rather than to tighten discipline. In essence the life remained voluntary, temporary and informal.[35]

Relationship with the Church

The Beguines went through four distinct phases of development which reflect their changing relationship with the institutional Church. The initial period was one of individual initiative where Beguines lived with their families or autonomously without any kind of withdrawal from normal lay life. These women were referred to as *beguinae singulariter in saeculo manentes* or simply as *mulieres sanctae*. The second period, in the early part of the thirteenth century, saw many of the Beguines gathering together to follow some form of common life for mutual spiritual support and also, possibly, for economic reasons. In this period there was much support from clergy, such as Jacques de Vitry, and from reformed religious, such as the Cistercians, but the movement remained essentially informal. The third period dates from the 1230s when houses or associations of Beguines were granted indirect and quasi-legal recognition by, for example, the bull of Gregory IX in 1233, *Gloriam Virginalem*. 'Closed' beguinages emerged which were completely self-contained. Episcopal and civic protection was growing and local statutes began to be written. The final stage, by the fourteenth century, was to constitute beguinages as autonomous parishes. This was also the period of greatest episcopal organisation and saw the granting of certain privileges, such as exemption from taxation, similar to religious houses. Even in the later stages, autonomous Beguines did not die out but such women were not encouraged and did not gain the same privileges as the communities.[36]

It is easy to assume with McDonnell, the standard authority in English, that the growing formalization of the movement was in the best interests both of the Beguines and of the wider Church. The latter sought a firm bulwark against the dangers of heresy and the new urban classes needed an answer to their spiritual needs which was organized and within canonical prescriptions. McDonnell refers to the process of development as 'regularizing' and cites Bishop Henry of Guelders who was concerned to safeguard the Beguines from attacks by seeking a closer definition of their status within the Church. For this reason he censured those Beguines who remained autonomous and recommended statutes of observance for several houses.[37]

A more critical perspective suggests that far from being a purely natural development, to the unquestionable advantage of the Beguines, the growing formalization was either imposed by Church authority, as a means of greater control, or adopted by the Beguines in self-defence against suspicion and even persecution. Certainly, the third and fourth periods of development were marked by greater clerical control and supervision of the spiritual life as well as by the curtailment of freedom of movement by a degree of enclosure. Undoubtedly, the granting of parish status continued to mark the Beguines out from religious orders and, in a sense, to affirm their status as laypeople. However, it also separated them from *ordinary* parish life and placed them directly under the control of diocesan authorities. It seems that the Beguines were at their most dynamic in the first two stages before the time of formal recognition and greater control.

Why did prominent Churchmen support the Beguines? Jacques de Vitry saw them as a means of spreading what was best in the spirituality of the *vita apostolica* and also as an effective barrier against heresy. In England, the reform-minded Bishop of Lincoln, Robert Grosseteste, and the Benedictine chronicler Matthew Paris, were most impressed by Beguine simplicity and poverty which, Grosseteste suggested, in some ways outshone even the Franciscans. It is interesting, however, that even someone as close to the movement as de Vitry saw the Beguines in institutional terms and sought (in vain as it transpired) to regularize their status by having them incorporated into normal religious life.[38] He seems to have valued their spirituality more than their flexible organization, even though these two dimensions cannot really be distinguished because the chosen organization that evolved was an expression of their deepest values. Thus, in certain ways de Vitry failed to grasp their essential spirit. In this context the distinction made by Church authorities between 'good Beguines' and others often referred not to heresy but to the degree of ecclesiastical control. In a bull of Gregory IX in 1233, recognition was granted to 'good' Beguines or *beguinae clausae* (that is, semi-cloistered), in contrast to those who remained autonomous or in informal groups. McDonnell's study seems to accept uncritically this official distinction. In his description of the condemnation for heresy of the Beguine Marguerite Porete, he assumes that she 'must have been an unattached beguine, with no fixed residence, regarding mendicancy as a means of livelihood, pursuing a life of moral laxity, and refusing to submit to authority'.[39]

It has been assumed that the persecution of the Beguines by Church authorities on suspicion of heresy was often justified. This understanding has come under critical scrutiny in recent years. The accusations of heresy were inextricably linked to issues of control and approval by Church authority. For example, in his *De Scandalis Ecclesiae* of 1274, Gilbert of Tournai focuses on the use by Beguines of vernacular translations of the Bible and their interpretation of Scripture in meetings.[40] The translations were unauthorised and interpretation of Scripture by laypeople, and especially women, encroached on the prerogatives of clergy. The issue of Scripture was as much one of authority as of real or potential heresy. The opposition of one bishop, Bruno of Olmutz, in 1273 is revealing. He condemned the Beguines on three counts. Firstly, their way of life lacked proper approval. Secondly, they used their freedom to escape the obedience due to local clergy. Thirdly, large numbers of women became unavailable for marriage! His conclusion was that women should be content either to enter traditional convents or to get married. The same fear of lack of control by Church authority is echoed in the criticisms of Pope Clement V in 1311. The status of the Beguines was the crucial issue for him and the only category within which he was able to judge was that of traditional religious life.[41]

The condemnation of the Beguines at the Council of Vienne (1311–12) combined the question of authority with suspicions of heresy. Because the Beguines wore distinctive dress yet were not religious, did not owe explicit obedience to Church authorities and had no approved rules, it seemed that they refused to accept the hierarchy, were indifferent to the sacraments and were morally lax. Their 'heresy' was described more specifically as idle speculation about the nature of God and the sacraments. This may have been an extrapolation, in terms of some classical heretical type, from official suspicion of the Beguines' avoidance of the formalism of religious life and their attempts to offer an alternative to ordinary parochial life. Some modern commentators share the assumption that the lack of traditional monastic structures inevitably made the Beguines susceptible to the contagion of heresy.

Were the accusations of heresy justified? Recent scholarship suggests that the word 'Beghards', the title given to male equivalents of the Beguines, was also used by contemporaries for the heretics of the Free Spirit. It seems likely that the Beguines were indescriminately taken under the umbrella of so-called heresy by many observers. Popular stories which link the heresy of the Free Spirit with the Beguines point to an important assumption about free associations of women in particular. Women were seen as fundamentally weak and therefore likely to be subverted (both sexually and doctrinally) unless they were subject to proper control and to the protection of enclosure.

An interesting case is that of Marguerite Porete, generally thought to have been a Beguine, who was burned as a heretic in Paris in May 1310. Her writings were condemned for two doctrines: autotheism (that the soul can become one with God), and antinominianism (as a consequence of union with God, we can ignore the moral law). Both doctrines were associated with the heresy of the Free Spirit. However, the strange thing is that Marguerite's book survived in monastic circles. By the fifteenth century some people thought that it was by (the orthodox) Ruusbroec and in modern times it was translated into English as *The Mirror of Simple Souls* under the auspices of the English Benedictines! Modern reassessment of her heresy is based largely on the fact that her little book, while ambiguous, is open to orthodox interpretation and was, in fact, believed to be sound both by several significant contemporary ecclesiastics, who had seen the whole text, and by later editors. The theologians who condemned her had only seen extracts taken out of context.[42]

To sum up, the suspicion of heresy cannot be disassociated from the issue of authority. Beguines did not fit a pattern of well-regulated religious life. It was difficult for church authorities to obtain information about them and to control them. They were not approved religious and sought to satisfy the religious needs of their age without much formality and by maintaining a certain independence from normal authority structures. There was a suspicion of the *vita apostolica* movement as a whole because of its association with criticisms of the laxity of some clergy. In an atmosphere of heresy-hunting, any group which looked like a private conventicle was likely to be seen as disordered and charges of moral laxity were closely associated with lack of official surveillance. The Beguines were seen as too pious or as fanatics. Any excess, real or assumed, led to accusations of hypocrisy and a desire to show that they were falsely motivated. Finally, the Beguines appeared similar to the mendicant orders and those who disapproved of the latter attacked the Beguines because they lacked the protection enjoyed by the mendicants and were easier game.[43] In summary, the persecution of the Beguines, while complex in origin, involved, in part, a desire to preserve traditional ecclesiastical structures and the accepted norms of religious behaviour.

Conclusion: an assessment

To assess the Beguine movement as a whole would be a complex task. However, three general questions arise from the development and progress of the movement. Were the Beguines original or derivative? Were they traditional or radical critics? Finally, can they be said to have succeeded or failed? With regard to originality, Ernest McDonnell suggests that the Beguines and the Cistercian nuns were so intertwined that their contemporaries often thought of them as equivalent. There were similarities in the spirituality of Beguines and Cistercian nuns especially in their common mystical tendencies and there were undoubtedly close relations between the two groups. However, they were so different in important respects that the older interpretation must be seriously questioned.

The fact that the Beguines were not religious and had no fixed rule or central organization cannot be thought of as incidental. They did not look back to a saintly founder or normative 'stories of origin' as did religious. They sought no formal authorization or patrons. Their vows were not those of religious life and were a statement of intention (which was always provisional) rather than an irreversible commitment to a fixed discipline and way of life, ultimately enforced by authority. The Beguine ethos was to continue to work in the world even if there was, at times, a contemplative and even a mystical element to their spirituality. Their version of the apostolic life was characteristic of lay rather than religious attitudes and this is especially true of poverty. The emphasis was not on spiritual poverty alone but on a materially simple life-style linked to self-support by the work of their hands. Finally, unlike the Cistercian nuns, the Beguines may validly be described as a women's movement in the sense that they were not a feminine appendage to a monastic reform that owed its original impetus to men.[44]

In summary, the Beguines were original in the sense that they were not merely a version of another spiritual tradition such as the Cistercians. Equally, they offered something new – an organized way of life for lay women which was informal and not constrained by the canonical regulations of traditional religious life. On the other hand, they did not arise in isolation but were part of a much wider spiritual movement, the *vita apostolica*, and reflected many of the values which the different elements of that movement (whether new or reformed religious communities or lay groups) had in common.

Several writers present the Beguines as fairly traditional and mainline (except in those cases where they fell into heresy) and distinguish them from other elements of the *vita apostolica* movement by suggesting that they avoided threatening the institutional Church by not 'turning the virtue of poverty into a vice by attacking the ecclesiastical power structure'. They lived their lives but minded their own business, gave example but eschewed overt criticism and, most importantly, remained humble and obedient to Church authority. Contemporary witnesses, such as de Vitry, have been cited in support of their obedience and humility.

Such a view is questionable because one-sided. The very *existence* of the Beguines was an implicit criticism and consequently a threat. This would explain the strength of the accusations against them and their widespread persecution. They set out to reform the ecclesiastical order as it affected laypeople and women in particular, even if in a low-key manner, precisely because traditional structures were not adequate for their needs. The secular clergy were frequently enmeshed in temporal affairs and, despite reform groups, monasticism was declining as the predominant spiritual force in the Church. Not only did the Beguines create an alternative life-style but they placed a great premium on two things which were not generally favoured by Church authority: biblical translations and vernacular preaching of a radical kind. Their attitude to poverty may not have been strident, but such an emphasis could not but be contentious because it presupposed the dispensability of temporal possessions and recommended a life-style based on individual labour.

[margin note: RADICAL CLAIM]

It is also inaccurate to suggest that Beguines never explicitly criticized the clergy and the institutional Church. Mechtild of Magdeburg, in her only work, *The Flowing Light of the Godhead*, denounced the abuses in the Church and the laxity of the clergy in rather strong terms. She spoke of 'corrupt Christianity', of the Church as a maiden who was unclean and unchaste and referred to the cathedral clergy as 'goats'! When criticized, her reaction was to fight back fearlessly and to label her critics 'pharisees'.[45] Having said this, it does not seem to me justifiable at the other extreme to describe the Beguines as radical reformers and forerunners of the Reformation. Their critique of the Church, if such it may be called, was not doctrinal, but ascetical or devotional, and should be judged within its own age rather than in terms of issues and movements current two or three hundred years later.

Were the Beguines a success or a failure? Obviously the first thing to note is that they survived, despite persecution and institutionalization. In this sense they accomplished two important things. Firstly, they managed to create an alternative life-style, in line with many of the values of the *vita apostolica*, which gained patronage and support from sufficient reforming clerics that it could live in the mainstream of the Church. Secondly, their spirituality fitted the needs of the thirteenth century in that women could live an apostolic life and seek perfection while remaining free of strict enclosure. However, the price they paid was greater institutionalization and control.

The authorities hoped that the best aspects of the *vita apostolica* could be brought within stable Church structures as a defence against even greater extremism and possible heresy. This motive was part of the reason for the acceptance of the mendicant orders and for attempts by Pope Innocent III to bring radical groups, such as the Humiliati in Italy, within the mainstream. It has been suggested that Innocent's flexibility with regard to the Humiliati, while pragmatic and apparently effective, sowed the seeds of their decline as a radical evangelical movement. Much the same comment could be made of the Beguines. Outside the official structures they were valuable critics and in a strong position to respond to non-institutional needs among laywomen. Once regulated, they seem to have declined in devotional fervour and to have lost their early spontaneity and, therefore, attraction.[46] Viewed in developmental terms, the movement began as relatively radical and ended as more traditional. The Beguines are a striking symbol of the fate of the *vita apostolica*. The Church was unable to cope with such fervour except by reacting against it or by trying to channel some features into well-established patterns. A case can be made for saying that the original Beguine movement was too radical for the official Church and, through revision and increasing structure, changed to such a degree that eventually it neither provoked opposition nor continued to attract large numbers of fervent recruits.

Notes

1. Cited by François Vandenbroucke in Louis Bouyer, ed., *The Spirituality of the Middle Ages* (ET, London 1968), pp. 353–7.

2. R. W. Southern, *Western Society and the Church in the Middle Ages*, (Harmondsworth, 1970), p. 301.

3. For stimulating overviews of this period and revised interpretations of the movements of reform, see Southern, ibid., ch. 7 and espec. pp. 300–8 and George Tavard, 'Apostolic Life and Church Reform' in Jill Raitt and John Meyendorff, eds, *Christian Spirituality: High Middle Ages and Reformation* (London 1987), pp. 1–11. In her brief but helpful introduction to *Beguine Spirituality: An Anthology* (London/New York 1989), Fiona Bowie includes an overview specifically of the situation of women in society and Church immediately prior to the emergence of the Beguines.

4. See Ernest McDonnell, *The Beguines and Beghards in Medieval Culture: With Special Emphasis on the Belgian Scene* (New York reprinted 1969), pp. 141–2. This remains the standard work on the Beguines in English although dated in some respects. A number of more recent essays and other studies have served to revise some of his perspectives. Many of these are cited in the following notes. Also Brenda Bolton, 'Innocent III's Treatment of the Humiliati' in G. J. Cuming and Derek Baker, eds., *Popular Belief and Practice*, Studies in Church History 8 (Oxford 1972), p. 73.

5. Southern, *The Church in the Middle Ages*, pp. 323–4.

6. For McDonnell's comments, see *Beguines and Beghards*, p. vii.

7. See McDonnell, *Beguines and Beghards*, pp. 120–21. The *Vita Mariae Oigniacensis* by Jacques de Vitry appears in the Bollandists' *Acta Sanctorum* in the volume *Iunii, IV* (Antwerp 1707), pp. 636–66. Cited subsequently as *VMO*.

8. McDonnell, *Beguines and Beghards*, pp. 86–8.

9. See McDonnell, *Beguines and Beghards*, pp. vii–viii.

10. See Brenda Bolton, *'Mulieres Sanctae'* in Derek Baker, ed., *Sanctity and Secularity*, Studies in Church History 10 (Oxford, 1973), pp. 86–7.

11. Brenda Bolton, *'Vitae Matrum*: a further aspect of the Frauenfrage' in Derek Baker, ed., *Medieval Women*, Studies in Church History, Subsidia 1, (Oxford 1978), p. 261. See also *VMO*, pp. 643.28 and 662.95 for references to a maid, and pp. 639.11 and 646.37 for Mary's dress.

12. McDonnell, *Beguines and Beghards*, p. 71 and pp. 97–99.

13. The archives are cited in Robert Lerner, *The Heresy of the Free Spirit in the Later Middle Ages* (Berkeley, 1972), pp. 231–2.

14. Bishop John is quoted in Lerner, p. 231. Bishop John's deposition appears in Stephanus Baluzus, *Vitae Paparum Avenionensium*, G. Mollat, ed., vol. III (Paris 1921), pp. 353–6. On social anxiety, see Caroline Walker Bynum, 'Religious Women in the Later Middle Ages' in Raitt, *Christian Spirituality*, pp. 124–6.

15. The tract *'Daz ist Swester Katrei'* is quoted in Lerner, *Free Spirit*, p. 232 and n. 17. For a survey of the social and cultural context of the heresy of the Free Spirit which has some application to the Beguines who were frequently treated as adherents, see Lerner, pp. 228–43. On the socio-economic motives behind the Beguines, see also McDonnell, *Beguines and Beghards*, pp. 81–6.

16. See for example, Bolton, *'Mulieres Sanctae'*, pp. 77–84.

17. Southern, *The Church in the Middle Ages*, pp. 309–18.

18. See Bolton, *'Mulieres sanctae'*, p. 85.

19. See Bynum, 'Religious Women', pp. 123–30.

20. See F. I. Dunn, 'Hermits, Anchorites and Recluses: A Study with Reference to Medieval Norwich' in Frank Dale Sayer, ed., *Julian and her Norwich: Commemorative Essays and Handbook to the Exhibition 'Revelations of Divine Love'* (Julian of Norwich 1973 Celebration Committee, Norwich), pp. 18–27.

21. On the importance of locality, see the comments by Southern, *The Church in the Middle Ages*, pp. 318ff.

22. Bynum, 'Religious Women', p. 123.

23. See Bolton, *'Vitae matrum'*, p. 260.

24. McDonnell, *Beguines and Beghards*, pp. 146–53 and Part 2, chapter XVI.

25. Cited in Dennis Devlin, 'Feminine Lay Piety in the High Middle Ages: the Beguines' in John Nichols and Lillian Thomas Shank, eds, *Distant Echoes: Medieval Religious Women* (Kalamazoo 1984), pp. 186–9. See also *VMO*, p. 646.

26. On social renunciation see Bynum, 'Religious Women', pp. 125–6. On the threat posed by poverty movements, see Devlin, 'Feminine Lay Piety', p. 188. On the link between penitential movements and imitation of Christ see, for example, John Henderson, 'The Flagellant Movement and Flagellant Confraternities in Central Italy, 1260–1400' in Derek Baker, ed., *Religious Motivation*, Studies in Church History 15, (Oxford 1978), pp. 147–60.

27. On the eucharistic and mystical devotion of the Beguines, see McDonnell, *Beguines and Beghards* pp. 310–33.

28. De Vitry quoted in McDonnell, *Beguines and Beghards*, p. 330. See also *VMO*, pp. 637–8. On Beguine mysticism in general, see Elizabeth Petroff, ed., *Medieval Women's Visionary Literature* (Oxford 1986), pp. 171–8; Lerner, *Free Spirit*, pp. 62–3; and Caroline Walker Bynum, *Jesus as Mother: Studies in the Spirituality of the High Middle Ages* (Berkeley 1982), ch. 5, 'Women Mystics in the Thirteenth century: the Case of the Nuns of Helfta'. For a recent edition of Hadewijch in English, see Columba Hart, ed., *Hadewijch: The complete Works* (New York/London 1980). For Hadewijch's bride mysticism, see for example Vision 12, 'The Perfect Bride'.

29. Quoted in McDonnell, *Beguines and Beghards*, pp. 155–6.

30. On bypassing clerical authority, see McDonnell, *Beguines and Beghards*, pp. 319, 343–4 and 382. On the balance of personal and collective elements, see for example McDonnell, p. 479 and n. 14.

31. Petroff, ed., *Medieval Women's Visionary Literature*, p. 175.

32. On relations between Beguines and Tauler and Ruusbroec, see Oliver Davies, *God Within: the Mystical Tradition of Northern Europe* (London 1988), p. 73 and ch. 5.

33. On property and the Beguines see McDonnell, *Beguines and Beghards*, pt 2, ch. 3 *passim*, and also pp. 60–2 and p. 99 for example.

34. Lerner, *Free Spirit* p. 114 and pp. 139–40.

35. On the development of distinctive dress, see McDonnell, *Beguines and Beghards*, pt 2, ch. 3; and rules pp. 3–7, 120–27 and 134–5.

36. For a description of the stages, see McDonnell, *Beguines and Beghards* pp. 3–7. There is a somewhat more critical assessment of the stages of development in Devlin, 'Feminine Lay Piety', pp. 183–96.

37. McDonnell, in *Beguines and Beghards* pp. 162–3.

38. Grosseteste and Matthew Paris cited in Southern, *The Church in the Middle Ages*, pp. 319–20. On de Vitry's attempts to gain formal recognition for the Beguines, see Bolton, '*Mulieres sanctae*', pp. 84–5. See also *Lettres de Jacques de Vitry*, R. B .C. Huygens, ed., (London 1960), pp. 73–4.

39. McDonnell, *Beguines and Beghards*, p. 367.

40. Cited by Vandenbroucke in Bouyer, *The Spirituality of the Middle Ages*, pp. 353–7.

41. For Bruno of Olmutz see Southern, *The Church in the Middle Ages*, p. 329. Clement V cited in McDonnell, *Beguines and Beghards*, p. 124.

42. On the indiscrimate accusations of heresy levelled at the Beguines, see Lerner, *Free Spirit*, p. 10. On assumptions about women, see ibid., p. 11. The English edition of Marguerite Porete is C. Kirchberger, ed., *The Mirror of Simple Souls*, London 1927. On doubts about Marguerite's condemnation, see Lerner, *Free Spirit*, p. 1 and pp. 68–78.

43. See Lerner, *Free Spirit*, pp. 36–54.

44. On the connections between Beguines and Cistercian nuns and on the differences between them, see McDonnell, *Beguines and Beghards*, p. 438; Devlin, 'Feminine Lay Piety', pp. 183–96 and Southern, *The Church in the Middle Ages*, pp. 319–22.

45. John Howard, ed., 'Mechtild of Magdeburg' in Katharina Wilson, ed., *Medieval Women Writers* (Manchester 1984), pp. 154 and 168 for extracts from this work.

46. For an assessment of the effect of regulation on the Humiliati, see Bolton, 'Innocent III', pp. 73–82.

PART THREE

Interpreting Texts and Traditions

CHAPTER SEVEN

Interpreting Spiritual Texts

At times in the past, when Christians had little sense of historical distance from the origins of the spiritual traditions of which they were a part, questions of interpretation were not a major issue. Our own age is different in several respects. We can no longer take for granted that all those who seek to use the spiritual classics have much familiarity with the Christian tradition. Even within the Christian community, there is a greater pluralism, both theological and spiritual, than twenty years ago. And, in general, we live in a historically conscious age – at least in the sense that the world of the past, and consequently much that is present in classical texts, seems strange to us. These factors inevitably raise the question as to what is going on when a text, created within different historical horizons, encounters a twentieth-century person. More graphically, what does it mean when a successful city business person buys a paperback edition of *The Cloud of Unknowing* at a railway station bookstall and claims to have found wisdom and meaning in it?

The theory of textual interpretation (or what is technically called 'hermeneutics') has been at the centre of the debate about how Christians are to read the Bible. This is obviously a crucial issue because biblical texts have the status of 'revelation' for Christian, as opposed to other, readers. The later tradition of theological writings, and spiritual classics in particular, are obviously not 'revelatory' in this fundamental sense. Yet, for many Christians, the foundational texts of their particular theological or spiritual tradition have a normative status and (for example in the case of the Rules or Constitutions of religious orders) may be closely bound up with issues of present identity. Thus, the question of what a text 'means', as opposed merely to whether we agree with a text's teaching, is of great importance. For this reason, the issue of hermeneutics has become of increasing importance in scholarly circles when the interpretation of spiritual texts is addressed. The concept of 'hermeneutics', and debates about it, have also found a home in recent years in the vocabulary of secular historians and

171

philosophers of history. It cannot, therefore, any longer be limited purely to the world of biblical scholarship.

Spiritual classics

Obviously not all spiritual texts travel well from age to age. Those that do, while not losing their historically conditioned nature, seem to offer something of perennial value about the spiritual journey. How do we recognize a spiritual classic? Perhaps we experience that 'certain expressions of the human spirit so disclose a compelling truth about our lives that we cannot deny them some kind of normative status.'[1] Undoubtedly, classics have a capacity to surprise and challenge. Most importantly, I feel, classics are those texts that bring us into transforming contact with what is enduring and essential in our religious tradition. To put it another way, a classic is what may be called a 'wisdom document'. Its practical value is not that it opens up the *past* (although it may indeed do this) nor that it offers detailed laws by which we may infallibly regulate our spiritual quest. The value of a classical text is not so much that it bridges the gap between the present and a normative past as that it makes the presence of divine truth accessible in our world.[2]

Finally, the success of particular spiritual classics has a great deal to do with their literary genres. The genres within which spirituality is presented are important indicators in explaining why particular works have a wide appeal, even if the ideas they contain are quite conventional. Content and teaching cannot be separated from genre when examining the effectiveness of a text. In general terms, classics succeed in not merely teaching but also in persuading and moving the reader to a response. *The Spiritual Exercises* of St Ignatius, for example, are not particularly stimulating as spiritual reading – no more, perhaps, than the maintenance manual of a car. The language, too, is dry and thoroughly conventional. However, as a text which seeks to provide a framework for an experience, the book has proved remarkably effective over many centuries. Again, the *Showings* of Julian of Norwich, although written by a fourteenth-century woman, still have the power to move many people as well as to teach. There is an intimacy of language, and almost poetic use of imagery, which invite the reader into the heart of contemplative experience. It touches emotions by attending to individual need rather than simply to objective formulations of teaching. In other words, both texts are *pastoral* works rather than manuals of technical spiritual theology.

An analysis of popular devotional manuals, such as *The Imitation of Christ*, by Thomas à Kempis, or *Pilgrim's Progress*, by John Bunyan, reinforces the perception that spiritual classics, with a wide following, have certain common characteristics. They avoid technical language, provide practical advice (especially for self-help), and effectively translate Christian ideas into life-style so that the connection between theory and practice is made explicit. Such texts give an accessible map for charting life's depths, whether with verbal imagery or pictures to stimulate the imagination. They also draw clearly on the author's own experience and values.[3]

Naiveté and classical texts

In reading a classical spiritual text, we will notice that, in crucial respects, its perspective is different from our own. This means that we cannot avoid the question of how far we can respect a text's conceptual framework, structure or dynamics as appropriate for our own encounter with God's grace. Certain responses to this dilemma may be naive. The most negative solution would be to reject the text entirely as the product of a past that is only of spectator interest. We may be historically conscious and at the same time reject history as irrelevant. Less radically, we may feel that the relevance of a text is limited to those parts which are immediately compatible with the present. Thus, I may in effect ignore the horizons of the author and simply use a text as it suits me. There is a tendency these days to seek spiritualities that are immediately attractive.

The opposite naiveté would be to say that the text simply means what its words convey without any further question. This would be to confine 'meaning' to the literal sense of the words and to maintain that this is self-evident. A more sophisticated version of this approach would be to link the meaning of the text essentially to the intention of the author. This subordinates our own horizons to a past that is normative in its 'pastness'. This may involve an escape into an idealized past in reaction to a present age which seems inimical to spiritual values. All of these approaches assume that to arrive at the 'meaning' of a text is a relatively simple matter. Either it is what the author intended or it is what I can get out of it. As we shall see, I neither believe that we can afford to reject the past nor that we can reproduce spiritual texts uncritically. What is needed is a receptive and at the same time critical dialogue with a spiritual text in order to allow the wisdom contained in it to challenge us and yet to accord our own horizons their proper place.

Necessary background

Leaving aside for the moment the precise relevance of an author's intention to our present circumstances, it is a fallacy to believe that we can know this without any background. Spiritual texts were intended for a specific audience. Their authors expressed themselves in language different from our own and sought to be intelligible primarily for their own age. To decipher what an author meant demands some historical knowledge, for example of the horizon of the author, the concerns which the text addresses and the nature of the audience. We will also need some awareness of the basic insights of literary criticism. For example, words change their meaning over the centuries and the fact that a word seems familiar to us can be misleading. Equally, texts belong to different literary genres some of which, for example parable, myth or epic, may be unfamiliar. Without some understanding of how these function, a text may be confusing if not misleading.

The genre of a text often appears obvious but with some texts the problem is more complex. One example is *The Constitutions of the Society of Jesus*. A general knowledge of the Constitutions of religious orders, and a cursory reading, could mislead us into assuming that this is essentially, or solely, a legal document. We may be surprised that the preamble shows a preference for the 'interior law of charity' over written Constitutions; we may note that the Constitutions are, unlike some others, not binding 'under the pain of sin'; we may further note that there is an in-built flexibility that allows adaptation with due regard to 'times, places and persons'. Yet the overall genre seems clear enough.[4]

However, contemporary commentators agree that the intelligibility of these Constitutions is dependent on an understanding of the prior experience of the early Jesuits concretely embodied in another text that lies behind the Constitutions: *The Spiritual Exercises*. The organic relationship between the two texts means that to read the Constitutions in isolation would be dangerous. The Constitutions essentially seek to enable an *experience* and consequently, even if they are something of a hotch-potch of spiritual principles and pragmatic directions, they are not to be understood merely as laws that prescribe in detail what must as a rule be done even though a superficial examination of the structure and language appears to indicate this. It is significant, in this regard, that, while practical arrangements have changed considerably in the groups that use the Constitutions, the text, like the classical monastic Rules, has never been altered but is retained as a basic wisdom document. A realization that the meaning of a text cannot be confined to what is present in it in isolation, is important for our appreciation of spiritual classics in general.[5]

As a consequence of these issues, the understanding and use of a spiritual text involves what both historians and theologians refer to as 'hermeneutics'. That is, we need a theory of interpretation that will offer us an understanding of the unfamiliar in terms of the familiar. The assumption is that the 'meaning' of a text consists of more than its literal sense. There is a disclosure of something of truth and value which challenges us in different ways, depending on the contexts within which we dialogue with a text from the past.

The historical context

If the interpretation of a classical spiritual text involves a dialogue between its horizons and our own, it is apparent that an understanding of the text's historical context is an important starting point. Yet our contemporary horizons produce the questions that enable us to understand the past and therefore to read a classical text. Another factor is our understanding of the nature of time itself. In approaching a text we are not dealing simply with two quite disconnected moments, that is the historical moment of the text's creation and the moment in which we read it. Any two moments are linked as well as separated by what comes between them – in this case the subsequent history of the text and of its interpretation. Our moment of reading is not isolated but on a continuum which may broadly be called the tradition. So we 'receive' not merely the original text but also its subsequent history and the effect of that on our moment of reading.

In our attempts to get to grips with a spiritual tradition its foundational texts have a two-fold function. They articulate something distinctive about Christian identity, and they provide a source of precedents against which to judge our options, now and in the future. Both conservatives and innovators tend to argue from precedent to present conviction. It is here that issues of faithfulness and betrayal arise. We need to be cautious because to return to sources does not mean to reject a present which we judge negatively in order to recover some original purity. Among the historical deviations present in Catholic theological thinking in the past was a sense (expressed sharply, for example, in the document on faith at Vatican I) that modern history was a story of progressive corruption. This view of history was decisively rejected by John XXIII and Vatican II. The use of historical sources in the present is not an attempt to reconstruct a golden age.[6] A return to sources is based on a belief that the great spiritual figures of Christian history were graced by God not merely for their own day but in order that the grace may be available to subsequent generations. An understanding of the context of a text is vital because while a text may have levels of meaning beyond the limitations of the original author, it may not have any and every meaning.

History and present application

In order to understand the normative role of historical knowledge, it may be helpful to distinguish between a 'classical' (or essentialist) and a 'creative' (or a historical and interactive) approach. In the classical account, what is essential in a tradition is only the original intention. True, we should adapt this to contemporary needs but this is merely an application of 'essentials' that always remain the same, and are simple and perennial indications of what we are allowed to do with a tradition. In this case, problems concerning objective historical knowledge are an inconvenience. In contrast, the creative or historical approach suggests that we may be transformed in the present by an imaginative use of tradition. In other words, insights into the past have value precisely to the degree that they dispose us to respond to God's self-communication in the present. The meaning of a text or tradition is discovered within our present experience through its particular symbols or teachings and its history. This way of understanding the process more easily allows for shifts in historical knowledge and does not limit meaning to unchanging essentials which we reproduce from age to age.[7] It is worth noting that there is a substantial difference between reading historical texts creatively from within the community which is the bearer of the texts, and of subsequent interpretation, and reading from outside that community.

There are limits to the objectivity of historical knowledge.[8] It is important to remember that, when we read a text, we encounter not pure facts or the direct experience of another age but what the text *claims*. For example, spiritual texts employ the spiritual categories of their age, most notably in their images of personal holiness. We also need to make proper allowance for the fact that there is a gap between original experiences and the texts which build upon them. Thus, classic texts are filtered through the memory, bias and hindsight of those who write them. A good example would be the *Showings* of Julian of Norwich, where the Long Text is explicitly presented as the result of years of reflection on Julian's visions, while the Short Text seems to be much closer in time to her experience. Does this make the Short Text more 'true'?[9]

To allow for the interpreted nature of texts does not necessarily involve rejecting the truth value of what results. Indeed, the reflections of an author on earlier experience may be more interesting and relevant to our purposes than the original event or experience alone, even assuming that we can disentangle it from the other layers in the received text. It is worth remembering that *the* classical texts for Christians, the gospels, are themselves based on creative reworkings of pre-existing traditions about Jesus. The writers of the gospels felt free to allow these traditions to interact with their own contexts and selected, ordered and interpreted material in the light of the needs of their audiences. A classical or essentialist approach, based on a kind of historicism, would demand a precise reconstruction of the life of Jesus as it 'really was' behind the literary conventions of the gospel authors and their interpretations. On the other hand, the gospels' creative approach to traditions is part of the value for readers in subsequent ages.

Those who write spiritual texts are rarely able to see themselves within a process of historical development because they lack the necessary distance. Therefore authors usually express their ideals imperfectly. They will be more aware of their continuity with the past than of the ways in which they are innovative. Sometimes practical politics may make it advisable to stress traditional features. For example, Ignatius of Loyola felt bound to compare the different stages mapped out in his *Spiritual Exercises* to the traditional language of the purgative, illuminative and unitive ways, while contemporary commentators agree that this comparison is neither particularly accurate nor helpful.[10]

A historical perspective also helps us to grasp the way texts work. Firstly, what is their purpose? In some cases, they are explicitly intended *as* performance. The *Spiritual Exercises* are a case in point. Because they map out a route for an experience they cannot be fully appreciated at a distance, even though we may be helped by prior knowledge of what Ignatius Loyola intended, what certain words mean, and structures imply. If we attempted to read *The Spiritual Exercises* as an evocative spiritual classic (comparable to the poetry of John of the Cross, or the *Showings* of Julian of Norwich) we would miss much of what the text had to offer. The same would be true if we read the Authorised Version of the Bible, the poetry of John of the Cross or John Bunyan's *Pilgrim's Progress* for literary or antiquarian reasons. A scholarly interest in *The Spiritual Exercises* as an example of Catholic Reformation piety, as an insight into social habits, or as background to the life of some important figure influenced by them is, of course, valid within its limits. But this process will not reveal the full potential of meaning.

Secondly, an understanding of the structure is an important key to how a text works because structure is closely allied to the dynamic which the text seeks to embody. We need to see the parts of a text in organic relationship. In such a delicately balanced text as Ignatius Loyola's *Spiritual Exercises*, the purpose, which is to aid a movement towards inner freedom before God, is closely associated with the way that the text is organized. This does not exclude a creative approach to the text but we need to know how it works before deciding, in particular situations, to vary the given structure. Experience teaches that thoughtless tinkering or selection is not merely an abstract issue of faithfulness but may do damage by ignoring the human wisdom which is embodied in the text. We cannot get to the heart of a text, and what it has to offer, without attention to, and respect for, the medium the author has chosen. 'It was as though someone took *King Lear* and extracted the great speeches and lyrical passages, arranged them in some rough logical order, dismembered the text, dislocated the dramatic structure and destroyed the story. And then said, there you have the essence of *King Lear*.'[11]

While historical knowledge is valuable we must not overstress its importance. Historians can provide useful answers to some questions but this is not sufficient when it comes to interpreting spiritual texts in the present. The American theologian, David Tracy, questions whether theology is 'effectively a matter of obedience to an external norm rather than an acceptance based on a risk and a personal recognition of the authority of a living religious tradition'. To approach our traditions as a matter of external acceptance and simple repetition is not to *interpret* them at all.[12] The interpretation of a spiritual text would therefore be unsatisfactory if it distinguished rigidly between the meaning of a text and its significance for today. An over-emphasis on historical consciousness limits meaning to the original intention, context and audience. Broadly speaking, this was the understanding of inter-pretation or hermeneutics in the last century and it remained the conventional approach until relatively recently. The basic principle was that the prejudices, new knowledge or different experiences that a reader brings to a text were a problem for a correct understanding.

In spirituality, this understanding of interpretation has also played a role even in some modern editions of spiritual texts published in the generally excellent series, The Classics of Western Spirituality. For example, in the introduction to *The Cloud of Unknowing*, the editor commented: 'Many years' acquaintance with *The Cloud of Unknowing* has convinced the present editor that any *true appreciation* [my italics] of this work depends on a knowledge of its author's background: that is, of the spiritual climate in which he writes and of the sources essential or helpful to this environment.'[13] Certainly, such knowledge is vital but a true appreciation cannot simply stop here. The essay therefore examines the status of the author, the audience addressed, the influences, sources and basic doctrinal content and the structure. The reason for the emphasis is clear: 'the several recent attempts to pan-syncretize the author's method of contemplative prayer, and to tear it loose from its traditional roots and Western monastic context, encourage such an effort.'[14] Certainly, historical naiveté is a problem to be avoided, but ultimately this conventional approach to meaning, unless complemented by other perspectives, leaves important questions unanswered. There does not seem to be an engagement in conversation with the text from the editor's own engagement in the present. More recently, hermeneutics has sought a broader interpretation of a spiritual text whose possibilities may be evoked in a new and creative way by the new cultural-religious world in which it finds itself.[15] We cannot escape from history into timeless truth, but history in itself is not the focus for our loyalty. Rather, history opens up new possibilities for every person who dialogues with it.

What is the precise relationship between historical knowledge and an appropriate application of a text in the present? The example of the performing arts may be helpful. For example musicians, in their performances, are interpreting a text. It is possible to be faithful to the composer in a limited sense simply by being technically faultless and by a literal observance of the composer's instructions. Yet a 'good' performance seeks to be more than technically correct. It is also creative. Faithfulness certainly involves technique, but linked to imagination, because the composer did not merely describe how to produce certain sounds but sought to create an experience in the listener. However, a 'good' performance *is* true to the score in that the players cannot do simply anything with Mozart and still call it 'his' symphony. Some knowledge of the *limits* of the text (the score) is therefore prior to a 'good' performance. In the case of music, this is provided by a reconstruction of the best text available and some sense of the history of interpretation. Just as performers do not usually do this for themselves, but rely on the researches of experts, so in spirituality those who seek to use a spiritual classic rely indirectly on the expertize of others, and to the degree necessary to avoid the obvious pitfalls.[16]

The process of interpretation

The image of 'performance' leads us to the heart of the interpretative process. There is no single, true interpretation of a spiritual classic. Without ignoring the historical context, we reveal new and richer truths which the author never knew, by bringing a text into contact with new questions. The pursuit of meaning undoubtedly begins with a prior understanding of what the text is about. However, in dialogue with it, our understanding is enlarged. We put questions to the text which are, in turn, reshaped by the text itself. This is what is often referred to in theology as the 'hermeneutical circle'. *The dance* The German philosopher and theologian, Hans-Georg Gadamer, who has been highly influential in the development of a broader theory of interpretation, stressed that the text must 'break the spell' of our presuppositions which initially gave us a point of entry. The text corrects and revises our preliminary understanding:

> I must allow the validity of the claim made by tradition, not in the sense of simply acknowledging the past in its otherness, but in such a way that it has something to say to me. This too calls for a fundamental sort of openness. Someone who is open in this way to tradition sees that the historical consciousness is not really open at all, but rather, if it reads the texts 'historically' has always thoroughly smoothed them out beforehand, so that the criteria of our own knowledge can never be put in question by tradition.[17]

In Gadamer's terms, the text has an 'excess of meaning' beyond the subjective intentions of the author. What the text embodies enters different periods of history in distinctive ways. The text comes alive in the present. The present situation, as experienced by the reader, affects the meaning of a text *and* a text alters the reader's understanding of the present. Gadamer further concludes that understanding, interpretation and application are a unified process. In Gadamer's view, the earlier hermeneutics, which detached the application of a text (for example in preaching) from interpretation, was inadequate. But we come to a fuller understanding of a text in applying it to the present situation.[18]

Interpreting a text may therefore be thought of as a conversation between the text and the reader. Genuine conversation allows the question or subject matter to have primacy. We are carried along by the to and fro of conversation to a point of new understanding. Gadamer further believes that the time distance between a historical text and the present moment forces the reader to recognize his or her horizons and, consequently, the pre-understanding of a text created by the tradition of which the reader is a part. Yet, the claim made by a text and its horizons invites the interpreter to begin a conversation with the text. Our aim is thus to fuse horizons in an interpretation which, because of our own historicity, is always new. Neither the text nor the interpreter are static realities. A classic is something that provokes a genuine and different interpretation. The reader is also provoked into a new self-understanding because of the encounter. Thus, both text and reader shift horizons in the fusion.

Does this fusion of horizons imply an unhistorical approach? Certainly, understanding takes place in the present but it happens as I face the question mediated from the past. Even if I accept that there is an 'excess of meaning' in a text beyond the author's original and time-bound intention, this is nevertheless part of a classical text which is rooted in its own time and yet calls on my time and situation as well. Thus a classical text is not a timeless moment that demands mere repetition. Understanding implies a constant reinterpretation of a text by people who question and listen within their own historical circumstances.[19]

A good example of what such a conversation means is provided by the normative documents of particular religious communities such as the Jesuit Constitutions or the Rule of St Benedict. The Constitutions and the Rule seek to pass on something. The 'something' is not a series of unchangeable rules which demand literal observance but the *experience* of the first generation of monks or Jesuits which was reflected upon before being put into written form. For example, the Jesuit Constitutions offer a model, for all who seek to use them, of a process rather than specific actions. This process, which lies behind the creation of the text and which is to be mirrored by the reader's response, is three-fold. Firstly, there is an experience, of God, the world and the Church. Secondly, there is reflection in the light of the gospel and of the specific values of the tradition. Finally, there is a discernment of what response is appropriate. This is the only way in which the text may be understood and interpreted, because the purpose of the Constitutions is explicitly to facilitate a self-understanding that will result in a way of life and action.

We need to be in tune with the text and its related documents, the language, culture and theological presuppositions, but the Constitutions also demand of every reader, by their basic principles, an awareness of the contemporary world, its cultures, theologies and concrete needs. Beyond the knowledge of these facts is the need to be effectively *involved* in them, for the process of the Constitutions demands that we learn their meaning by living them in a world of concrete circumstances.[20] Thus, conversation is not merely a dialogue of ideas but is an insertion into the 'way of being in the world' held up by the text.

It has already been suggested that the origins of a text continue to exert some kind of normative role which prevents us from exploiting a text for our own ends. Gadamer therefore talks of a kind of 'consent' to a text in the necessary fusion of the horizons of the text and of the interpreter.[21] In other words, while our presuppositions and questions provide our initial route into an understanding of a text, the horizons of the text reflect back on us as interpreters so that what is distinctive and perennial about the message of the text will just as effectively question us and our values. An illustration is provided by Caroline Walker Bynum, in her essay on medieval women's religious experience, when she considers the danger of excessively 'presentist' perspectives tempting us to adopt a highly selective and critical approach to items in historical texts which we instinctively find distasteful to contemporary sensitivities. We must let the strangeness touch and challenge us.[22]

This vital 'hermeneutics of consent' implies that our interpretations of a text are, to a degree, constrained by the authority retained by the author. If we believe that a particular text continues to have a value now, and is not merely of antiquarian interest, we are saying effectively that the question which the text seeks to address has continued significance and that, through the medium of this text, an answer may be reached. Our present-day questions and horizons mean that we will always tell the story differently (or play the music score in a creative way) but, if we use *this* text, we cannot tell a different story or play another tune.[23]

A second way in which a text and its tradition exert some

normative role on our interpretation and use of it is that any valid interpretation will always refer to the *whole* of that tradition, which includes the consensus of previous and present interpretations and uses. Interpretation is not a solitary affair but a collective one. So an important criterion for a valid interpretation of a spiritual text will be whether this is in harmony with that of other readers, especially the community 'of capable readers over centuries', or is at least not radically out of tune with this community of experience.[24]

A critical interpretation

While a hermeneutics of consent gives a certain priority to the text in the process of interpretation there is also a necessary hermeneutics of suspicion. This involves a recognition that the questions provoked by our contemporary situation may well be critical of the text and its theological and social assumptions. In interpreting texts nowadays, we are more aware of their conditioning and the need to expose the hidden ideologies in our spiritual past. However, we need to pay attention not only to questions suggested by our intellectual horizons but also to the concerns of those who have been marginalized by the past and who now seek a history which liberates. They help us to read the past more fully and to realize that, even in spirituality, there never is a golden age. The dark side of our past continues to influence our present biases.

History, as we have seen, has marginalized groups and traditions and our use of history may subtly perpetuate this. Those who are spiritually (and perhaps also socially) marginal inevitably relate to the past differently from those who operate from a position of dominance. Consciously or not, the latter tend to exploit the past in order to underpin their status. When the interpretation of spiritual texts remains in the hands of an intellectual élite, it frequently takes place within post-Enlightenment assumptions. One example would be the belief that the human subject is able to develop his or her potential autonomously. This assumption is socially conditioned because it is associated with relative prosperity. In other words, it is material possessions and the power that stems from them that enable us to experience ourselves as autonomous. The socially powerful and autonomous use material prosperity to shape their relationships. A similar attitude may also characterize those with spiritual status.

Such assumptions make it difficult to recognize that life is essentially a gift. Those who are used to directing their own lives tend to relativize a redemption offered 'from without'. Thus, one problem in interpreting spiritual texts is a possible clash between a sense of autonomy or power and the kind of hope offered by Christian tradition. Those who experience themselves as self-sufficient may control their relationship to the past by remoulding it in accordance with their own interests. In other words, a particular danger for those who have power is to read a text in ways that justify the status quo.

This conditioned approach to texts works in two related ways. Firstly, it adopts a reductive exegesis. In other words, it is selective and tends to retain only that part of a text which is 'appropriate' to modern conceptions of reality. The incomprehensible or unacceptable is discarded in such a way as to prevent a text from transforming the present. Secondly, this approach seeks an objective or 'pure' meaning which may be distilled from the whole. While I would not want to suggest that this is universal or conscious, such dangers are inevitably involved in the present-day popularity of selections from spiritual classics which offer 'The essential John of the Cross' or 'The message of the mystics', for example.

The standpoint of powerlessness and poverty, whether spiritual, social or both, offers a different hermeneutic which is less likely to subject a text to dominant intellectual values. The poor are those who can only approach a text with their hopes or needs and, therefore, their desire to receive something from it rather than to impose something upon it. The experience of powerlessness is more likely to acknowledge that we are dependent on the past. This contrasts with those approaches which imply that we can dominate the past and thus turn it into little more than a vague religious heritage incapable of provoking repentance or of revising our present attitudes and practice.[25]

Two classical texts

It would be helpful, briefly, to illustrate aspects of interpretation, as a dialogue between different horizons, by reference to some classical spiritual texts which have been much in vogue in recent years. I have opted for two which, while they arise from what may broadly be termed 'the Catholic tradition', have found favour well beyond the limits of the Roman Catholic Church, namely *The Cloud of Unknowing* and *The Spiritual Exercises*. What I hope to underline by doing this is that we can neither take such texts on face value, without critical evaluation, nor simply be selective in our approach to texts by subordinating them entirely to our own unquestioned assumptions.

The wide popularity of a fourteenth-century mystical text, probably written in a monastic environment and certainly addressed to someone desiring the solitary life, may seem particularly strange. Of course, like the writings of Julian of Norwich which are also popular, the text is easily available in a number of modern English versions, unlike other fourteenth-century spiritual writings, such as those by Walter Hilton or Richard Rolle. The latter, while also reflecting a contemplative and solitary environment, appear to have been more consciously aware than *The Cloud* of a wider readership among secular clergy or devout laypeople. In their own day, Hilton and Rolle seem to have been more attractive than *The Cloud* among people who sought to bring together contemplative and active life-styles in what was known as the 'mixed life'. Indeed, the teaching of these texts seems to have been widely disseminated by reforming clergy, in the North of England, who were concerned to improve pastoral care, to combat the attractions of heretical groups, such as the Lollards, and to provide a spirituality that would be suitable for working clergy and devout laypeople alike. This, of course, begs the question as to why it is *The Cloud*, rather than Hilton or Rolle, that has attracted so much popular attention in our own day. Perhaps it is that, in an age when the search for spiritual meaning is once again of increasing interest, *The Cloud*, on the face of it, appears to offer a map of the journey which is encouragingly simple.[26] Other aspects have a contemporary attraction. Superficially, it seems to avoid both detailed methods of prayer or questionable devotion, in favour of stark simplicity, and the complexities of dogma and public worship, in favour of the personal and experiential. In western culture, when the institutional Church is viewed by many as unreliable, the fact that *The Cloud* seems to bypass its piety further commends it. Further, despite passing references to Christ, the tone of the text does not appear to demand a full commitment to Christian dogma in order to benefit from its wisdom. Finally, for those concerned with interiority alone, *The Cloud* seems to offer an inward way, detached from outward activity. Such a superficial impression of the text, and of its contemporary relevance, would be quite dangerous. *The Cloud* undoubtedly does offer the reader great riches but it also challenges some of our modern presuppositions.

The Cloud does not teach a medieval equivalent of the technique of Transcendental Meditation aimed at inner harmony and stillness. In other words, it is not a quick route through method to experience.

185

Indeed, experience in isolation is not what the book is about at all. It emphasizes first of all that what it has to say is not for everyone but only for those who have progressed a certain way on the spiritual journey (Prologue and chapter 1 for example), and it presupposes the companionship of an experienced spiritual guide (for example chapters 2 and 4). This challenges some aspects of contemporary egalitarianism when it reminds us that, in practice, not everyone is a contemplative and that becoming one is not a simple question of personal whim or adjustment to our methods of prayer. *The Cloud* reminds us that contemplation is not an optional *style* of prayer but a gift, a response to a call (chapter 15). It cannot be produced nor does it depend on merit (chapters 34–5). At its heart is a desire for union with a personal God. *The Cloud* is not a doctrinally agnostic text. Its portrayal of the spiritual journey reflects a particular understanding of the way God reaches out to humans in love through Jesus Christ. Nor is contemplation an easy way. The frequent use of the word 'work' underlines that such a way is one of striving (chapters 21 and 29) and perseverance (chapters 26 and 71). It makes demands and involves hardship as we struggle with our ambiguities and lack of freedom.

Because it is a Christian text, our contemporary spiritual and theological horizons also demand that our interpretation and use of it be critical. I offer four examples. Firstly, the tone of *The Cloud* is somewhat individualistic and contrasts with a more explicit emphasis these days on the ecclesial and social dimensions of spirituality. Secondly, the text seems to assume that contemplation is an élite experience and this contrasts with a present-day sense that contemplation is a possibility for all Christians. Thirdly, there appears to be a suspicion of the body and of the created world which contrasts not only with the insights of modern psychology but also with a renewed theology of the human person and creation. Finally, *The Cloud* conceives the spiritual journey in terms of distinct stages and an ascent away from the material world, which is questionable in the light of our different theological assumptions.

True, there are understandable reasons for the individualistic tone in the nature of the text itself, quite apart from its religious horizons and social context in an insecure period of English history. It is written for a solitary and is, overtly at least, addressed to a single person seeking personal direction. It may be argued, too, that an ecclesial dimension is presupposed even if adverted to only infrequently. It speaks of the sacrament of penance (chapters 15, 28, 35 and 75) and fidelity to the Liturgy of the Hours (chapter

37). Charity to others is described at one point as a 'good and holy business' (chapter 17) and yet, more often than not, it is seen primarily as part of the active life which is lower than the contemplative. Contemplation is the 'better part' of the gospels chosen by Mary the sister of Martha (chapters 18 and 21). So, at best, the approach to the Church as community is implicit rather than explicit and the attitude to engagement ambivalent. We would nowadays question the medieval tendency to detach aspects of the teaching of Pseudo-Dionysius (the anonymous sixth-century writer who influenced *The Cloud*) from its context in the Christian life as a whole, and would, in contrast, favour a reintegration of mysticism with the universal 'insertion into the Mysteries of Christ' offered by the sacramental life of all Christians. Equally, contemporary attempts to integrate mysticism and politics (for example by Thomas Merton or some theologians of liberation) provide a different mental horizon within which to reinterpret such a text as *The Cloud*.

Even if contemplation is, in practice, limited to a few people, is such a way *open* to all or only to those who live a privileged life-style of solitude and silence? As we have seen, the text was most likely written by a monastic solitary. In this sense the assumptions of the author would be those of traditional monasticism. The text seems to imply that mystical union is open only to those who lead the contemplative life under a Rule (chapter 21). The active life is a lower stage and the contemplative (by implication, silent and solitary) a higher level (chapters 1 and 8). Yet, there is some ambiguity over this issue as the author also suggests in the Prologue that the active life is not to be disdained and that, in its inward dimension at least, it is a participation in the life of contemplation. However, what is clear is that there is a considerable gap between the mentality of the author, concerning the relative merits of monastic solitary life and active engagement in the world, and our contemporary perspectives. Further, when we realize that even the positive remarks made in the Prologue about the active life are a reference to religious and clergy, then the gap that separates this text from a contemporary emphasis on the contemplative potential of all Christians becomes even more striking. Clearly, the teaching on the contemplative life may be separated from assumptions about privileged life-styles (this is precisely one of our contemporary insights) and so we do not have to accept these in order to use the text.

The élitism of *The Cloud* is based partly on a fairly negative evaluation of the world and the body (including sexuality) and therefore of important aspects of people's everyday lives. Only those free from involvement with 'sinful creatures' could therefore hope to attain contemplation. In *The Cloud* the way of perfect contemplation is one of negation in which the first task is to separate the self from the world and created things by leaving them behind in a cloud of forgetting. The tone of the text at least suggests a depreciation of the human and an alienation from the world. Although it is possible to argue that such language was simply conventional and should not be taken to imply a thorough-going dualism, to image the self as a 'filthy, nauseating lump of sin' (chapter 40) could be psychologically damaging and certainly causes resistance in some contemporary readers. A modern reading with very different theological and spiritual horizons would want to detach the contemplative journey from the text's ambivalent attitude towards the created world. Thus, while chapter 48 reflects, 'God forbid that I should part what he has joined, the body and spirit. For God wants to be served with body and soul both together,' chapter 47 affirms, 'By its nature every physical thing is farther from God than any spiritual.'

Finally, the assumption behind *The Cloud*, and other medieval mystical or contemplative texts, is that the spiritual journey is an ascent towards God and away from the world and that it can be divided into distinct stages which are conceived as consecutive. This notion of successive and distinct stages was part of a wider tendency (developed most notably in medieval scholastic theology) to divide and to distinguish. It is true that the concept of some kind of three-fold structure of spiritual development is present in almost all writers from the patristic period onwards and appears in some of the first-hand declarations of mystics. However, there are critical questions which it is helpful to ask. In examining these writings, how far can we distinguish what is part of the original experience (for example, of mystics) and what is dependent on subsequent interpretation based on theological assumptions? How far is the traditional notion of stages based on one, neo-Platonic, concept of the created world and the human person – a philosophical system which is no longer favoured? How far is it the case that this approach reflects male rather than female ways of experiencing? Theological speculation was dominated by men, even if mystics belong to either sex.

Spiritual development is very much part of our present horizons. In this context, Margaret Miles suggests that the metaphor of 'ascent' retains a certain value in that it emphasizes taking personal responsibility as opposed to mere passivity, the dynamic quality of

Christian life against a static view, and continuity within a spiritual journey rather than a succession of quite disconnected experiences. However our problems with the traditional understanding of development may be summarized in several ways.

An over-emphasis on separate, successive stages, with universal application, conflicts with a sense of the uniqueness of each person's spiritual journey as well as with the freedom of God and unpredictability of grace. Equally, the experience of spiritual guidance suggests that the characteristics which give names to the traditional three stages (purgative, illuminative, unitive), that is repentance, enlargement of vision, growth in selfless love for God and neighbour, are present in different proportions at *every* point on our journey. Again, by focusing exclusively on union with God as the final stage, we may miss the point that union with God is not so much a stage above and beyond all others as the precondition of all spiritual growth. There is also a danger that we see union as the result of human effort. Further, the traditional approach to stages really reflected a division between the active (lower) and contemplative (higher) ways of life which contrast with our renewed sense of the universal Christian call to perfection. The latter emphasis would conceive the two levels or ways as part of the same dynamism, or as two ways of experiencing the same life and the unity of Christian experience. Finally, such a metaphor of ascent exaggerates the separation and contrasting values of the world of the senses and the spiritual realm. A hierarchy of values soon gives way to a hierarchy of life-styles whereby professionally spiritual people have a greater share in God's being.

It is worth noting that, beyond the qualifications voiced by such as Margaret Miles, some theologians such as Karl Rahner question the very concept of distinct stages at all as based on a neo-Platonic anthropology, derived from Origen, in which the pivotal point is total detachment from all human passions. He rejects the traditional approach which he sees as involving the concept of an objective, continual and inevitable increase of grace or the limitation of higher moral acts to one stage rather than another.[27]

When we turn to another popular spiritual classic, *The Spiritual Exercises* of St Ignatius of Loyola, there are many questions of linguistic, historical or theological interpretation for the contemporary reader, given the cultural and theological distance between the sixteenth century and our own.[28] If we focus on key areas of the Exercises, some of Ignatius's fundamental theological presuppositions may affect both the way in which the Exercises are presented and how they are received by a retreatant. Ignatius has a strongly personal, if not individualistic emphasis, for example in his understanding of salvation, sin and the relationship of God's will to each and every person. In such central images as 'The call of the King', the emphasis is, to some degree, out of harmony with contemporary perspectives. Discernment is presented in supernaturalist language. Finally, the tension of prayer and action is not fully resolved in Ignatius's formulae. These elements of the Exercises need to be translated into terms that are compatible with contemporary theological insights, especially about grace and the human person.[29]

Major developments within the Ignatian spiritual tradition have led to an interpretation of the Exercises in social justice terms. The fact, of course, is that such a modern concept was alien to Ignatius and to the sixteenth century in general. The text should not be made to say what could never have been present. This, however, is quite a different matter from suggesting that we do not need to adopt a completely individualistic understanding of the text in order to do justice to Ignatius's own horizons. It is also legitimate to re-read the text from a different theological standpoint in order to provide for interconnections with social justice as long as this does no damage to the text's basic dynamic or central values.[30]

Interpretation-through-use is crucial to *The Spiritual Exercises*. I would like to outline three present-day issues of interpretation which are central to the way in which *The Spiritual Exercises* are now presented, as illustrations of the possibility of re-reading a classic text. Firstly, who may make the Exercises and what degree of adaptation is valid? Secondly, are the Exercises possible only on a one-to-one basis? Thirdly, are the Exercises only viable in solitude or may they be made in the midst of life?

The Spiritual Exercises themselves (Exx 18–20) suggest that the full Exercises should only be given to a few outstanding persons yet we know that Ignatius and the early Jesuits gave exercises in some form to a wide range of people. The first Annotation (Exx 1), at the beginning of the text, perhaps provides the key. There is a distinction between 'spiritual exercises', which cover a wide range of activities, and the Spiritual Exercises as the full range of exercises, in a particular order and with a specific dynamic, as laid out in the text as a whole. Early practice shows that there was a variety of ways in which elements of the text could be put to use. So 'making the Exercises' was a spectrum of activity, derived from the text, yet not always the full experience. This broadens the range of people who could be touched in some way by the spirit of *The Spiritual Exercises*. There is a wisdom in the text, and in the wider Ignatian tradition, about the kinds of people to make the Exercises and about principles of adaptation. It would be foolish to ignore this. However, it would be equally foolish to be fundamentalist about the precise details, as they appear in the text or in what we know of early practice, for these are historically conditioned. For example, the experience of some contemporary spiritual directors is that, with patience and proper preparation, it is possible to offer the full Exercises in an inner-city environment where the criteria of 'the more educated' as well as that of 'freedom from daily affairs' hardly apply.[31] It is important to remember that adaptation to different categories of people is inherent to the methodology of the Exercises and is not a concession on rare occasions.

May the Exercises be given only on a one-to-one basis? This is increasingly the current practice and there is no doubt that in this lies a recovery of the more original tradition. However, the fact that there were some early concessions on this matter does raise the question as to whether individual guidance is vital rather than simply ideal. My previous comment about the use of 'some exercises', as opposed to the full 'Spiritual Exercises', leaves open the possibility of retreats for groups 'in the Ignatian spirit'. For some, this may be preparatory to making the full Exercises at a later date. We should, however, take note of the considerable resistance on the part of Ignatius and even the generation after him to giving the full Exercises to more than one person at a time, and the principle reason. This was that the adaptation proper to the full Exercises was based on close attention to inner spiritual movements. This could only be effective in a personal dialogue.[32]

Finally, do the full 'Spiritual Exercises' depend on solitude or may they be made in everyday life? The latter is increasingly common at the present time, and people's instincts are always to look for a precedent in the tradition. However, the evidence is ambiguous. In a recent collection of essays on the subject, two writers took quite different positions on what the tradition offered to the present.[33] It is not clear that Annotation 19 of the text (which has led to the popular terminology, '19th Annotation retreat') actually describes current practice – that is, the *full* Exercises in daily life. So we may have to come to terms with the possibility that, as interpretation-through-use, contemporary practice is a re-interpretation. Yet, the text itself and the earliest interpretations of it place greatest emphasis on respecting the personal aspects of the Exercises-as-experience (or the dynamic brought about by the Exercises rather than simply the structure of the Exercises). Consequently, we can trust that to respect the dynamic of *The Spiritual Exercises*, in present usage or adaptation, is not *essentially* about the selection and ordering of a sequence of certain exercises. These merely serve the way the Spirit acts within the individual and how the individual responds. The text, therefore, according to its own deepest principles, is always subordinate to an inner and more personal dynamic.[34]

Conclusion

It may seem that the strength of my emphasis on the complexity of the issues surrounding our interpretation and use of spiritual texts involves a kind of mystification, or an élitism that denies to the non-scholar any immediate access to the riches of our spiritual heritage. My response to the criticism is that it is the reverse which is the case. That is, the more dangerous élitism, not to say arrogance, is to refuse to see the importance of giving ordinary Christians, and others, a popular slice of the hermeneutical cake. Scholars, or those with some knowledge of critical issues, are not some 'stewards of private mysteries', the new gnostics, with privileged access to information that places them higher than most people on some spiritual ladder or in an otherwise more advantageous position. Those with specialist knowledge and wider background, to whatever degree, have a duty of service and a task of translation. My belief is that any course or workshop on spirituality which draws upon the riches of the Christian spiritual tradition should not limit itself to practical questions but should seek to mediate the insights of scholarship in a way that is not only relevant, but accurate and intelligible as well.

Notes

1   See David Tracy, *The Analogical Imagination: Christian Theology and the Culture of Pluralism* (London/New York 1981), ch. 3, 'The Classic', espec. p. 108.

2. On wisdom documents see Howard Gray, 'What Kind of Document?' in a collection of studies on 'The Ignatian Constitutions Today', published as *The Way Supplement* 61 (1988). Margaret Miles suggests that such classical documents rather than philosophical theology are the medium by which most people have shaped their lives around Christian attitudes. See her *The Image and Practice of Holiness: a Critique of the Classic Manuals of Devotion* (London 1989), p. ix.

3. For an analysis of the attractiveness of the genre of devotional manuals, see Miles, *Image and Practice of Holiness*, p. ix and pp. 4–15. For interesting reflections on literary genres in reference to Erasmus' spirituality, see John W. O'Malley, ed., *Collected Works of Erasmus* 66 (Toronto/London 1988), pp. xxviii–xxx.

4. See George Ganss, S J, tr. and ed. *The Constitutions of the Society of Jesus*, (Institute of Jesuit Sources, St Louis, 1970), paras 134, 136 (and cross refs), 602. The editor, writing nearly twenty years ago, seems to give the impression that the legal dimension of the Constitutions is more central than would, perhaps, nowadays be thought. See pp. 119–20, n.2.

5. For useful analyses of what kind of document the Constitutions is, see Joseph Veale, 'How the Constitutions Work' and Gray, 'What kind of Document?' in *The Way Supplement* 61 (1988), pp. 3–20 and 21–34 respectively.

6. See, for example, the comments of Giuseppe Ruggieri in 'Faith and History' in Giuseppe Alberigo et. al. eds, *The Reception of Vatican II* (E T, Washington D C 1987), pp. 95–8.

7. See Philip Endean, 'Who Do you Say Ignatius is? Jesuit Fundamentalism and Beyond', *Studies in the Spirituality of Jesuits* 19: 5 (1987), 3. A slightly different, but closely related, distinction concerning our approach to traditions (in this case the 'classical' mentality and the 'historical' mentality) was analysed by Ladislas Örsy in 'The Future of Religious Life', *The Way* 14: 4 (1974), pp. 311–20.

8. Endean helpfully summarizes four common 'traps for the unwary' in terms of the search for historical knowledge in reference to spiritual texts in his article cited above.

9. The critical edition is Edmund Colledge and James Walsh, eds, *The Book of Showings of the Anchoress Julian of Norwich*, Toronto 1978. A recent edition in modern English is Edmund Colledge and James Walsh, eds, *Julian of Norwich: Showings* (New York 1978). See also the modern study by Grace Jantzen, *Julian of Norwich: Mystic and Theologian*, London/New York 1987.

10. See Exx 10. *The Spiritual Exercises*, Louis Puhl ed., (Chicago 1951).

11. Veale, 'How the Constitutions Work', p. 9. The whole article touches on a number of the issues raised here.

12. See Tracy, *The Analogical Imagination*, p. 99.

13. James Walsh, ed., *The Cloud of Unknowing* (New York 1981), foreword, p. xxv.

14. ibid., p. 1.

15. On the limitations of conventional textual interpretation, see David Tracy, *Blessed Rage for Order: the New Pluralism in Theology* (New York 1978), ch. 4, espec. Christian texts: the possibility of their interpretation', pp. 72ff; and Nicholas Lash, *Theology on the Way to Emmaus* (London 1986), ch. 6, 'What Might Martyrdom Mean?'

16. Lash, *Theology on the Way to Emmaus*, ch. 3, 'Performing the Scriptures', suggests a musical image for interpretation-through-performance.

17. Hans-Georg Gadamer, *Truth and Method* (London 1979), pp. 324–5. On interpretation and Gadamer's theory see Andrew Louth, *Discerning the Mystery: an Essay on the Nature of Theology* (Oxford 1983), pp. 29–43; Tracy, *Analogical Imagination*, ch. 3; Michael O'Sullivan, 'Towards a Social Hermeneutics of the Spiritual Exercises: an application to the Annotations', in *The Spiritual Exercises of St Ignatius Loyola in Present-Day Application* (Rome 1982), *passim*. On hermeneutics in reference to the appropriation of our spiritual past in the present, see William Thompson, *Fire and Light: the Saints and Theology* (New York 1987), pp. 68–73.

18. See Gadamer, *Truth and Method*, pp. 274–5.

19. See Gadamer, *Truth and Method*, pp. 325–41; also Tracy, *Analogical Imagination*, ch. 3.

20. See Veale, 'How the Constitutions Work', pp. 15–16.

21. Gadamer, *Truth and Method*, pp. 325–41.

22. Caroline Walker Bynum, 'Religious Women in the Later Middle Ages' in Jill Raitt and John Meyendorff, eds, *Christian Spirituality: High Middle Ages and Reformation* (London/New York 1987), pp. 136–7.

23. See for example Lash, *Theology on the Way to Emmaus*, ch. 3, 'Performing the Scriptures'.

24. Tracy, *Analogical Imagination*, p. 116.

25. For a much fuller treatment of these issues, see Ottmar John, 'The Tradition of the Oppressed as the Main Topic of Theological Hermeneutics', *Concilium* 200 (1988), pp. 143–55. In reference to spiritual classics, Margaret Miles writes both of a 'hermeneutic of suspicion', or what she calls active disobedient reading, and a hermeneutic of generosity, or avoiding anachronistic criticisms, in *The Image and Practice of Holiness*, p. 10 and ch. 1.

26. *The Cloud of Unknowing* has been reprinted almost annually since its publication by Penguin Classics, London, in the mid-1960s. Another recent edition in modern English is that edited by James Walsh SJ in the Classics of Western Spirituality series published in the USA by Paulist Press and in the UK by SPCK. A critical edition is *The Cloud of Unknowing and Related Treatises*, Phyllis Hodgson, ed., Analecta Cartusiana 3, Salzburg 1982. There are plans to publish some of the works of Walter Hilton in the same series and there has recently appeared Rosamund S. Allen, ed., *Richard Rolle: The English writings*, (New Jersey/London 1989). On the dissemination of the teachings of Hilton and Rolle beyond monastic circles, see Jonathan Hughes, *Pastors and Visionaries: Religion and Secular Life in Late medieval Yorkshire* (Woodbridge, Suffolk/Wolfeboro, New Hampshire 1988), chs 2, 4 and 5.

27. See Miles, pp. 74–9 and also Karl Rahner, 'Reflections on the Problem of the Gradual Ascent to Perfection', *Theological Investigations* 3 (London 1967).

28. The best available text in English is that edited by Louis Puhl SJ, Loyola University Press, Chicago, and frequently reprinted. This

translation is based on the so-called Spanish Autograph text which appears in *Sancti Ignatii de Loyola, Exercitia Spiritualia* New Edition, *Monumenta Historica Societatis Jesu*, vol. 100 (Rome 1969), on even pages, column 1, between pp. 140–416. My references are to the standard paragraph numeration in modern editions (e.g. Exx 1).

29.   The American Jesuit theologian, Roger Haight, tackles some of these topics in 'Foundational Issues in Jesuit Spirituality', *Studies in the Spirituality of Jesuits* 19/4, (1987).

30.   On individualism and the Exercises see Philip Sheldrake, *Images of Holiness* (London/Notre Dame 1987), ch. 4, 'Discipleship and the Cross'; on a social hermeneutic for reinterpreting the Exercises, see Michael O'Sullivan, 'Towards a Social Hermeneutics'.

31.   See, for example, Martha Skinnider's article in *The Way Supplement* 49 (1984). The whole Supplement is dedicated to the Exercises as given 'in daily life' rather than in a closed retreat.

32.   See Michael Ivens, 'The Eighteenth Annotation and the Early Directories', *The Way Supplement* 46 (1983), pp. 3–10. This provides an interesting discussion on the early Ignatian tradition concerning the difference between 'the full Exercises' and 'some exercises', the adaptation of elements of the Exercises for a wider public and the issue of preached versus individual direction.

33.   See *The Way Supplement* 49, essays by Brian Grogan and Ian Tomlinson.

34.   See, for example, Joseph Veale, 'The Dynamic of the Spiritual Exercises', *The Way Supplement* 52 (1985), pp. 3–18.

CHAPTER EIGHT

Types of Spirituality

As we have seen earlier in this book, historians employ a number of conventional frameworks, such as chronology, to assist them in organizing material in an intelligible way. Some organizing frameworks, however, are more contentious. In spirituality there have been a variety of attempts to differentiate spiritual traditions into 'types'. This has a value in that it helps us to analyse the contrasts between different traditions. However, all typologies have their limitations because they rely on certain assumptions. In this chapter I want to evaluate four of the more common ones, both traditional and contemporary.

Spirituality or spiritualities?

Firstly, however, to speak of 'types' implies that Christian spirituality is plural. This itself has been a matter of debate. Until about twenty-five years ago it was generally assumed that all spirituality was essentially the same. The basis for this viewpoint was really theological. As was described in chapter 2, there had been a move towards a systematic spiritual theology particularly in the late nineteenth century. This theology had two characteristics that are relevant to the question of unity or plurality. Firstly, the approach was deductive, that is, it proceeded from universal principles to particular instances and used revelation and rational knowledge rather than experience as its principal sources. Secondly, such distinctions as were made were associated with different stages of spiritual growth or even higher and lower levels of Christian life. This approach, combined with the tendency to categorize in a hierarchical fashion, affected the understanding of different 'schools' of spirituality. Thus the monastic life was understood as higher, or more perfect, than the active or apostolic life.

In reflecting on the ways we have used our spiritual traditions (chapter 4), some approaches to history were noted which predominated in Church circles until recent years and which reflected the priority of theological presuppositions over historical considerations. Thus, history as 'mere instances of enduring truths' made spiritual experience something that transcended historical conditions. Again, the assumption that spirituality was a 'transcultural phenomenon' in fact created a single model of spirituality and of its constituent parts such as 'holiness'.[1]

In recent years, as we have seen, a major shift has taken place in spirituality which has influenced the question of unity and diversity, that is that human experience was increasingly accepted as a valid context for serious theological reflection. The acceptance of experience means that spirituality has moved away from a deductive process (from first principles to specific instances) towards a realization that spiritualities arise within particular and therefore different contexts.

The influence of these changes was reflected in the debate in France, concerning 'spirituality or spiritualities', that took place in the early 1960s. Louis Bouyer's Preface to his multi-volume history of spirituality, which continued to emphasize the unity of spirituality, was further debated by Bouyer and Jean Daniélou in the French journal *Études* and by Maurice Giuliani in *Christus*.[2] Further articles, available in English, appeared in 1965. François Vandenbroucke, while not excluding a common core in all spiritual traditions, emphasized the multiplicity of spiritualities and analysed their origins in terms of temperament and social milieux, the creative influence of individuals within particular traditions and the needs of different groups within the Christian community. He also admitted that the spiritualities of different traditions evolved in the light of concrete situations and did not simply repeat themselves in line with the original formulae. Hans Urs von Balthasar offered a different perspective by arguing that the fundamental unity of all spirituality in Christ is prior to a diversity of charisms. Christologically, all possible forms of spirituality meet and flow together. 'The spirituality of the gospel' was the norm against which all particular traditions must be measured.[3]

In one sense the debate about unity or diversity reflected a struggle to break free from a monolithic theology and spirituality while continuing to maintain that, for the Christian, Jesus Christ is the one way to the Father. In practice the question of unity or diversity is a matter of viewpoint. By affirming that all meaning must be judged in reference to a set of contingent facts surrounding the person of Jesus in first-century Palestine, Christian spirituality has two distinct levels. On the level of origin and revelation, there can be only one spirituality. On the other hand, Christianity is a religion of incarnation and thus cannot retreat from history or the particular into 'timeless truth'. Each Christian, or group of Christians, is confronted by the gospel message from the past, which nevertheless demands a response within the concrete circumstances of today. In one sense, therefore, there are as many spiritualities as there are Christians but some of these responses come to exercise a formative influence in the course of history.[4]

Typologies of Christian spirituality

Having established, from one point of view, that there are different yet equally valid spiritualities we may go on to ask whether there are a number of definable types. Of the four approaches to this question which I want to evaluate, three of them have become fairly common: classification by 'schools'; apophatic and cataphatic 'ways'; and the division between Protestant and Catholic spiritualities. Finally, in recent years, some authors have sought to distinguish spiritualities according to their theological emphases. Perhaps most interesting, in a book concerned with history, are two typologies which focus specifically on attitudes to human history and the world.

Schools of spirituality

The division of Christian spirituality into schools is common in traditional histories and is often used without comment or evaluation. This typology takes two forms, which either organize spiritualities according to institutional expressions (e.g. Benedictine or Franciscan) or according to periods and countries considered to have a common spiritual vision (e.g. the seventeenth-century French school).

The 'institutional' typology has a certain validity in that particular schools share a number of common central features even though they cross cultural boundaries and extend across a period of time. For example, those who are described as representing the Benedictine school undoubtedly share a sense of common origins, history and identity. Schools in this form usually have agreed foundational texts, a common focus provided by certain images, themes and values, and a similar purpose expressed in a way of life. However this also has limitations, particularly if it is used as the *sole* framework for describing spiritualities. Firstly, it is exclusive because it is applicable only to traditions with well-developed institutional expressions. In practice this usually means religious orders. Secondly, it formulates spirituality primarily in terms of articulated ideas. Thirdly, the criteria for evaluating schools are usually purely *internal*, that is, in terms of faithfulness to a foundational vision without external criteria for judging the tradition as a whole in relation to gospel values. Finally, this approach seems to suggest that particular traditions are simple rather than complex. In fact, every tradition is subject to internal tensions, phases of historical development and cultural variation.

The second form of schools typology is framed in terms of period and place. I have already mentioned the example of the seventeenth-century French school but sometimes the ambit is much broader, such as 'Counter-Reformation spirituality'. This framework is the product of later historians rather than of contemporary self-consciousness. Some of these organizing structures are generally accepted to have some validity for historical interpretation. However the limitations are also apparent. Such a framework does not necessarily express any profound common identity. Would Ignatius Loyola and John of the Cross have understood themselves to belong to an identifiable common tradition (apart, perhaps, from a sense of being 'Catholic' rather than 'Reformed')? And, in seventeenth-century France, how would quietists and Jansenists have reacted to suggestions of a common identity and purpose? In fact the common roots, if they exist, seem to be confined to a general religious consciousness. This form of the school typology is too inclusive to be finally convincing as it covers a spectrum of values and expressions, the unity of which is not easily quantifiable.

Apophatic and cataphatic 'ways'

The words 'apophatic' and 'cataphatic' have often been used to describe *different* spiritual paths: apophatic, emphasizing silence, darkness, passivity and the absence of imagery; and cataphatic, emphasizing by contrast the way of images and the positive evaluation of creation or human relationships as contexts for God's self-revelation. In their use of the terms, writers across the centuries in the West, whether medieval or modern, have usually claimed a connection with the writings of the anonymous late fifth- or early sixth-century writer commonly known as Pseudo-Dionysius. Do his writings, and the use made of them in medieval western mystical theology, justify the use of 'apophatic' and 'cataphatic' as a typology for different spiritualities?

Probably the best-known texts of Pseudo-Dionysius, and certainly those which exercized the greatest influence on later western writers and mystics, are the *Divine Names* and the *Mystical Theology*. Fortunately for the general reader these, and other works, are available in a new English translation with notes and introductory essays by an international team of recognized scholars.[5]

Although the writings of Pseudo-Dionysius are associated primarily with the so-called apophatic way, he writes about both 'apophatic' and 'cataphatic' theologies. Cataphatic theology is what we affirm about God and apophatic theology reflects the fact that when in the presence of God we are reduced to silence. It is thus a process of negation whereby what we affirm must also ultimately be denied. It is also important to realize that Pseudo-Dionysius' theology is not concerned with subjective religious experience but with how we praise God, our response to the love of God made manifest. The fundamental link is liturgy and Scripture, as it was for all the patristic writers, a fact often forgotten when his *Mystical Theology* is taken out of context and too much emphasis is placed on his use of neo-Platonic language.[6] Recent commentators have revised the previously widely accepted western interpretation of Pseudo-Dionysius as a neo-Platonist. There is clearly a difference between using neo-Platonic categories and adopting wholesale the platonism of Proclus on whom Pseudo-Dionysius was thought to be dependent. Orthodox theologians in particular, such as Vladimir Lossky, have been critical of such an interpretation of Pseudo-Dionysius and eastern mysticism in general.[7]

How are cataphatic and apophatic 'theologies' related? The whole of creation is brought into being by God to show forth divine glory. Pseudo-Dionysius therefore has a positive view of the cosmos as the self-revelation of God's goodness. There is a 'procession', emanation or outflowing of Divine life into the cosmos whose motive force is goodness. This 'goodness' is the first affirmation about God discussed in the *Divine Names*, a work which may be described as 'cataphatic' as it explores the manifestation of God in creation. The Trinity is first discussed in terms of 'distinctions' whereby we can know something of God, but behind these lies a unity which is ultimately incomprehensible. The theology of the Trinity is cataphatic because it affirms something about God yet, *at the same time*, it is apophatic because the affirmation we make takes us beyond what we can grasp. In other words, the Trinity reveals God as *unknowable*. Through our relationship to the manifestations of God and in our affirmations we come to realize that God never becomes our possession, an object of knowledge. Consequently, we must 'deny' what we are affirming. Thus cataphatic theology provides those affirmations through whose denial (apophatic) we find the path to a deeper knowledge of God.[8] Or, to put it another way, cataphatic theology is concerned with God's movement outwards, or self-manifestation, in the cosmos as well as in Scripture and liturgy, and our involvement in it. Apophatic theology concerns a 'remanation', or return of all things into the One, our movement inwards to God which takes place in a process of denial. But the point is that we are involved in *both* and so cataphatic and apophatic ways are inextricably linked.[9] There is an essential paradox: the whole of creation reveals God yet at the same time no one has ever seen God. So God will receive many names and yet will ultimately remain above every name. Indeed the potential 'infinity' of names for God itself indicates the ultimate unnameable quality of God.[10]

For Pseudo-Dionysius, therefore, cataphatic theology is *vitally necessary*. The apophatic way is not an alternative to it but grows out of it and may be said to succeed it. More properly, these are two sides of the same coin whereby the cosmic cycle of God's outpouring into creation, and the return of all into the One, demands both an affirmation of the meaningfulness of symbols and, at the same time, a destruction of all symbols for the naked knowledge of unknowing.[11] Pseudo-Dionysius is not systematic and is therefore always in danger of being misunderstood. For example, he uses the word 'ascent' for our movement back to God (or divinization). 'The fact is that the more we take flight upwards, the more our words are confined to the ideas we are capable of forming so that now as we plunge into that darkness which is beyond intellect, we shall find ourselves not simply running short of words but actually speechless and unknowing.'[12] But it would be misleading to understand this as affirming that we come closer to God the higher we ascend. In fact, for Pseudo-Dionysius, every creature is immediate to God by virtue of creation. Union, therefore, does not create an immediacy which does not previously exist but *realizes* it.

There seems to be no justification, in Pseudo-Dionysius himself, for understanding the cataphatic and apophatic ways as *alternative* spiritualities. Does however, the development of his thought in the medieval West move us further in that direction? In the West, apart from a translation of Pseudo-Dionysius by the Irishman John Scotus Eriugena in 862, Dionysian influence was largely indirect until the twelfth century. Even then, Jean Leclercq suggests, Dionysian influence was very slight in the monastic context. It was through the work of some canons regular, the Victorines of Paris, that Pseudo-Dionysius passed into scholastic theology. The notable figures were Hugh of St Victor (d.1141), Richard of St Victor (d.1173) and Thomas Gallus (d.1246). Subsequently, in the thirteenth century, Robert Grosseteste (later Bishop of Lincoln) and the Dominican theologians Albert the Great and Thomas Aquinas translated or wrote commentaries on several Dionysian works. The Dionysian corpus also influenced the great Franciscan theologian of mysticism, St Bonaventure, but the greatest influence was on the so-called Northern mystics of the fourteenth and fifteenth centuries especially Meister Eckhart and John Tauler.[13]

It is important to bear in mind that, after the twelfth century, a unified vision of human knowledge began to break down into a distinction between head and heart – that is, the intellectual and affective faculties. This tended to lead to a rejection of *knowledge* of God and a concentration on the apophatic dimension of Pseudo-Dionysius in isolation. This is very apparent once we come to a work such as *The Cloud of Unknowing*, in the fourteenth century, which drew a great deal on the thought of Pseudo-Dionysius, yet subtly changed its meaning in offering a mystical theology of darkness and unknowing. In this, *The Cloud* appears to be dependent on the Victorine, Thomas Gallus, who had reinterpreted Dionysian language about the limitations of reason in terms of the supremacy of affectivity to all forms of knowing in the human ascent to God. Chapter 4 of *The Cloud* distinguishes between 'knowing power' and 'loving power' and it is by the latter that God is 'known'. Chapter 6, for example, goes on to suggest that, by the abandonment of thought, God comes to be known by love. Thus the central message of the work is that God is known by love and not through conceptual reasoning which must be buried under a cloud of forgetting.[14]

Apart from this distinction between love and knowledge, another emphasis in medieval spiritual theory affected the way in which the teaching of Pseudo-Dionysius was 'received' and used. There was a tendency to subject the spiritual journey to analysis and distinctions and there developed a hierarchy of levels, for which 'ascent' by means of 'ladders' became a central image (for example, Walter Hilton's *The Ladder of Perfection*). This reflected a sense that one needed to move beyond the world of the senses as well as concepts. The way of images (cataphatic) thus gradually came to be seen as the stage *before* and *below* the way of unknowing or imagelessness (apophatic). Both Hugh and Richard of St Victor continued to insist that knowledge of invisible divine things is first mediated through the symbolic significance of material reality.[15] However, Meister Eckhart and John Tauler, the Dominican mystical theologians of the fourteenth century, placed their greatest emphasis on the negative way and described union with God in terms of detachment whereby a person is no longer occupied with material things, abandons all that is 'not God' and enters a kind of divine darkness.[16] Gradually the apophatic way, in some writers, became almost coterminous with 'mystical' or 'contemplative'. The active life was necessarily associated with involvement in the material world and the contemplative, or higher way, was to be reached by withdrawal as well as the negation of images. *The Cloud of Unknowing* in chapter 8 links this movement from images to darkness to a distinction between the active life, which is lower, and the contemplative life which is higher. In the former, active life there is also a lower and higher part. The higher 'consists of good spiritual meditations and earnest consideration of a man's own wretched state with sorrow and compassion, and of the wonderful gifts, kindness, and works of God in all his creatures, corporeal and spiritual with thanksgiving and praise'. However, higher contemplation is entirely darkness and the cloud of unknowing.

The great Flemish mystic, Jan Ruusbroec, seems to employ Eckhartian language in his insistence on the need to transcend all creatures and images in order to attain an imageless state of naked being. He also wrote in terms of three stages, moving from the lower to the higher. The 'active life' was for beginners and consisted of 'union with God by intermediary'. The 'interior life' was higher and more inward and union with God was 'without intermediary'. The third stage, the 'contemplative life', was the highest point and union was 'without distinction'. However, a closer analysis indicates that Ruusbroec departed significantly from the stark emphasis of Eckhart on the negative way. For Ruusbroec each stage is indispensable. They form a continuum in which one does not supplant another. Nothing is lost as one moves inward. In *The Spiritual Espousals* Book 1: Part 4, at the end of a section on 'the active life', Ruusbroec asserts that ultimately God must transcend all concepts, yet at the same time he offers a more positive appreciation of the naming of God than other more 'negative' mystical writers. In his consideration of 'the contemplative life' in Book 3, in the final Part 4, the darkness of which he writes differs strikingly from Eckhart or what some have called 'pure Dionysianism'. There is an active meeting with the Trinity in eternal love and thus a dialectical relationship between a resting in darkness and activity.[17] Ruusbroec, it appears, retains a more balanced approach to the relative values of the 'positive' and 'negative' ways than Eckhart. And while he uses the language of stages his relegation of the positive and active to a 'lower' or more preliminary stage is less absolute and more sophisticated than *The Cloud*.

Although there are differences of emphasis between Eckhart and Ruusbroec, they are not distinguishable in terms of apophatic and cataphatic ways. However, the noted scholar of Franciscan spirituality, Ewert Cousins, argues that a distinction between two kinds of religious consciousness did develop in the thirteenth century. Up to the twelfth century, western spirituality had been dominated by an emphasis on the risen Lord or eternal Logos rather than the humanity of Jesus. This tended to support a spirituality which sought ultimately to move upwards from the level of creatures rather than to be engaged in the historical and material. Gradually, from Anselm onwards and inspired in part by the monastic *lectio divina*, there developed a devotion to Christ's humanity. Before Francis of Assisi, the most notable exponents were the Cistercians Bernard of Clairvaux and Aelred of Rievaulx.[18]

Cousins suggests that Francis of Assisi's devotion to the humanity of Christ and Christ-centred visionary mysticism ushered in a major trend in western spirituality. He describes this as a 'mysticism of the historical event'. The current of spirituality to which this gave birth tended to be rooted in an attention to the Jesus of history as well as an appreciation of God's self-revelation and gift of divine life in and through the created world. It contrasted with the a-historical and world-transcending emphases of other schools of mysticism by concentrating on the historical, the concrete and the human.[19] Through the *Tree of Life* of St Bonaventure and the anonymous *Meditations on the Life of Christ* in the late thirteenth century, this new religious consciousness passed into the writings of the Carthusian, Ludolph of Saxony, and thence into the spirituality of St Ignatius of Loyola.[20] This kind of spirituality produced an emphasis on 'imitation of Christ'. Francis and Bonaventure concentrated their attention on the nativity and passion. Ignatius of Loyola developed this ideal of imitation further by focusing on Jesus's mission and public ministry. The resulting spirituality, consequently, sought to share in Christ's building of the Kingdom of God and thus, from a different perspective, in Christ's poverty and sufferings.

Cousins's distinction between two kinds of spirituality is important but does not correspond to apophatic and cataphatic ways. For
example, in St Bonaventure's *The Soul's Journey into God*, the
Franciscan emphasis on the 'mysticism of the historical event' and
Christocentric spirituality mingle with more 'apophatic' elements
which Bonaventure had inherited, possibly from the direct influence
of the Dionysian works. From chapter 1, when he explores God
as reflected through the material world, to chapter 6 where he
contemplates the Trinity as the mystery of the self-diffusive God,
his approach may be described as cataphatic. However, chapter 7
moves beyond this to the unknowing of the *via negativa*. Strangely
enough it is here, where Bonaventure draws on the *Mystical Theology*
of Pseudo-Dionysius, rather than in earlier chapters, that he finds
the essential point of union with St Francis's mystical visions of
Christ.[21]

Rather than adopt an apophatic-cataphatic distinction, it would
be more accurate to see the distinction between the two streams
of spirituality in terms of the degree of Christocentrism, especially
emphasis on the humanity of Jesus, and the degree to which
spiritualities stress either a world-transcending view or the experience of God in the concrete and human. In fact, all spiritualities
focus ultimately on the God who is 'Other' and recognize the
danger of becoming fixated with created reality. For example, in
the writings of Ignatius of Loyola, who stressed so strongly 'finding
God in all things', the important preamble to his *Spiritual Exercises*,
entitled the 'Principle and Foundation', recognises the importance
of detachment from all created things and that one must be rid of
all that hinders 'the end for which we are created', which is 'to
praise, reverence and serve God our Lord'.[22] However, the more
world-transcending spiritualities, such as *The Cloud of Unknowing*,
place a different emphasis on the negative effects of created reality
on the contemplative journey. Thus, there will be a tendency to
insist on the danger of created things as intermediaries in our
relationship with God. Those spiritualities, such as the Franciscan
or Ignatian and the mysticism of Julian of Norwich, which place
more emphasis on the concrete and human in our relationship with
God will focus more on the generosity of God, or God's immanence
in creation and in human experience.

Finally, in our contemporary context, a stress on the methodology
of prayer and on subjective religious experience has led to the
language of apophatic and cataphatic ways becoming more narrowly
associated with methods of prayer. The apophatic way is understood

by many as coterminous with still, imageless or even truly *contemplative* prayer. For a variety of reasons which need not detain us here, this way of prayer has found a great deal of favour in recent years. So much so that some writers, reacting against it, have suggested an 'apophatic bias'. This way of employing the terms apophatic and cataphatic, while retaining some connections with its original usage, is far more subjective and limited in scope.[23]

It does not seem to me to be helpful to see the two 'ways' as in any sense mutually exclusive or as absolute alternatives. If one returns to the works of Pseudo-Dionysius on which so much later theory depends, it would be incorrect to describe him and his mystical theology as *purely* apophatic. The doctrine of the Trinity, as revelation of the Divine, and the Incarnation both affirm that God always reveals and offers divine life in and through the cosmos, the world and human experience, including liturgy and Scripture. As Raimundo Panikkar suggests, 'iconolatry' is a normal dimension of human religious life and of the manifestation of God to us. Indeed, religion cannot come into being without at least some traces of it. The world and human experience is where the encounter with God must always begin. Even if the icon as 'sign' is necessarily provisional, in that it must yield to the underlying reality in due time, it nonetheless stands in a vital way for the possibility of encounter and is the condition of the binding together of God and humankind. For if God were totally other there would be no room in such extreme impassibility for love, knowledge or prayer.[24] The two-fold movement of divine manifestation to us and our arduous return to God is recognized in what Panikkar calls 'true iconolatry' (as opposed to idolatry which stops with the image in itself). 'Man is the image of God, the world a divine "vestige" and the presence of the absolute is always that of incarnation.'[25]

Protestant and Catholic

Histories of western spirituality have often made a sharp distinction between the Protestant and Catholic traditions as a whole, and some writers have consequently adopted this distinction as an explicit typology. The concepts 'Protestant' and 'Catholic' were born of a separation of communities which gave birth to a sectarian mentality that persists even today. The two parts of western Christianity developed distinctive forms of religious consciousness and this, in turn, led to an *assumption* that the differences were fundamental. The challenge of ecumenism, has irrevocably changed the agenda.

We are slowly learning not to define ourselves (whether 'we' are Protestant or Catholic) essentially over and against 'the other'. This progressively frees us to recognize more of ourselves in the spiritual traditions of each part of the Christian family. The new situation also invites us to ask critical questions concerning the ways in which we define and evaluate differences.

In fact, until relatively recently, the world 'spirituality' was viewed with some suspicion by Protestants. They preferred terms such as Godliness, piety, holiness of life or the devout life because these seemed less tainted than 'spirituality' with the erroneous doctrine of works-righteousness.[26] This situation has changed substantially. The Lutheran theologian Wolfhart Pannenberg suggests that every major historical type of spirituality implies a complete interpretation of the world which will relate to whatever aspect of Christian doctrine is central to the religious consciousness of the time.[27] Despite suspicion of the term, Protestant theology was from the start concerned with spirituality because it sought to articulate the human-divine relationship and to work out concrete ways in which it might be expressed. This is especially clear in Luther who sought to reintegrate the division which scholastic theology had effected between theology and spirituality.[28]

In what ways have Protestant and Catholic spiritualities been distinguished? One approach points to a historical difference between the *condition* which each tradition chose for attaining the end and purpose of Christian life by focusing on the presence of religious life in the Roman Catholic Church, its absence in classical Protestantism, and what this implies about the very nature of the spiritual life. Thus, Catholic spirituality has been characterized by a double standard whereby the highest kind of spirituality is to be found in religious communities or, at least, in some adaptation of their way of life to people forced to live 'in the world'. This was associated with a total concentration on God which necessitated detachment from worldly concerns. In contrast, Protestantism rejected not only the 'works-righteousness' of monasticism but also the associated idea of a double standard in spirituality in favour of a single standard for holiness, based simply on justification by God.

As we have seen in earlier chapters, there is some justification for the criticism of a double standard in Catholic spirituality. However, there are problems about suggesting that this indicates a permanent or essential difference between Protestantism and Catholicism. First of all, such a double standard was rejected by

Vatican II's teaching on the single call to holiness and, secondly, developments in the theory and practice of Catholic religious life, as well as the rebirth of monasticism in a number of the Churches of the Reformation, indicate that neither a works-righteousness nor a double standard of spirituality is *necessarily* implied by the presence of religious life in the Christian community.[29]

A more substantial attempt to distinguish Protestant and Catholic spirituality focuses around the contrasting emphases on word or sacrament and possibly, as a consequence, between the individual 'hearer of the Word' and member of a sacramental *community*. This distinction is suggested by two representatives of the Reformed tradition, the Swiss biblical scholar Franz Leenhardt and, more recently, the Dutch pastoral psychologist Hieje Faber.[30] Leenhardt identifies Protestant and Catholic spirituality with two strands of the biblical tradition. First of all there is what he calls the 'Abrahamic' strand which stretches from Abraham through the prophets and Paul towards the Protestant reformers for which the symbol is 'the word'. Then there is the 'Mosaic' strand which stretches from Moses, through the Israelite priesthood and Peter, towards the papacy for which the symbol is 'the burning bush'. Faber, while not adopting precisely the same terminology, also detects two basic forms of spirituality, with Old Testament origins, which diverge and stand in a kind of relationship of tension with each other. There are considerable similarities between the contents and symbols of Leenhardt's and Faber's two types and so I propose to treat them together.

The Protestant type of spirituality, for Leenhardt, emphasizes dependence solely on God, hearing the call of God's word, repentance, and moving forward to the eschatological Kingdom in hope (or what Faber calls prophecy and pilgrimage). Faber points to further elements of this type. God is experienced as distant, transcendent and as a figure of authority. God is heard (thus the word is central) but invisible. God is essentially free, intervenes, is critical and continually calls humans to a response. Both Leenhardt and Faber identify similar forms of cult. Images or ritual forms which get in the way of dependence on the word, or become substitutes for security in God alone, are questioned or rejected. For Leenhardt, ethical purity replaces ritual purity, for Faber the expounding of Scripture and meditation on the Law demand essentially a reaction of faith. For both Leenhardt and Faber, the New Testament figure who best expresses this spirituality is Paul, for whom the central task is receiving the word and for whom God remains the God of law even if this is a new law. In addition Faber suggests that, historically, this spirituality emphasizes a fundamental gulf between God and humankind, is anti-syncretistic and tends to criticize 'religion'.

The Catholic type of spirituality, by contrast, also involves a journey of faith but in the context of a people and a tradition. This spirituality is one in which the gospel is mediated through concrete, sacramental instruments and is expressed by mutual love in community. Faber further suggests that, in this tradition, God is essentially *present* and revelation is bound up with specific contexts, priesthood, cult and holy places. The stress is on the glory of God rather than on his name and this glory is capable of being made visible and tangible. Both writers agree about the cultic implications. The medium is not the ear but the eye. Ritual is not seen as getting in the way of our relationship with God but actualises it. The sacraments fulfil what the word proclaims. Ethical purity and ritual purity flow from the same source which is the presence of God among us. In addition, this spirituality values the natural world and experiences human life as being taken up into a holy order. While for Leenhardt the New Testament figure is Peter, for Faber it is John, the theologian of glory. Historically, this spirituality emphasizes the unity of the community, images and mysticism and has an openness to natural theology.

Leenhardt and Faber are able to point to some distinctive characteristics of each tradition without, it seems to me, justifying an absolute or exclusive division between the two. It would be invalid to suggest that, in biblical terms, 'Abrahamic' religion has no place for external signs or theophanies or that 'Mosaic' religion does not place its ultimate trust and hope in the promises of God. In looking particularly at Leenhardt's thesis, many Protestants will recognize something of themselves in the 'Mosaic' strand and many Catholics will identify themselves with the Pauline and prophetic. There is a danger that, if applied too rigidly or exclusively, these distinctions will force historical personalities into preconceived models which do damage to their complexity. Historically speaking, Protestantism and Catholicism have always been plural phenomena. Faber indeed makes the distinctions less absolute and recognizes that the most important fact is that *both* Catholic and Protestant spiritual traditions are firmly biblical, and each admits that God's presence is ultimately elusive. Faber further points out that there are mixed forms of spirituality which contain elements of both emphases.[31]

Another way of approaching how Protestant and Catholic traditions differ in their understanding of human communion with God has been in terms of the alternatives of 'mediation' and 'immediacy'. Wolfhart Pannenberg admits that the spirituality of the Middle Ages encompassed 'a piety concerned with the immediacy of God' and not simply a system of mediation through Church, sacraments and the intercession of saints. He suggests that nonetheless the distinctive quality of Reformation spirituality was that it adopted a particular representation of immediacy and contrasted this critically with the whole ecclesiastical system of mediation. The most classical expression was Luther's treatises on the freedom of the Christian. Luther highlighted the tension between the foregiveness of sins and redemption from the power of sin by the death of Jesus Christ on the one hand, and a sense, on the other, that Christians still live under the power of sin. For Pannenberg, it is the underlying awareness of separation from God that explains the medieval desire for mediation particularly through the saints and the sacraments, especially that of confession. In contrast the Reformation message was *total liberation* from sin and guilt and thus from the uncertainties of endless mediations such as Luther had experienced as an Augustinian friar. This liberation depended, of course, on sharing Luther's basic intuition of 'mystical participation' in Christ by faith.[32] It is worth noting that the Anglican Church, while subscribing to the classic Reformation doctrines of salvation and grace, retained many of the traditional *structures* associated with mediation such as Saints days, the cycle of the liturgical year and ancient liturgical forms.

Although there are notable differences of emphasis between the great reformers Luther and Calvin, both accepted what may be described as *the* fundamental mark of Reformation spirituality: the principle of divine monergism, that God initiates and accomplishes everything in the work of salvation. The depravity of the human will confronted by the unconditional love of God are the two vital elements which together enable us to understand Reformation spirituality.[33] In the light of God's sovereign initiative, the theological bases for Reformation spirituality, as opposed to traditional Catholic spirituality, may be reduced to four classical slogans: grace alone, faith alone, Christ alone and Scripture alone. These, it has been argued, are stronger than merely alternative emphases because the Reformers believed that humans were quite incapable through sin of even *desiring* to be reconciled. God, therefore, completely overrides corrupt human will in order to redeem. In other words,

while traditional Catholic and Protestant spirituality both agree
that salvation is by grace and through Christ, the foundations are
substantially different. For the Reformers, God forgives sin once
and for all and salvation is assured solely by a gracious God in a
completely free act. Traditional Catholic spirituality, by contrast,
suggested that by grace God makes human actions worthy in his
sight. The sacraments communicate grace that really sanctifies our
incomplete good works. Thus room is left for human action in the
salvation process, even if essentially aided and even initiated by
grace. The 'God emphasis' of the Reformers therefore completely
reverses the conventional ideas of spirituality whereby the soul
seeks God, ascends to the spiritual plane and the sinner can and
must strive to come to God. On the contrary, God alone seeks,
strives and descends to us.[34]

While it is important not to fudge these distinctions, the attempt
to use 'Protestant' and 'Catholic' as absolute types for distinguishing
different spiritualities is nowadays complicated by a number of
factors. Firstly, and perhaps most significantly, there is a much
greater realization of the continuities between the Reformers
and medieval spirituality. A detailed analysis of these is not
necessary here but it is worth noting that the second volume on
Christian spirituality, in the continuing series, World Spirituality:
an Encyclopedic History of the Religious Quest, deliberately places
the spiritualities of the major reformed traditions together with a
consideration of the spirituality of the High Middle Ages. This
choice of division is justified in the Introduction.[35] Pannenberg,
as we have already noted, draws attention to a strand in medieval
spirituality which was concerned with the immediacy of communion
with God and which was continued in a different form by the
Reformers. Further continuity, with reference to views of salvation
and of the relationship between God and humankind, is noted in
the volume by Veith.[36] In general, it is now admitted quite freely
that the reformers had a great esteem for *some* medieval spiritual
thinkers such as St Bernard, Meister Eckhart, Tauler and à Kempis.
Previously sharp distinctions between a Protestant emphasis on the
word as opposed to sacraments are now recognized to be simplistic.
Sacraments continued to play a more important role in Reformation
spirituality than was previously admitted. Equally, the emphasis on
the rugged individualism of Protestant spirituality has now been
tempered by a greater appreciation of the role of the Church as
a community of faith, whether in its established forms, in folk
Churches, or even in 'gathered' groupings of the 'pure' (e.g.

Puritans) and groups for the mutual cultivation of Godliness (e.g. the Pietists or Methodist 'class' meetings). Both Luther and Calvin denied that they were innovators and in particular they were concerned, in their different ways, for the renewal and revitalization of the Christian *community* and not just of individuals.[37]

A second factor is the greater realization that Reformation spirituality in the strict sense and later developments in Protestantism must be distinguished. The thought of the reformers was much closer to their medieval predecessors than it is to some, at least, of the contemporary brands of Protestantism. Thus 'Reformation spirituality' and 'Protestant spirituality' are not simply coterminous. On the one hand, Protestantism developed in many different directions and, on the other, Reformation *spirituality*, as opposed to ecclesiastical positions and structures, may even be found in elements of later Roman Catholicism. The same medieval roots found expression both in the reformers and in some aspects of post-Reformation Catholicism. *The Spiritual Exercises* of St Ignatius Loyola, for example, have been seen by some as part of an Augustinian and Pauline revival which predates the Protestant Reformation. On the question of the divergences between later Protestantism and the early Reformers, it is worth noting that the issue of the role of human action and choice in salvation re-emerged quite soon. The monergism espoused by Luther and Calvin alike was confronted by a renewed emphasis on synergism (that is, human co-operation with God) in Lutheranism (for example, Melanchthon) and in Calvinism, (for example, Arminius).[38]

Finally, the rather monolithic interpretation of both Protestantism and Catholicism has been replaced by a greater appreciation of the plurality at the heart of both traditions. Indeed it is better to see both as clusters of traditions which have a sense of shared history. It is important to understand that, from the very start, there were serious differences between Luther and Calvin despite the things which they held in common. In turn both differed substantially from the proponents of the so-called 'radical reformation' which has largely been omitted from traditional portrayals of Protestant spirituality until fairly recently.[39] It is hard to define 'Protestant' or 'Catholic' spirituality in one-dimensional terms if one considers, on the one hand, the contrast between the poetry of George Herbert and the Ranters or Levellers of the English Civil War period, or, on the other, that between Ignatius of Loyola, John of the Cross and Pascal. In more contemporary terms, Protestantism encompasses the High Church Lutheranism of Sweden and the fundamentalism of the 'Bible Belt' in the United States and Catholicism contains Gustavo Gutiérrez, Hans Küng, John Paul II and charismatic renewal.

While it is important to preserve the *particularity* of, for example, the spiritualities of Luther and Ignatius of Loyola and to accept that there are substantially different assumptions behind each there are, for the reasons I have touched upon, real problems about such all-embracing terms as 'Protestant spirituality' and 'Catholic spirituality' as a helpful typology. Perhaps, in the end, it is safer to talk in terms of 'the spirituality of Luther' or the 'spirituality of Ignatius of Loyola'. On the one hand, this preserves the notion that these are distinctive traditions and yet, on the other, admits that there is a plurality within the wider Protestant and Catholic traditions, continuities between both and their medieval forebears, and finally, for all the differences, some degree of overlap between them.

Theological world-views

Despite the limitation which I have suggested, the attempt to create a typology for spiritualities in terms of 'Protestant' and 'Catholic' highlights the importance of theological assumptions. Two recent attempts to classify spiritualities have adopted theological criteria. This seems likely to be particularly fruitful because, as Pannenberg suggests, 'in the more important forms of Christian spirituality we encounter the substructures of theology'.[40] As always, a rigid classification of every spiritual tradition would, of course, be unhelpful and often inaccurate, yet a theological framework may assist a degree of differentiation. The two recent attempts are focused in terms of attitudes to 'the world' and 'human history'.

The American Jesuit, Edward Kinerk, identifies four types of spirituality which relate not to an acceptance or rejection of the world and history in general but to how these contexts are interpreted as 'potential loci for expressions of the authentic'.[41] By 'authentic', Kinerk understands the ultimate fulfilment of the human person which he describes as self-transcendence – the purpose of all forms of spirituality. The 'inauthentic', therefore, is self-centredness which is also self-alienation. The assumption is that all spirituality is concerned with growth from the inauthentic to the authentic, a growth which is dialectical because it involves a 'yes' to what assists the process, and a simultaneous 'no' to what inhibits growth. In other words, Kinerk focuses on the degree to which the world and history are seen as contexts for *self-transformation*.

Kinerk's first type of spirituality says 'no' to the world and history. His subtitle for this type is 'apophatic'. This is not a question of understanding the world as evil, and history as meaningless. For Kinerk, the classical expression of this type lies in mystical spiritualities such as *The Cloud of Unknowing* or John of the Cross. The journey to the authentic is through negation of specific images or through darkness. The second type is the opposite: 'yes' to the world and to history. This he subtitles 'apostolic'. Here, both the world and history are the places of self-transformation. Spiritualities which fall into this category are concerned not only with the conversion of individuals but also with the transformation of history, by involvement in the world. Kinerk's classical example is Ignatius of Loyola. The third type of spirituality says 'yes' to the world but 'no' to history. This is subtitled 'City of God' spirituality. The context for transformation is one special place, outer or inner, to the exclusion of others – this place is a reflection of the Kingdom of God in a privileged way. For Kinerk, the classical expressions are monasticism, which seeks to build a Kingdom community (outer), and *The Imitation of Christ*, which finds the Kingdom in the human heart (inner). The fourth and final type says 'no' to the world but 'yes' to history. This Kinerk calls the 'prophetic'. It is not a spirituality of gloom but of challenge, for prophecy interprets history and judges the world. The classical expressions include martyrdom, the radical poverty of Francis of Assisi and contemporary peace spirituality or social disobedience. The main point to note about Kinerk's typology is that all four categories are positive and therefore, in Christian terms, equally valid.

The Methodist theologian, Geoffrey Wainwright, provides a more complex analysis with five types of spirituality which he adapts from Richard Niebuhr.[42] While also attending to attitudes to the world and human history, Wainwright's types are framed, more specifically than Kinerk's, in terms of eschatology, that is, the balance of 'now' and 'not yet' in our understanding of the coming to be and location of the Kingdom of God. In other words, in their attitudes to world and history, are spiritualities more centred on the present or on the future?

The first type is entitled 'Christ against culture'. Here the world is hostile and in conflict with the Kingdom of God. The basic attitude, therefore, is renunciation and escape. The eschatology is one of conflict, with the Kingdom *replacing* this world. This may take one of two directions. The more common is that the Kingdom of God is 'not yet' or, even more strongly, 'never', for the world of human history is beyond redemption. The less common, and more paradoxical, is that the Kingdom is over-realized in the present, in particular privileged communities which are set apart. Some embodiments might be martyrdom, primitive monasticism, Pentecostalism. The danger of such a type is that it tends simplistically to underestimate the world as the object of God's love.

Wainwright's second type is the exact opposite: the 'Christ of culture'. Its characteristic is a simplistic affirmation of the world as it is. In terms of eschatology, this type either completely identifies the Kingdom with the world or, in its liberal form, avoids the language of eschatology altogether because there has been no Fall. The embodiments, in general terms, may be either politically conservative or liberal. Specific examples would be the Imperial Christianity of the late Roman Empire, the Reich Church of Nazi Germany, or Harvey Cox's 'secular city'. Wainwright also suggests that, paradoxically, Puritan theocracies, which sacralize society as opposed to secularizing religion, might fit this type. Like the first type, this is interpreted as cripplingly deficient.

Wainwright then suggests three more types which are more balanced in their attitudes to world and history, although they may be more or less positive towards them. The first is 'Christ above culture'. This emphasizes a positive view of humanity and culture, but also recognizes the need for purification. Grace builds on nature and there is a high valuation of the incarnation. Eschatologically, this type values creation as such, but adds that Christ raises the whole of creation in his redemptive action. This tends to favour the present effectiveness of the Christ-event over a future-oriented completion. As possible embodiments, Wainwright chooses, among others, Thomas Aquinas, Karl Barth and Charles Wesley as well as the aesthetic spirituality of icons and much Orthodox theology in general.

The second 'balanced' type is 'Christ and culture in paradox'. This Wainwright calls 'dualist' because it is more on the world-negating side of centre. God reveals, but is also hidden, saves, but also judges. Spiritualities of this type are 'paradoxical' and emphasise struggle and conflict. Thus the eschatology will tend to be both 'now' and 'not yet' at the same time. There is often an apocalyptic tone. Among the interesting and varied examples Wainwright suggests are Luther and, more recently in this tradition,

Bonhoeffer and Dag Hammarskjöld. He also places the holy fools of Syria, Ireland and Russia in this category as well as the seventeenth-century Jesuit, Jean-Joseph Surin.

The third and final middle type is 'Christ the transformer of culture'. The main characteristic is an emphasis on transformation – that the world should be viewed positively and that its radical corruption is not inherent but a perversion of the good. Thus, transformation, conversion and rebirth play a central role. Spiritual growth and development are very much part of this type – not in a bland way, but interpreted as following the pattern of Jesus's death and resurrection in a radical dependence on God. The eschatology of this type certainly suggests that the beginnings of the Kingdom lie in history, through the process of dying to sin and living to God. However, this process awaits completion and thus there is always an impulse to press on towards a final goal with urgency. St Augustine may be placed in this type, although some commentators would take a less positive view, along with sacramental spirituality and missionary spirituality at its best. Historical groupings would be early Methodism (and 'Wesleyanism' in general) as well as 'developed' religious life (as opposed to primitive monasticism), such as the mendicants and the Jesuits. Wainwright also finds a place here for the Salvation Army (which he suggests is sacramental, while having no sacraments) and the liberationist spirituality of the Latin American Basic Communities.

While the basic theological framework used by Kinerk and Wainwright seems to offer quite useful typologies, and while there is common ground between them, in their adoption of attitudes to world and history as criteria for differentiation, there are a number of important points to note. Firstly, it is reasonable to question some of the embodiments which are suggested for the various types. This is especially the case with Wainwright who is prepared to list far more examples. To place particular spiritualities in one type rather than another always implies an *interpretation* of these traditions, rather than merely a value-free observation of incontrovertible characteristics. Secondly, while mysticism is a varied phenomenon, and cannot be placed as a single 'tradition' within one type, it is almost entirely ignored by Wainwright. Because his typology is based, to some degree, on the observation of specific instances, as well as on theological categories, the absence of mysticism from serious consideration actually affects the typology which he establishes. Thirdly, the typologies of Kinerk and Wainwright differ in an important way. Kinerk's is entirely positive and views each type as equally valid. There is no evaluation of relative strengths and weaknesses. By contrast, Wainwright's types are inherently value-laden. The first two, 'Christ against culture' and the 'Christ of culture', are characterized as essentially unbalanced and thus deficient. In a sense, Wainwright's ideal is a balance point between 'yes' and 'no' to the world and history. The three acceptable types are all somewhere in the middle, although the 'Christ above culture' type is characterized as more towards the 'yes' side of centre, and the 'Christ and culture in paradox' type as on the 'no' side of centre. By implication, the final type, 'Christ transformer of culture', is understood to be the most balanced type.

This difference makes it difficult to fit the typologies of Kinerk and Wainwright together even though they begin from a similar theological starting point. For example, Kinerk's first type, 'No to history and world', is not the same as Wainwright's 'Christ against culture'. For Kinerk the 'No' does not necessarily imply a *rejection* of either the world or history as evil. Indeed, Kinerk's assumptions are quite different because, for him, this is the 'mystical' type par excellence. In some respects it bears comparison with aspects of Wainwright's second balanced type, the 'paradoxical'. Equally, Kinerk's second type, 'Yes to history and world', has quite different assumptions from Wainwright's 'Christ of culture' type, although there are very superficial similarities. For Kinerk this is the 'apostolic' type whose key is 'transformation' and thus relates more closely to Wainwright's favoured type: 'Christ transformer of culture'. Finally, neither of Kinerk's 'balanced' types (but his 'balance' is not a category of evaluation) fit easily with any of Wainwright's. Elements of each may be found in all the types of Wainwright, both those he considers adequate and those he rejects as deficient. Overall, this difficulty of comparison points not only to substantially different assumptions behind each typology but also reminds us of the danger of adopting too readily any *one* typology for differentiating spiritualities, even if they are of an apparently straight-forward theological kind.

Conclusion

Do typologies have any value? I believe that they do, for they help us to preserve the particularity of specific spiritual traditions and to appreciate the rich plurality at the heart of Christian spirituality. In the chapter on the use of spiritual history, it was suggested that an over-emphasis on the sameness of spirituality often resulted in a lack of nuanced awareness of the differences between traditions, and even of the plurality within them. Spiritual traditions are not merely accidental 'instances of enduring truths', but arise and develop in accord with historical circumstances. This is, if you like, a theological as well as an historical truth for the realm of spiritual experience, in Christian terms, is not cut off from the concreteness of the world and history. It is always 'heaven in ordinary'.

Yet, undoubtedly, there are dangers. No single typology is complete or perfect as all are based on relative values and limited perspectives. We must take care not to make our distinctions absolute and not to force the complexities of historical personalities and movements into the constraints of over-simple frameworks. An even greater danger would be if we used typologies, not as ways of reinforcing our sense of the unfathomable riches of God's encounter with the human condition, but as a means of establishing that certain ways are 'right' or 'wrong', 'more perfect' or 'less perfect'.

The question of typologies is relevant not merely to those interested in deepening their historical understanding but equally so to those engaged in a personal spiritual quest. On the one hand, if our typologies exaggerate or distort for the sake of definition, they can raise barriers which make it difficult for Christians to understand one another, or to learn from traditions which initially seem alien. On the other, any attempt to ignore differences, in favour of some universal or generic spirituality, is not only unrealistic but dangerous. In practice, contemporary Christians are increasingly crossing traditional sectarian boundaries in their spiritual quest. This, I believe, is one of the hopeful 'signs of the times' which deepen faith and hope in the face of centuries of entrenched bigotry, as well as institutional conservatism. And yet, in this movement outwards, it is not helpful to be rootless or to wander aimlessly from one spiritual culture to another in a search for somewhere to be at home. To enter fruitfully into the unfamiliar one needs a real sense of where one belongs. If this is true of travel, and exposure to other cultures, it is equally true of the spiritual pilgrimage. In this context, typologies may help us not only to ground ourselves more surely in what is particular to our own tradition but also to discover the same loving God in the diversity that lies beyond our familiar horizons.

Notes

1. For the treatment of unity versus diversity in some classical histories, see P. Pourrat, *La Spiritualité Chrétienne*, 4 vols (Paris 1918), especially the preface to vol. 2 and 3; Louis Bouyer et al., *A History of Christian Spirituality*, ET 3 vols (London 1968) especially the preface; Jean Leclercq adopts a broader view but nevertheless continues to emphasize the unity of spirituality more than its diversity: see his introductions to two volumes edited by E. Rozanne Elder, *The Spirituality of Western Christendom*, Cistercian Studies 30 (Kalamazoo 1976) and *The Roots of the Modern Christian Tradition*, Cistercian Studies 55, (Kalamazoo 1984).

2. See *Études* 94 (1961), pp. 170–4 and 411–15; and *Christus* 8 (1961), pp. 394–411.

3. See the articles by Vandenbroucke and von Balthasar in *Concilium* 9 (1965).

4. See Rowan Williams, *The Wound of Knowledge* (London 1979), pp. 1–2; and Josef Sudbrack, 'Spirituality' in Karl Rahner ed., *Encyclopedia of Theology: a Concise Sacramentum Mundi*, London 1975.

5. Colm Luibheid and Paul Rorem, trs and eds, *Pseudo-Dionysius: The Complete Works* (London/New York 1987) in the Classics of Western Spirituality series. For recent introductions to the thought of Pseudo-Dionysius, see Andrew Louth, *The Origins of the Christian Mystical Tradition from Plato to Denys* (Oxford 1981), ch. 3, and *Denys the Areopagite* (London 1989); also Paul Rorem, 'The Uplifting Spirituality of Pseudo-Dionysius' in Bernard McGinn and John Meyendorff, eds, *Christian Spirituality: Origins to the Twelfth Century* (London/New York 1986), pp. 132–51.

6. See Louis Bouyer, 'Mysticism: an Essay on the History of the Word' in Richard Woods, ed., *Understanding Mysticism* (London 1981), pp. 52–3.

7. The classical view is expressed by the once influential but now dated work of Cuthbert Butler, *Western Mysticism*, London 1922. For an Orthodox critique, see Vladimir Lossky, *The Mystical Theology of the Eastern Church* (Cambridge 1957), ch. 2, and *Vision of God* (London 1963), ch. 7, espec. pp. 99–100.

8. See Louth, *Origins*, pp. 164–8.

9. See Louth, *Origins*, pp. 170–8, and *Denys*, pp. 87–8.

10. See, for example, René Roques in Luibheid and Rorem, *Pseudo-Dionysius*, pp. 6–7.

11. See Guntrum Bischoff, 'Dionysius the Pseudo-Areopagite: the Gnostic myth' in Elder, *The Spirituality of Western Christendom*, pp. 22–34. While accepting the cataphatic dimension of Pseudo-Dionysius, Lossky still maintains that there is a fundamental 'antinomy between the two theologies' and that the apophatic way is the true way of eastern mysticism. See *Mystical Theology*, p. 26.

12. Luibheid and Rorem, *Pseudo-Dionysius*, ch. 3, 'The Mystical Theology', p. 139.

13. See Jean Leclercq, 'Influence and non-influence of Dionysius in the Western Middle Ages', in Luibheid and Rorem, *Pseudo-Dionysius*, pp. 25–32. Also Alois Haas, 'Schools of Late Medieval Mysticism', in Jill Raitt and John Meyendorff, eds, *Christian Spirituality: High Middle Ages and Reformation* (London/New York 1987); Brant Pelphrey, *Love Was His Meaning: the Theology and Mysticism of Julian of Norwich* (Salzburg 1982), pp. 57–66.

14. A critical edition is *The Cloud of Unknowing and Related Treatises*, Phyllis Hodgson, ed., Analecta Cartusiana 3, Salzburg 1982. For a recent modern edition of the text, see James Walsh ed., *The Cloud of Unknowing*, New York 1981. On the influence of Gallus see Rosemary Ann Lees, *The Negative Language of the Dionysian School of Mystical Theology: an Approach to the Cloud of Unknowing* Analecta Cartusiana, 107. Salzburg 1983.

15. For example, 'The Mystical Ark', book 2, ch. 17, Grover Zinn, ed. *Richard of St Victor: Works*, London 1979.

16. For comments see Oliver Davies, *God Within: the Mystical Tradition of Northern Europe* (London 1988), chs. 2 and 3. On union with God in Tauler, see Maria Shrady, ed., *Johannes Tauler: Sermons* (London/New York 1985), for example, Sermon 21, pp. 77–8; in Eckhart, see Edmund Colledge and Bernard McGinn, eds, *Meister Eckhart: The Essential Sermons, Commentaries, Treatises and Defense*, (London/New York 1981), for example, sermon 48, p. 198, and sermon 83, pp. 207–8.

17. See James Wiseman, ed., *John Ruusbroec: The Spiritual Espousals and Other Works*, New York 1985. For helpful comments on Ruusbroec, see Davies, *God Within*, pp. 135–52.

18. Ewert Cousins, 'The Humanity and the Passion of Christ', in Raitt, *Christian Spirituality*, pp. 375–80.

19. Ewert Cousins, 'Francis of Assisi: Christian Mysticism at the Cross-roads', in Steven Katz, ed., *Mysticism and Religious Traditions*, Oxford 1983.

20. Cousins, 'The Humanity and Passion', pp. 386–9. A recent author has, incidentally, argued for Tuscan authorship of *The Meditations* – specifically, the friar Giovanni de Caulibus. See, Daniel R. Lesnick, *Preaching in Medieval Florence: the Social World of Franciscan and Dominican Spirituality* (Athens, Georgia/London 1989), p. 143 and note.

21. Ewert Cousins, ed., *St Bonaventure: The Soul's Journey into God; The Tree of Life; The Life of St Francis*, London 1978.

22. Louis Puhl, tr., *The Spiritual Exercises of St Ignatius* (Chicago 1951), no. 23.

23. For an overview of the features of apophatic and cataphatic 'mysticisms' in the modern sense of subjective experience and approaches to prayer, as well as an attempt to draw the two ways together, see Harvey Egan, 'Christian apophatic and kataphatic mysticisms', *Theological Studies* (September 1978), pp. 399–426. While useful in some respects, Egan's article does not really provide an adequate

treatment of the two 'ways' because it does not deal with the patristic background nor with the ways in which the terms have changed their usage.

24. Raimundo Panikkar, *The Trinity and the Religious Experience of Man* (London/New York 1973), pp. 11–19.

25. ibid., p. 18.

26. See Jill Raitt, 'Saints and Sinners: Roman Catholic and Protestant Spirituality in the Sixteenth Century' in Raitt, *Christian Spirituality*, especially p. 454.

27. Wolfhart Pannenberg, *Christian Spirituality and Sacramental Community* (ET, London 1984), pp. 14–15.

28. See Frank Senn ed., *Protestant Spiritual Traditions* (New York 1986), introduction.

29. Such a distinction is made in Henry Rack, *20th Century Spirituality* (London 1969), p. 9 and ch. 3.

30. Franz Leenhardt, *Two Biblical Faiths: Protestant and Catholic* (ET, London 1964); Hieje Faber, *Above the Treeline: Towards a Contemporary Spirituality* (ET, London 1988), chs. 1 and 6.

31. Faber, *Above the Treeline* p. 21.

32. Pannenberg, *Christian Spirituality and Sacramental Community*, pp. 15–22. See also Don E. Saliers, 'Introduction, II' pp. xxi–xxiii, in Louis Dupré and Don E. Saliers, eds, *Christian Spirituality: Post-Reformation and Modern*, New York 1989/London 1990.

33. See, for example, Gene Edward Veith, *Reformation Spirituality: the Religion of George Herbert* (Toronto/London 1985), ch. 2, '"Sinne and Love": the Two Poles of Reformation Spirituality'.

34. Veith, ibid., pp. 19 and 24–8; also Rack, *20th Century Spirituality*, ch. 3.

35. See Raitt, *Christian Spirituality* Specific details of continuities are discussed in the essays on Luther, Calvin and the Radical Reformation in the same volume. See also the essays on Lutheran and Reformed spirituality in Senn, *Protestant Spiritual Traditions*

36. Veith, *George Herbert*, p. 25.

37. See for example, Senn, *Protestant Spiritual Traditions*, Introduction, and Veith, ibid., p. 19.

38. Veith, *George Herbert* pp. 26–8. On the Pauline basis for Ignatian Spirituality, see also John O'Malley, 'Early Jesuit Spirituality: Spain and Italy', in Dupré and Saliers, *Christian Spirituality: Post-Reformation and Modern*, p. 19.

39. See the illuminating essay by Timothy George in Raitt, *Christian Spirituality*.

40. Pannenberg, *Christian Spirituality and Sacramental Community*, p. 14.

41. Edward Kinerk, 'Towards a Method for the Study of Spirituality', *Review for Religious* 40:1 (1981), pp. 3–19.

42. Geoffrey Wainwright, 'Types of Spirituality', Cheslyn Jones et al., *The Study of Spirituality* (London/New York 1986), pp. 592–605.

Conclusion

Hopefully, this study has established clearly two fundamental points. Firstly, the process by which spiritualities emerge in history, and subsequently are developed or marginalized, is not value-free nor a simple question of progress. The story of religious movements is not, any more than history in general, a record of the triumph of progressive forces, or a 'survival of the fittest'. The attempts to describe and interpret this process in historical accounts are also created within particular horizons and are affected by our assumptions, whether spiritual or socio-cultural ones. Secondly, it is possible to look at the history of spirituality in ways which are quite different from what has generally been the case in the past. However, this reconsideration, or revision, cannot take place effectively unless we devise more adequate frameworks and more critical questions. The source for these will be found in the new approaches to historical knowledge that have developed in recent decades, in a reconsideration of what we understand by spirituality, and, because history involves interpretation, in the contemporary values or commitments we bring to our study and reflection.

Because 'power' is basic to much of what we have considered, this seems a useful concept within which to summarize some of the principal questions and conclusions of this book. Power is an uncomfortable word. What the history of spirituality discloses, both in its actual process and in its subsequent interpretation, is that the dynamism of many kinds of power, which operates throughout all that is human, does not cease in some unique way because this is spiritual history. Of course, in one sense, this means that all that has been described is normal in terms of human history. Equally, it is not possible to avoid power, nor is it necessarily bad in all possible circumstances. For example, we talk of empowering those who are powerless, through education or through a more equitable distribution of wealth or greater access to the world's resources. A similar idea of empowerment is, as we have seen, appropriate in the context of spirituality. In this sense, we think of power as a potential for good and for individual or collective development. However, the fact that power is normal, and that it has potential as well as

222

problems, does not mean that it should not be subjected to critical scrutiny or that we are not free to make conscious choices about it.

The historical process, within which spiritual traditions emerge and develop, inevitably creates groups who predominate and others who are subordinate or are actively marginalized. It does not seem unfair to reflect upon the Christian tradition in terms of those who seek to control, produce and then dispense spirituality and those who are made into the recipients of spiritual bequests that originate with others. This is an issue of power: who has it, how it is used (whether consciously or not), and what the effects are, in different contexts, on those who are, at different times, a spiritually dependent underclass. Of course, authentic spiritual experience can never ultimately be controlled by those who hold power in the Church. Yet, it would be naive to pretend that distortions in how spirituality is viewed, particularly if these distortions are 'canonised' by ecclesiastical authority over centuries, have not disabled many people spiritually and led them to seriously underestimate important elements of their personal or collective encounters with the divine. The underside of history has been one of the concerns of this study. However, we should remember that all of us, in fact, have access to a genuine spiritual experience which is uniquely our own. The point about power is not so much that it inhibits such an experience in some people, as that it controls how this is valued or even recognized for what it is.

It is true that the story of Joseph Malan and his family, described in André Brink's novel, *Looking on Darkness*, and noted in chapter 4, existed apart from the official history of South Africa. In spirituality, as much as in any kind of history, judgements are made by chroniclers about what is significant and what, therefore, is to be recorded. Those with power record as the story of their time what accords with their own perceptions of importance. Joseph was aware that the story of his people was what he called 'the shadow-side of history'. But it was a real story, a real history, nonetheless. There has always been, I believe, an obscure sense that 'history' is more than the significant events of the privileged. Or, to put it another way, we catch a glimpse, in different ways, of two histories which run on parallel tracks and intersect from time to time.

For example, popular legends abound, in different cultures, of famous people who disguise themselves, or find themselves off the beaten track, and who, for a time, abandon their place in privileged history to join the common story. Kings or popes leave their palaces to mingle with the crowds to catch, briefly, the whiff of 'ordinary life'. King Alfred, on the run from the Danish invaders of Saxon Wessex, found hospitality at a simple hearth where he was berated for allowing the cakes to burn. He was thus reminded that ordinary people see the real story of life in the ordinary daily round. In this legend, privileged history is subtly expanded, for a moment, to include a homely detail as a symbol of the great mass of human experience which such history does not usually encompass. Sometimes, however, the narrowing of historical consciousness, which gives priority to the world stage over the domestic hearth, does not limit its powerful effect to the privileged participants. It is those on the margins who begin to identify themselves and their experience as inherently insignificant. It was told of the Duke of Wellington, victor of the battle of Waterloo and prime minister that, as he stepped from his church pew to make his Communion, a woman in front of him curtsied and moved aside in order to give him first place. The Duke insisted sharply that she maintain her place and cease to show deference, 'At this table, Madam, we are equals.'

The point, surely, is that the process of history produces a gap between the story of the powerful, or those who act in and upon history, and those whose story merits no significant record or who are merely acted upon. Further, this fact inevitably plays a role in establishing or submerging the identity of individuals and groups not only for future historians but for those who inherit the results. It is not surprising, therefore, that the recovery of a proper history is vital for the liberation, in the present, not only of the relatively powerless but also of those whose unbalanced possession of power has, in its own way, circumscribed their experience. Certainly, when it comes to the question of writing historical accounts, there is a danger that we interpret events and personalities in terms of well-established, and often unconscious, power-structures. The writing of history too often serves élites and continues to deny a story, and therefore an identity, to many individuals and groups. Historians need to be aware of their own power in this respect. Equally, those of us who read spiritual classics need to be exposed to the challenging strangeness of different horizons rather than to be confirmed in our assumptions, through a selective reading.

There is, as we have seen, no such thing as naked history. The writers of historical accounts have their own values and commitments, whether these are historical ones or not, and these find inevitable expression in the kinds of stories they tell. It is perfectly valid, therefore, to direct critical questions at the assumptions which historians bring to their task and to seek to re-read history from a different perspective. This may well involve a commitment to give a story, and thus a voice, to those groups who have been disenfranchized not only by the process of history but also by the way in which historical accounts have traditionally been constructed. Such a commitment should be all the more striking in our approaches to the history of Christian spirituality. The equality of all people and of their experience before God, irrespective of gender, culture and life-style, is fundamental to the gospel and should therefore be the bedrock on which the Christian spiritual tradition rests. Sadly, as we have seen, this has often been obscured as the result of conditioning by other social values.

Bibliography

Alberigo, Giuseppe; Jossua, Jean-Pierre; Komonchak, Joseph A., eds: *The Reception of Vatican II*. ET, Washington DC 1987.

Alberigo, Giuseppe, 'New Frontiers in Church History', *Concilium* 7: 6 (1970), pp. 68–84.

Alberigo, Giuseppe, 'The Local Church in the West (1500–1945)', *The Heythrop Journal* 28: 2 (1987), pp. 125–43.

Alexander, Jon, 'What do Recent Writers Mean by Spirituality?', *Spirituality Today* 32 (1980), pp. 247–56.

Allen, Rosamund S., ed., *Richard Rolle: The English Writings*. New Jersey/London 1989.

Angle, Siddika, 'Beyond Familiar Shores: New Age Spirituality', *The Way* (April 1993), pp. 138–47.

Anson, Peter, *The Call of the Desert*. London 1964.

Aquinas, Thomas, *Summa Theologiae*. London/New York 1963 onwards.

Arbuckle, Gerard; 'Suffocating Religious Life: a New Type Emerges', *The Way Supplement* 65 (Summer 1989), pp. 26–39.

Armstrong, Regis and Brady, Ignatius, eds, *Francis and Clare: The Complete Works*. London/New York 1982.

Aumann, J., *Spiritual Theology*. London 1980.

Babinsky, Ellen, ed., *Marguerite Porete: The Mirror of Simple Souls*. Classics of Western Spirituality. New York 1993.

Baker, Derek, ed., *Medieval Women*, Studies in Church History, Subsidia 1. Oxford 1978.

    ed., *Religious Motivation*, Studies in Church History 15. Oxford 1978.

    ed., *Sanctity and Secularity*, Studies in Church History 10. Oxford 1973.

Baluzus, Stephanus, *Vitae Paparum Avenionensum*, ed. G. Mollat, volume III. Paris 1921.

Bischoff, Guntrum, 'Dionysius the Pseudo-Areopagite: the Gnostic Myth', in E. Rozanne Elder, ed., *The Spirituality of Western Christendom*. Kalamazoo 1976.

Blumenfeld-Kosinski, Renate and Szell, Timea, eds, *Images of Sainthood in Medieval Europe*. Ithaca/London 1991.

Bolton, Brenda, 'Innocent III's Treatment of the Humiliati', in G. J. Cuming and Derek Baker, eds, *Popular Belief and Practice*, Studies in Church History 8. Oxford 1972.

'Mulieres sanctae' in Derek Baker, ed., *Sanctity and Secularity*, Studies in Church History 10. Oxford 1973.

'Vitae Matrum: a Further Aspect of the Frauenfrage', Derek Baker, ed., *Medieval Women*, Studies in Church History, Subsidia 1. Oxford 1978.

Bolton, Brenda and Gerrard, Paul, 'Clare in Her Time', in *Contemporary Reflections on the Spirituality of Clare, The Way Supplement* 80 (Summer 1994), pp. 42–50.

Bouyer, Louis et al., *A History of Christian Spirituality*, ET, 3 vols. London 1968.

An Introduction to Spirituality. ET, New York 1961.

'Mysticism: an Essay on the History of the Word', in Richard Woods, ed., *Understanding Mysticism*. London 1981.

Bowie, Fiona, *Beguine Spirituality: an Anthology*. London/New York 1989.

Breisach, Ernst, *Historiography: Ancient, Medieval and Modern*. Chicago 1983.

Brennan, Margaret, 'Women and Theology: Singing of God in an Alien Land' in *The Way Supplement* 53 (Summer 1985), pp. 93–103.

Brink, André, *Looking on Darkness*. London 1982.

Brooks, Peter, ed., *Christian Spirituality: Essays in Honour of Gordon Rupp*. London 1975.

Brown, Peter, *Society and the Holy in Late Antiquity*. London 1982.

The Body and Society: Men, Women and Sexual Renunciation in Early Christianity. New York 1988/London 1989.

'The Notion of Virginity in the Early Church', Bernard McGinn, John Meyendorff and Jean Leclercq, eds, *Christian Spirituality: Origins to the Twelfth Century*. London 1986.

Burnham, Frederic B., ed., *Postmodern Theology: Christian Faith in a Pluralist World*. New York 1989.

Burton-Christie, Douglas, 'The Literature of Nature and the Quest for the Sacred', in *Spirituality, Imagination and Contemporary Literature, The Way Supplement* 81 (Autumn 1994), pp.4–14.

Butler, Cuthbert, *Western Mysticism*. London 1922.

Bynum, Caroline Walker, *Jesus as Mother: Studies in the Spirituality of the High Middle Ages*. Berkeley 1982.

'Religious Women in the Later Middle Ages', in Jill Raitt ed.,

Christian Spirituality: High Middle Ages and Reformation. New York/London 1987.

Holy Feast and Holy Fast: The Religious Significance of Food to Medieval Women. Berkeley/London 1988.

Fragmentation and Redemption: Essays on Gender and the Human Body in Medieval Religion. New York 1992.

The Resurrection of the Body in Western Christendom, 200–1336. New York 1995.

Byrne, Lavinia, *Mary Ward: a Pilgrim Finds Her Way.* Dublin 1984.

Canivez, J.M., ed., *Statuta Capitulorum Generalium Ordinis Cisterciensis.* Louvain 1934.

Canning, Raymond, tr., *The Rule of St Augustine – With Introduction and Commentary.* London 1984.

Chadwick, Owen, 'Indifference and Morality', in Peter Brooks, ed., *Christian Spirituality: Essays in Honour of Gordon Rupp.* London 1975.

Chittister, Joan, *Women, Ministry and the Church.* New Jersey 1983.

Colledge, Edmund and McGinn, Bernard, eds, *Meister Eckhart: The Essential Sermons, Commentaries, Treatises and Defense.* New York 1981.

Colledge, Edmund and Walsh, James, eds, *The Book of Showings to the Anchoress Julian of Norwich.* Toronto 1978.

Colledge, Edmund and Walsh, James, eds, *Julian of Norwich: Showings.* New York/London 1978.

Collins, Mary, 'Daughters of the Church: the Four Theresas', *Concilium* 182 (1985) '*Women, Invisible in Theology and Church*', pp. 17–26.

Congar, Yves, 'Church History as a Branch of Theology', *Concilium* 7: 6 (1970), pp. 85–96.

Conn, Joann Wolski, *Spirituality and Personal Maturity.* New York 1989.

Cosin, John, *A Collection of Private Devotions*, ed. P. Stanwood. Oxford 1967.

Cousins, Ewert, 'Francis of Assisi: Christian Mysticism at the Crossroads', in Steven Katz, ed., *Mysticism and Religious Traditions.* Oxford 1983.

ed. *St Bonaventure: The Soul's Journey into Christ; The Tree of Life; The Life of St Francis.* London 1978.

'The Humanity and Passion of Christ', in Jill Raitt, ed., *Christian Spirituality: High Middle Ages and Reformation.* London 1987.

Cuming, G.J., and Baker, Derek, eds, *Popular Belief and Practice,*

Studies in Church History, 8. Oxford 1972.

Daniélou, J., 'Patristic Literature: Introduction', in J. Daniélou, A.H. Couratin and John Kent, *The Pelican Guide to Modern Theology* 2. Harmondsworth 1971.

Davies, Oliver, *God Within: The Mystical Tradition of Northern Europe*. London 1988.

De Cantimpré, Thomas, *The Life of Christina Mirabilis*. Trans. Margot King. Matrologia Latina. Toronto 1989.

The Life of Marguerite of Ypres. Trans. Margot King. Matrologia Latina. Toronto 1990.

De Certeau, Michel, *The Mystic Fable*. ET, Chicago 1992.

De Guibert, Joseph, *The Theology of the Spiritual Life*. ET, London 1954.

Deidun, Thomas, 'Beyond Dualisms: Paul on Sex, Sarx and Soma' in *The Way* (July 1988), pp. 195–205.

Delooz, Pierre, 'The Social Function of the Canonisation of Saints', *Concilium* 129 (1979) '*Models of Holiness*', pp. 14–24.

'Towards a Sociological Study of Canonised Sainthood in the Catholic Church', in Stephen Wilson, ed., *Saints and Their Cults*. Cambridge 1983.

Delumeau, Jean, *Catholicism Between Luther and Voltaire*. ET, London 1977.

D'Evelyn, Charlotte, ed., *The Latin Text of the Ancrene Riwle*, EETS. London 1944.

Devlin, Dennis, 'Feminine Lay Piety in the High Middle Ages: the Beguines', in John Nichols and Lillian Thomas Shank, eds, *Distant Echoes: Medieval Religious Women* 1. Kalamazoo 1984.

De Vitry, Jacques, *Vita Mariae Oigniacensis*, *Acta Sanctorum*, volume Iunii, IV. Antwerp 1707.

The Life of Marie d'Oignies and Thomas de Cantimpré, *Supplement to the Life of Marie d'Oignies*. Trans. Margot King and Hugh Feiss. Matrologia Latina. Toronto 1993.

De Waal, Esther, *Seeking God: the Way of St Benedict*. London 1984.

Dillard, Annie, *Pilgrim at Tinker Creek*. London/New York 1977.

Dinzelbacher, Peter, 'The Beginnings of Mysticism Experienced in Twelfth-Century England', in Marion Glasscoe, ed., *The Medieval Mystical Tradition in England*, Exeter Symposium IV, Dartington 1987. Woodbridge: Suffolk 1987.

Downey, Michael, ed., *The New Dictionary of Catholic Spirituality*. Collegeville 1993.

Duby, Georges and Perrot, Michelle, eds, *A History of Women in the West*. 5 volumes. Cambridge, Mass./London 1992–4.

Spirituality and History

Duffy, Eamon, *The Stripping of the Altars: Traditional Religion in England 1400–1580*. New Haven/London 1992.

Dulles, Avery, *Models of the Church*. Dublin 1974.

Dunn, F.I., 'Hermits, Anchorites and Recluses: a Study with Reference to Medieval Norwich', in Frank Dale Sayer, ed., *Julian and her Norwich: Commemorative Essays and Handbook to the Exhibition 'Revelations of Divine Love'*. Julian of Norwich 1973 Celebration Committee, Norwich.

Dupré, Louis; Saliers, Don E., eds, *Christian Spirituality: Post-Reformation and Modern*. London/New York 1989–90.

Dussel, Enrique, 'Was America Discovered or Invaded?', *Concilium* 200 (1988) '*Truth and its Victims*', pp. 126–34.

Egan, Harvey, 'Christian Apophatic and Kataphatic Mysticisms', *Theological Studies* (September 1978), pp. 399–426.

Elder, E. Rozanne, ed., *From Cloister to Classroom: Monastic and Scholastic Approaches to Truth*, Cistercian Studies 90. Kalamazoo 1986.

ed., *The Roots of the Modern Christian Tradition*, Cistercian Studies 55. Kalamazoo 1984.

ed., *The Spirituality of Western Christendom*, Cistercian Studies 30. Kalamazoo 1976.

Elkins, Sharon K., *Holy Women of Twelfth-Century England*. Chapel Hill/London 1988.

Endean, Philip, 'Who Do You Say Ignatius Is? Jesuit Fundamentalism and Beyond', *Studies in the Spirituality of Jesuits* 19: 5, November 1987.

Evans, G.R., ed., *Bernard of Clairvaux: Selected Works*. New Jersey 1987.

Evennett, H. Outram, *The Spirit of the Counter-Reformation*. Cambridge 1968.

Faber, Hieje, *Above the Treeline: Towards a Contemporary Spirituality*. ET, London 1988.

Fiorenza, Elizabeth Schüssler, 'Work, Spirit and Power: Women in Early Christian Communities', in Rosemary Ruether and Eleanor McLaughlin, eds, *Women of Spirit*. New York 1979.

Fontaine, Jacques, 'The Practice of the Christian Life: the Birth of the Laity', in Bernard McGinn, John Meyendorff and Jean Leclercq, eds, *Christian Spirituality: Origins to the Twelfth Century*. London 1986.

Fry, Timothy, ed., *The Rule of St Benedict in Latin and English with Notes*. Collegeville 1981.

Gadamer, Hans-Georg, *Truth and Method*. ET, London 1979.

Gannon, Thomas and Traub, George, *The Desert and the City*. Chicago 1984.

Ganss, George, ed., *The Constitutions of the Society of Jesus*. Institute of Jesuit Sources: St Louis 1970.

Garrigou-Lagrange, R., *Christian Perfection and Contemplation*. ET, St Louis 1937.

Gelber, Hester Goodenough, 'A Theater of Virtue: the Exemplary World of St Francis of Assisi', in John Stratton Hawley, ed., *Saints and Virtues*. Berkeley 1987.

George, Timothy, 'The Spirituality of the Radical Reformation', in Jill Raitt, ed., *Christian Spirituality: High Middle Ages and Reformation*. London 1987.

Gilchrist, Roberta, *Gender and Material Culture: The Archaeology of Religious Women*. London/New York 1994.

Glasscoe, Marion, ed., *The Medieval Mystical Tradition in England*, Exeter Symposium IV, Dartington 1987. Woodbridge: Suffolk 1987.

Gold, Penny Schine, 'Male/Female Cooperation: the Example of Fontevrault', in John Nichols and Lillian Thomas Shank, eds, *Distant Echoes: Medieval Religious Women*, 1. Kalamazoo 1984.

Goodich, Michael, 'Ancilla Dei: the Servant as Saint in the Late Middle Ages', in J. Kirshner and S. Wemple, eds, *Women of the Medieval World*. Oxford 1987.

Gossem, Garry H., ed., *South and Meso-American Native Spirituality*. New York/London 1993.

Gray, Howard, 'What Kind of Document?' *The Way Supplement* 61 (Spring 1988), pp. 21–34.

Gründler, Otto, 'Devotio Moderna', in Jill Raitt, ed., *Christian Spirituality: High Middle Ages and Reformation*. London 1987.

Gutiérrez, Gustavo, *We Drink from our Own Wells: the Spiritual Journey of a People*. London 1984.

Haas, Alois Maria, 'Schools of Late Medieval Mysticism', in Jill Raitt, ed., *Christian Spirituality: High Middle Ages and Reformation*. London 1987.

Haigh, Christopher, ed., *The English Reformation*, Revised edition. Cambridge 1987.

Haight, Roger, 'Foundational Issues in Jesuit Spirituality', *Studies in the Spirituality of Jesuits* 19: 4 September 1987.

Hanson, Bradley, ed., *Modern Christian Spirituality: Methodological and Historical Essays*. American Academy of Religion Studies in Religion no. 92. Atlanta 1990.

'Theological Approaches to Spirituality: A Lutheran Approach', *Christian Spirituality Bulletin* (Spring 1994), pp. 5–8.

Hart, Columba, ed., *Hadewijch: the Complete Works*. New York/ London 1980.

tr. (with Jane Bishop), *Hildegard of Bingen: Scivias*. New York 1990.

Hastings, Adrian, *A History of English Christianity, 1920–1985*. London 1986.

Hawkins, Jackie, ed., 'New Age Spirituality', *The Way* (July 1993).

ed., 'Interfaith Spirituality', *The Way Supplement* 78 (Autumn 1993).

Hawley, John Stratton, ed., *Saints and Virtues*. Berkeley 1987.

Heffernan, Thomas, *Sacred Biography: Saints and Their Biographers in the Middle Ages*. New York/Oxford 1992.

Henderson, John, 'The Flagellant Movement and Flagellant Confraternities in Central Italy, 1260–1400', in Derek Baker, ed., *Religious Motivation*, Studies in Church History 15. Oxford 1978.

Hodgson, Phyllis, ed., *The Cloud of Unknowing and Related Treatises*, Analecta Cartusiana 3. Salzburg 1982.

Hostie, Raymond, *Vie et Mort des Ordres Religieux: Approches Psychosociologiques*. Paris 1972.

Howard, John, 'Mechtild of Magdeburg', in Katharina Wilson, ed., *Medieval Women Writers*. Manchester 1984.

Hughes, Jonathan, *Pastors and Visionaries: Religion and Secular Life in Late Medieval Yorkshire*. Woodbridge: Suffolk/New Hampshire 1988.

Huygens, R.B.C., ed., *Lettres de Jacques de Vitry*. Leiden 1960.

Ivens, Michael, 'The Eighteenth Annotation and the Early Directories', *The Way Supplement* 46 (Spring 1983), pp. 3–10.

Janelle, Pierre, *The Catholic Reformation*. ET, Milwaukee 1963.

Jantzen, Grace, *Julian of Norwich: Mystic and Theologian*. London 1987.

John, Ottmar, 'The Tradition of the Oppressed as the Main Topic of Theological Hermeneutics', *Concilium* 200 (1988) *'Truth and its Victims'*, pp. 143–55.

Jones, Cheslyn, Wainwright, Geoffrey, and Yarnold, Edward, eds, *The Study of Spirituality*. London/New York 1986.

Kannengeisser, Charles, 'The Spiritual Message of the Great Fathers', in Bernard McGinn, John Meyendorff and Jean Leclercq, eds *Christian Spirituality: Origins to the Twelfth Century*. London 1986.

Katz, Steven, *Mysticism and Religious Traditions*. Oxford 1983.

Kent, John, *The Unacceptable Face: the Modern Church in the Eyes of the Historian*. London 1987.

Kieckhefer, Richard, 'Major Currents in Late Medieval Devotion', in Jill Raitt, ed., *Christian Spirituality: High Middle Ages and Reformation*. London 1987.

    Unquiet Souls: Fourteenth Century Saints and their Religious Milieu. Chicago 1984.

Kieckhefer, Richard and Bond, George, eds, *Sainthood: Its Manifestations in World Religions*. Berkeley/London 1990.

Kinerk, Edward, 'Towards a Method for the Study of Spirituality', *Review for Religious* 40:1 (1981), pp. 3–19.

Kirchberger, C., ed., *The Mirror of Simple Souls*. London 1927.

Kirshner, J. and Wemple, S., *Women of the Medieval World*. Oxford 1987.

Knowles, David, *Christian Monasticism*. London 1969.

    From Pachomius to Ignatius. Oxford 1966.

    The Monastic Order in England. Cambridge 1950.

Lane, Belden C., *Landscapes of the Sacred: Geography and Narrative in American Spirituality*. New York 1989.

Lash, Nicholas, *Theology on the Way to Emmaus*. London 1986.

Lawrence, C.H., *Medieval Monasticism*. London/New York 1984.

Leckey, Dolores, *The Ordinary Way: a Family Spirituality*. New York 1982.

Leclercq, Jean, *Aspects of Monasticism*. Michigan 1978.

    Contemplative Life. Kalamazoo 1978.

    'Introduction', in E. Rozanne Elder, ed., *The Roots of the Modern Christian Tradition*, Cistercian Studies 55. Kalamazoo 1984.

    'Introduction', in E. Rozanne Elder, ed., *The Spirituality of Western Christendom*. Kalamazoo 1976.

    'Monasticism and Asceticism: Western Christianity', in Bernard McGinn, John Meyendorff and Jean Leclercq, eds, *Christian Spirituality: Origins to the Twelfth Century*. London 1986.

    'Prayer and contemplation: Western', in Bernard McGinn, John Meyendorff and Jean Leclercq, eds, *Christian Spirituality: Origins to the Twelfth Century*. London 1986.

    The Love of Learning and the Desire for God. ET, New York 1974/London 1978.

    'The Spirituality of Medieval Feminine Monasticism', in William Skudlarek, ed., *The Continuing Quest for God*. Collegeville 1982.

Leech, Kenneth, *Soul Friend*. London 1977.

Leenhardt, Franz, *Two Biblical Faiths: Protestant and Catholic*. ET,

London 1964.

Lees, Rosemary Ann, *The Negative Language of the Dionysian School of Mystical Theology: an Approach to the Cloud of Unknowing*, Analecta Cartusiana 107. Salzburg 1983.

Le Goff, Jacques, 'Francis of Assisi Between the Renewals and Restraints of Feudal Society', *Concilium* 149 (1981) '*Francis of Assisi Today*', pp. 3ff.

Leonardi, Claudio, 'From "Monastic" Holiness to "Political" holiness', *Concilium* 129 (1979), '*Models of Holiness*', pp. 46ff.

Lerner, Gerda, *The Creation of Patriarchy*, Women and History, 1. New York/Oxford 1986.

Lerner, Robert, *The Heresy of the Free Spirit in the Later Middle Ages*. Berkeley 1972.

Lesnick, Daniel R., *Preaching in Medieval Florence: The Social World of Franciscan and Dominican Spirituality*. Athens, Georgia/ London 1989.

Leyser, Henrietta, *Hermits and the New Monasticism*. London 1984.

Liebowitz, Ruth P., 'Virgins in the Service of Christ: the Dispute over an Active Apostolate for Women During the Counter-Reformation', in Rosemary Radford Ruether and Eleanor Mc-Laughlin, eds, *Women of Spirit*. New York 1979.

Lossky, Vladimir, *The Mystical Tradition of the Eastern Church*. ET, London 1973.

Vision of God, ET, London 1963.

Louth, Andrew, *Denys the Areopagite*. London 1989.

Discerning the Mystery: an Essay on the Nature of Theology. Oxford 1983.

The Origins of the Christian Mystical Tradition from Plato to Denys. Oxford 1981.

Luibheid, Colm and Russell, Norman, eds, *John Climacus: The Ladder of Divine Ascent*. London 1982.

ed. (with Paul Rorem), *Pseudo-Dionysius: The Complete Works*. New York/London 1987.

McDonnell, Ernest, *The Beguines and Beghards in Medieval Culture: With Special Emphasis on the Belgian Scene*. New York 1969.

McGinn, Bernard, Meyendorff, John and Leclerq, Jean, eds, *Christian Spirituality: Origins to the Twelfth Century*. London 1986.

McGinn, Bernard, *The Foundations of Mysticism: Origins to the Fifth Century*. New York 1991/London 1992.

'The Letter and the Spirit: Spirituality as an Academic Discipline', *Christian Spirituality Bulletin* (Fall 1993), pp. 1–9.

ed., *Meister Eckhart and the Beguine Mystics*. New York 1994/London 1995.

The Growth of Mysticism: From Gregory the Great to the Twelfth Century. New York 1994/London 1995.

McNamara, Jo Ann, 'Muffled Voices: the Lives of Consecrated Women in the Fourth Century', in John Nichols and Lillian Thomas Shank, eds, *Distant Echoes: Medieval Religious Women* 1. Kalamazoo 1984.

Mack, Frances, ed., *The English Text of the Ancrene Riwle*, EETS. London 1963.

Megyer, Eugene, 'Spiritual Theology Today', *The Way* (January 1981), pp. 55–67.

Meyendorff, John, *Byzantine Theology*. London 1975.

Migne, J.-P. ed., *Patrologiae, Series Latina*, Volume 30, Paris 1865; volume 162, Paris 1889.

Miles, Margaret R., *Fullness of Life: Historical Foundations for a New Asceticism*. Philadelphia 1981.

The Image and Practice of Holiness: a Critique of the Classic Manuals of Devotion. London 1989.

Monumenta Historica Societatis Jesu: Epistolae et Monumenta P. Hieronymi Nadal V: 54. Rome 1962.

Monumenta Historica Societas Jesu: Sancti Ignatii de Loyola, Exercitia Spiritualia, new edition, 100. Rome 1969.

Moore, P.E. and Cross, F.L., eds, *Anglicanism: the Thought and Practice of the Church of England Illustrated from the Religious Literature of the Seventeenth Century*. London 1935.

Moorman, John, *The Anglican Spiritual Tradition*. London 1983.

Murray, Robert, 'The Features of the Earliest Christian Asceticism', in Peter Brooks, ed., *Christian Spirituality: Essays in Honour of Gordon Rupp*. London 1975.

Newman, Barbara, *Sister of Wisdom: St Hildegard's Theology of the feminine*. Berkeley 1987.

ed., *The Life of Juliana de Mont-Cornillon*. Matrologia Latina. Toronto no date.

Nichols, John and Shank, Lillian Thomas, eds, *Distant Echoes: Medieval Religious Women* 1, Kalamazoo 1984.

Norman, Edward, *Roman Catholicism in England from the Elizabethan Settlement to the Second Vatican Council*. Oxford/New York 1985.

O'Day, Rosemary, *The Debate on the English Reformation*. London 1986.

O'Donohue, John, 'A Return to Virtue', *Church* (Spring 1987), pp. 48–54.

O Laoghaire, Diarmuid, 'Celtic Spirituality', in Cheslyn Jones, Geoffrey Wainwright and Edward Yarnold, eds, *The Study of Spirituality*. London 1986.

O'Malley, John, ed., *Collected Works of Erasmus* 66. Toronto/London 1988.

    'Early Jesuit Spirituality: Spain and Italy', in Louis Dupré and Don E. Saliers, eds, *Christian Spirituality: Post-Reformation and Modern*. New York 1989/London 1990.

    'Priesthood, Ministry and Religious Life: Some Historical and Historiographical Considerations', *Theological Studies* 49 (1988), pp. 223–57.

    'To Travel to any Part of the World: Jeronimo Nadal and the Jesuit Vocation', *Studies in the Spirituality of Jesuits* 16: 2 March 1984.

Örsy, Ladislas, 'The Future of Religious Life', *The Way* 14: 4 (October 1974), pp. 311–20.

O'Sullivan, Michael, 'Towards a Social Hermeneutics of the Spiritual Exercises: an Application to the Annotations', *The Spiritual Exercises of St Ignatius Loyola in Present-Day Application*. Rome 1982.

Osuna, Javier, *Friends in the Lord*, Way Series 3. ET, London 1974.

Panikkar, Raimundo, *Blessed Simplicity*. New York 1982.

    The Trinity and the Religious Experience of Man. London 1973.

Pannenberg, Wolfhart, *Christian Spirituality and Sacramental Community*. ET, London 1984.

Peck, M. Scott, *The Road Less Travelled*. London 1983.

Pelphrey, Brant, *Love Was His Meaning: the Theology and Mysticism of Julian of Norwich*. Salzburg 1982.

    Christ Our Mother: Julian of Norwich. Wilmington, Delaware/London 1989.

Petroff, Elizabeth, *Consolation of the Blessed*. New York 1979.

    ed., *Medieval Women's Visionary Literature*. Oxford 1986.

    Body and Soul: Essays on Medieval Women and Mysticism. New York/Oxford 1994.

Pieris, Aloysius, 'Spirituality and Liberation', *The Month* (April 1983), pp. 118–24.

    'The Religious Vows and the Reign of God', *The Way Supplement* 65 (Summer 1989), pp. 3–15.

Pourrat, P., *La Spiritualité Chrétienne*, 4 vols Paris 1918.

Principe, Walter, 'Towards Defining Spirituality', *Sciences Religieuses* 12: 2 (Spring 1983), pp. 127–41.

'Pluralism in Christian Spirituality', *The Way* (January 1992), pp. 54–61.

'Broadening the Focus: Context as a Corrective Lens in Reading Historical Works in Spirituality', *Christian Spirituality Bulletin* (Spring 1994), pp. 1–5.

Progoff, Ira, ed., *The Cloud of Unknowing*. New York 1959.

Puhl, Louis, ed., *The Spiritual Exercises of St Ignatius*. Chicago 1951.

Rack, Henry, *20th Century Spirituality*. London 1969.

Rader, Rosemary, 'Christian Pre-Monastic Forms of Asceticism: *Syneisaktism* or Spiritual Marriage', in William Skudlarek, ed., *The Continuing Quest for God*. Collegeville 1982.

'Early Christian Forms of Communal Spirituality: Women's Communities', in William Skudlarek, ed., *The Continuing Quest for God*. Collegeville 1982.

Rahner, Hugo, *The Spirituality of St Ignatius Loyola*. ET, Chicago 1953.

Rahner, Karl, *The Dynamic Element in the Church*. ET, London 1964.

Theological Investigations 3. ET, London 1967.

Raitt, Jill, ed., *Christian Spirituality: High Middle Ages and Reformation*. New York/London 1987.

'Saints and Sinners: Roman Catholic and Protestant Spirituality in the Sixteenth Century', in ibid.

Riché, Pierre, 'Spirituality in Celtic and Germanic Society', in Bernard McGinn, John Meyendorff and Jean Leclercq, eds, *Christian Spirituality: Origins to the Twelfth Century*. London 1986.

Rogers, E.F., ed., *St Thomas More: Selected Letters*. New Haven/London 1976.

Roof, Wade C., *A Generation of Seekers: The Spiritual Journey of the Baby Boom Generation*. New York 1994.

Rorem, Paul, 'The Uplifting Spirituality of Pseudo-Dionysius', in Bernard McGinn, John Meyendorff and Jean Leclercq, eds, *Christian Spirituality: Origins to the Twelfth Century*. London 1986.

Rubin, Miri, *Corpus Christi: The Eucharist in Late Medieval Culture*. Cambridge 1991.

Ruether, Rosemary and McLaughlin, Eleanor, eds, *Women of Spirit*. New York 1979.

Ruggieri, Giuseppe, 'Faith and History' in Giuseppe Alberigo, Jean-Pierre Jossua and Joseph A. Komonchak, eds, *The*

Reception of Vatican II. ET, Washington DC 1987.

Russell, Robert J., 'Finite Creation Without a Beginning', in 'Mysticism, Spirituality and Science', *The Way* (October 1992), pp. 268–80.

Salu, M.B., trans., *The Ancrene Riwle*. London 1955.

Sandeman, Barnabas, 'Nuns and Monks: a Thousand Years of Change', *The Way Supplement* 40 (Spring 1981).

Schneiders, Sandra, 'Theology and Spirituality: Strangers, Rivals or Partners?', *Horizons* 13:2 (1986), pp. 253–74.

'Spirituality in the Academy', *Theological Studies* 50 (December 1989), pp. 676–97.

'Spirituality as an Academic Discipline: Reflections from Experience', *Christian Spirituality Bulletin* (Fall 1993), pp. 10–15.

'A Hermeneutical Approach to the Study of Christian Spirituality', *Christian Spirituality Bulletin* (Spring 1994), pp. 9–14.

Schoedel, William R., ed., *Ignatius of Antioch*. Philadelphia 1985.

Schulenberg, Jane Tibbets, 'Strict Active Enclosure and its Effects on the Female Monastic Experience (500–1100)', in John Nichols and Lillian Tomas Shank, eds, *Distant Echoes: Medieval Religious Women* 1. Kalamazoo 1984.

Senn, Frank, ed., *Protestant Spiritual Traditions*. New York 1986.

Sheils, W.J. and Wood, Diana, eds, *Women in the Church*, Studies in Church History 27. Oxford 1990.

Sheldrake, Philip, *Images of Holiness*. London/Notre Dame 1987.

'Some Continuing Questions: The Relationship Between Spirituality and Theology', *Christian Spirituality Bulletin* (Spring 1994), pp. 15–17.

'Spirituality and Theology', in Peter Byrne and Leslie Houlden, eds, *Companion Encyclopedia of Theology*. London 1995.

Living Between Worlds: Place and Journey in Celtic Spirituality. London/Boston 1995.

Shrady, Maria, ed., *Johannes Tauler: Sermons*. New York/London 1985.

Skudlarek, William, ed., *The Continuing Quest for God*. Collegeville 1982.

Southern, R.W., *Western Society and the Church in the Middle Ages*. London 1970.

Stanford, Michael, *The Nature of Historical Knowledge*. New York/London 1987.

Staudenmaier, John, *Technology's Storytellers: Reweaving the Human Fabric*. Society for the History of Technology/MIT: Cambridge, Mass., 1985.

Sudbrack, Josef, 'Spirituality', in Karl Rahner, ed., *Encyclopedia of Theology: a Concise Sacramentum Mundi*. ET, London 1975.

Symons, Thomas, ed., *Regularis Concordia*. London/New York 1953.

Szarmach, Paul, ed., *An Introduction to the Medieval Mystics of Europe*. New York 1984.

Tanquerey, A.A., *The Spiritual Life*. ET, Tournai 1930.

Tavard, George: 'Apostolic Life and Church Reform', in Jill Raitt ed., *Christian Spirituality: High Middle Ages and Reformation*. London 1987.

Thompson, Ross, 'Scientific and Religious Understanding', in 'Mysticism, Spirituality and Science', *The Way* (October 1992), pp. 258–67.

Thompson, Sally, *Women Religious: The Founding of English Nunneries after the Norman Conquest*. Oxford 1991.

Thompson, William, *Fire and Light: the Saints and Theology*. New York 1987.

Tosh, John, *The Pursuit of History*. New York/London 1988.

Tracy, David, *Blessed Rage for Order: the New Pluralism in Theology*. New York 1978.

The Analogical Imagination: Christian Theology and the Culture of Pluralism. London/New York 1981.

Vandenbroucke, François, 'Spirituality and Spiritualities', *Concilium* 9:1 (1965), pp. 25–33.

Van Engen, John, ed., *Devotio Moderna: Basic Writings*. New York 1989.

'The Christian Middle Ages as an Historiographical Problem', *American Historical Review* 91 (1986), pp. 519–52.

Van Ness, Peter H., 'Spirituality and Secularity', *The Way Supplement* 73 (Spring 1992), pp. 68–79.

Veale, Joseph, 'How the Constitutions Work', *The Way Supplement* 61 (Spring 1988), pp. 3–20.

'Ignatian Prayer or Jesuit Spirituality', *The Way Supplement* 27 (Spring 1976), pp. 3–14.

'The Dynamic of the Spiritual Exercises', *The Way Supplement* 52 (Spring 1985), pp. 3–18.

Veith, Gene Edward, *Reformation Spirituality: the Religion of George Herbert*. Toronto/London 1985.

Von Balthasar, Hans Urs, 'The Gospel as Norm and Test of All

Spirituality in the Church', *Concilium* 9:1 (1965), pp. 5–13.

Wainwright, Geoffrey, 'Types of Spirituality', in Cheslyn Jones, Geoffrey Wainwright and Edward Yarnold, eds, *The Study of Spirituality*. London/New York 1986.

Wakefield, Gordon, ed., *A Dictionary of Christian Spirituality*. London 1983.

Wall, John, ed., *George Herbert: The Country Parson, The Temple*. London/New York 1981.

Walsh, James, ed., *The Cloud of Unknowing*. New York 1981.

Ward, Benedicta, 'Julian the Solitary', *Julian Rediscovered*. Fairacres: Oxford 1988.

tr., *The Wisdom of the Desert Fathers*. Fairacres: Oxford 1986.

Warren, Ann, 'The Nun as Anchoress: England 1000–1500', in John Nichols and Lillian Thomas Shank, eds, *Distant Echoes: Medieval Religious Women* 1. Kalamazoo 1984.

Weiler, Anton, 'Church History and the Reorientation of the Scientific Study of History', *Concilium* 7:6 (1970), pp. 13–32.

Weinstein, D. and Bell, R., *Saints and Society: the Two Worlds of Western Christendom, 1000–1700*. Chicago 1982.

Williams, Rowan, *The Wound of Knowledge: Christian Spirituality from the New Testament to St John of the Cross*. London 1979.

Wilson, Katharina, ed., *Medieval Women Writers*. Manchester 1984.

Wilson, Stephen, ed., *Saints and Their Cults*. Cambridge 1983.

Windeath, B.A., tr., *The Book of Margery Kempe*. London 1985.

Winkler, Gabriele, 'The Origins and Idiosyncracies of the Earliest Form of Asceticism', in William Skudlarek, ed., *The Continuing Quest for God*. Collegeville 1982.

Wiseman, James, ed., *John Ruusbroec: The Spiritual Espousals and Other Works*. New York 1985.

Wolters, Clifton, ed., *The Cloud of Unknowing and Other Works*. New York/London 1961.

Woods, Richard, ed., *Understanding Mysticism*. London 1981.

Zinn, Grover, ed., *Richard of St Victor: Works*. London 1979.

'The Regular Canons', in Bernard McGinn, John Meyendorff and Jean Leclercq, eds, *Christian Spirituality: Origins to the Twelfth Century*. London 1986.

Index